Making Money, Making Music

Making Money, Making Music

History and Core Concepts

David Bruenger

UNIVERSITY OF CALIFORNIA PRESS

University of California Press, one of the most
distinguished university presses in the United States,
enriches lives around the world by advancing scholarship
in the humanities, social sciences, and natural sciences.
Its activities are supported by the UC Press Foundation
and by philanthropic contributions from individuals and
institutions. For more information, visit www.ucpress.edu.

University of California Press
Oakland, California

© 2016 by The Regents of the University of California

Library of Congress Cataloging-in-Publication Data

Names: Bruenger, David, author.
Title: Making money, making music : history and core
    concepts / David Bruenger.
Description: Oakland, California : University of California
    Press, [2016] | "2016 | Includes bibliographical
    references and index.
Identifiers: LCCN 2016012899 (print) | LCCN 2016014533
    (ebook) | ISBN 9780520292581 (cloth : alk. paper) |
    ISBN 9780520292598 (pbk. : alk. paper) |
    ISBN 9780520966062 ()
Subjects: LCSH: Music trade.
Classification: LCC ML3790 .B7767 2016 (print) | LCC
    ML3790 (ebook) | DDC 780.23/73—dc23
LC record available at http://lccn.loc.gov/2016012899

Manufactured in the United States of America

25 24 23 22 21 20 19 18 17 16

10 9 8 7 6 5 4 3 2 1

For Donna, source of inspiration and illumination now and forever more, without whom the music stops.

Contents

Introduction

Over the course of the twentieth century and (so far) in the twenty-first, musical experience and the means to monetize it have been fundamentally transformed—and more than once. At every stage, the system supporting the production, distribution, and consumption of music—whether based on records, radio, print publishing, and live shows, or downloads, streams, licensing, and live shows—involves many individuals, organizations, relationships, and processes. And, as new technologies, social behaviors, and economic conditions emerge, these systemic frameworks are inevitably affected, either adapting to change or collapsing into irrelevance, insolvency, or both.

This music production and distribution framework and its ongoing evolution exemplify a *complex system*. It is complex not only in the sense of "complicated" but also in the more technical meanings of the term. As broadly defined across multiple disciplines, a complex system is a network comprising many discrete components or agents that interact with one another at a local level and, though lacking any centralized control, produce coordinated results that go beyond the sum of their individual actions. While the workings of such a system tend to follow consistent, observable patterns, they are also organically adaptive to emergent changes in their environment.[1]

Such complex adaptive systems have been observed in nature, computer networks, and in social, legal, and economic contexts. So it is logical to consider that the business of creating and distributing music "can be described as a complex adaptive system in which legal, political, economic, socio-cultural, and technological subsystems converge, interact, and coevolve."[2]

Complexity theory offers two practical considerations for the study of the music business. First, a complex systems model can improve our understanding of music commerce, its agents, and processes. Second, applying that model to education illuminates particular challenges for aspiring music professionals and their teachers.

One consequence of teaching and studying such a complex subject as "the music industry" in a college or university setting is that content must be streamlined in order to fit the constraints of class time and comprehensibility. Often the streamlining process leads to a focus on "how it works today in the music business"—however "today" is defined. Because the music business is volatile, subject to changing technologies, legal frameworks, social behaviors, and economic conditions—not to mention the transient tastes of the listening public—it is challenging to keep studies of current practice "current."

This dilemma parallels challenges in the music marketplace, where participants must be able to respond to changing conditions. Consequently, the study of the music business should encourage development of an adaptive capacity if students are going to effectively participate and produce in the music marketplace.

To develop adaptive capacity, students need more than a detailed understanding of current practice. Of course, it is important to understand best practices. But in a complex market system, success depends also upon awareness of context, the capacity to see trends and recognize patterns, as well as the analytical skill to recognize pattern disruptions and the practiced ability to adapt existing, or create new, solutions.

This book is dedicated to the development of *adaptive expertise* in the study of music enterprise. It incorporates both "how it works" and "how it has worked" content, as well as opportunities to develop comparative analysis and pattern recognition skills. It explores not only how but also why a system or tactic works when it does and why it fails to work when it doesn't. The foundational method is to use contemporary and historical examples and comparisons to extract principles of operation that are consistent over time and adaptable across stylistic, social, technological, and economic contexts.

As the term is used here, a *core principle* is derived from a particular situation but is transferable to (potentially) every situation involving music, people, and money. A step beyond the core principle is the *operative dynamic.* Operative dynamics are not only descriptive. They are process models that show how something works. In its most fundamental form, an operative dynamic embodies a scalable, adaptive relationship or process, not just a concept or structure. But, like core principles, operative dynamics are transferable and can be used to explain piracy in 1899 and 1999 or the enterprises of Thomas Edison and Daniel Ek with equal validity.

In studying, applying, and learning how to develop their own core principles and dynamic models, students develop the capacity to analyze what is happening, recognize whether or not it has happened before, and what answers—familiar, adapted from another context, or entirely new—might work best in the emergent situation.

Through this learning process, students can develop a different kind of expertise in music business—an expertise that can be adapted to a variety of circumstances, used to solve "out of the box" problems, and create new processes and products. The person with those tools will not only be efficient with the complex yet routine processes of an established music industry, but also respond creatively and effectively when the unexpected arises.

In the first chapter, we begin with the most fundamental core principle—that all forms of music enterprise are based on a relationship between artist and audience; and an operative dynamic—that the musical experience is a transaction that is the basis for all meaning and value created through music.

Musical Experience as Transaction

The music of the soul is also the music of salesmanship.

—Herbert Marcuse

This is a book about making money, making music, and using the one to accomplish the other. It is not concerned with formal definitions of music or with practical music making. Nor will it provide specific guidance on how to promote your band, start a record label, or fill out a copyright registration form. This is an exploration of value in its many forms— artistic, social, cultural, and economic—and the capacity of music to create it. It is an examination of the human experience of music, why people place a value on that experience, and—perhaps most critically— how that value is measured.

One way to measure the value of music is by applying "aesthetic" criteria. If we define *aesthetic* as "being pleasing," then the simplest criterion would be, *does a given piece of music please the listener?* Since this kind of value is personal and entirely subjective, opinions will vary widely, and comparisons will be difficult. If, on the other hand, we define *aesthetic* as "a set of ideas or opinions about beauty or art," we have the basis for a system that can support comparisons between works of music and those who create them.[1]

By adopting formal aesthetic measures based on expert-established standards, musical artifacts—songs and larger compositions—can be ranked in terms of quality. The European classical music tradition is an example of this kind of value system. In it, music critics and scholars apply expertise gained from years of critical listening and study to evaluate and compare both established and new musical works and performances.

Outside of the classical tradition, musical quality tends to be measured in other ways, using criteria on the spectrum from high-level expertise to purely personal, in-the-moment reactions. These include various "Top 100" or "Best of" lists, such as Best Love Songs of All Time, Best Summer Anthems of the 2000s, or Best Dance Tracks of 2014, and so on. For lists like these, sometimes the public votes, or the list might be a compilation of a panel of pop music critics' opinions.

Collective judgments like these suggest that one can look at musical value through a social lens rather than a purely aesthetic one. The widespread practice of singing "Happy Birthday," playing Mendelssohn's "Wedding March" for weddings, singing carols at Christmas, "Take Me Out to the Ballgame" or "Rock and Roll, Part 2" for sporting events are all markers for musical value as measured by social adoption—popularity. Taken across a large enough sample and over time, this kind of popularity is a measure of the usefulness, familiarity, and "tradition value" of particular pieces of music for specific social events.

Ultimately though, whether value is assessed individually, by breadth of social adoption, by expert authority, in the moment, or over time, "goodness" in music is both situational and difficult to quantify. It is one thing to argue—either in the abstract or for a particular purpose— that Beethoven's Symphony no. 5 is "better" than Robin Thicke's "Blurred Lines." But answering the question "how much better?" is much more complicated. Aesthetic and popular assessments only underscore one's personal tastes.

There is, however, one system of measurement—a metric—that can quantify musical value objectively and consistently, and that supports comparative analysis across styles and contexts.

Money.

Purely as a measure of artistic quality or individual appeal, money has obvious limitations. The value and meaning of music is about more than the revenue it generates. It is commonly believed that art and commerce are mutually exclusive, that the people engaged in these aspects of the music enterprise are diametrically opposed, and that the artistic world is divided between creators, who are "good," and exploiters, who are "bad." This polarized view—expressed, for example, by the quote at the beginning of the chapter—powerfully shapes public perception and public policy about music and the arts.

However, virtually no music exists entirely outside an economic context. Even the greatest composers of the European classical music tradition were concerned with compensation; their survival depended upon it. Moreover, the economic constraints of classical music affected not only the lives of the musicians themselves but also the nature of their art. Thus, even though the study of classical music tends to avoid discussing money, a complete assessment of the productivity of iconic composers such as J. S. Bach, Franz Josef Haydn, Wolfgang Amadeus Mozart, or Ludwig van Beethoven is not possible without also considering the economic and social conditions in which their music was created.

The increasing professionalization and industrialization of music in the twentieth century amplified the importance of the economic realities that constrain and support the musical arts. In truth, while the value of music cannot be measured only in terms of money, we absolutely cannot talk about the music business or, more broadly, music enterprise, without talking about people who are making money while making music. Ultimately, a failure to understand and function within an economic context undermines the sustainability of any music enterprise, thus diminishing both the artistic and social value that it can create.

As a result, every music enterprise must be assessed in terms of its capacity to create multiple forms of value: good music, social purpose, and a sustainable economic model. Put another way, those metrics become a question: why and how do musicians, audiences, and economic opportunity come together?

MUSIC: SOCIOECONOMIC CONTEXT

Musical endeavors can be entirely personal and never intended for public ears, let alone commercial consumption. Yet more often than not, music occurs in a social setting. Most simply, music happens when someone is making it and someone else is listening. In that context, the experience of making and listening to music can be understood as an exchange, or transaction, between performer and listener. It is only when music is placed in such a social context—where the musical experience is an exchange between people—that its full potential to create value can be realized. This is the first core principle of the text.

> Music enterprise becomes possible when musical experience is an exchange between people.

The places—whether physical or technologically mediated—where musical artists, audiences, and economic opportunity come together are the marketplaces for music. Since musical experiences are as varied and diverse as the many different styles of music, multiplied by the number of performers and listeners, music marketplaces come in many forms. In addition, styles and tastes change and so do markets. Methods of production and delivery appear and permeate society or fade into obsolescence. New social behaviors emerge and traditions evolve.

Business models arise, are codified, and then, with the next wave of change, are rendered obsolete. As a result, the enterprise of creating value through music can be seen as cycling between bursts of innovation and periods of relative stability. On the one hand, this is an entertaining feature of studying the music business: things are not static. On the other hand, studying the music business can be frustrating; styles fluctuate, and the means of creation, production, and consumption are reinvented over and over again. And if it were your money and career at stake, it is easy to see how such volatility could be terrifying.

One thing that does not change, however, is that a musical experience can be understood as a relationship between people. Performers provide music and listeners provide their attention and, in that shared experience, there is an exchange of meaning and value, whether simple appreciation, admiration, money, or all of the above.

Framing musical experience as a transaction is a useful tool. It helps us to describe how musical value was created historically, to see how it is produced today, and to predict the contexts in which it is likely to develop in the future. It is the first *operative dynamic*—and the most foundational—of this text. Like all such dynamics (and core principles), it is scalable and applicable across different times, styles, business structures, and socioeconomic contexts.

The circles in the diagram in figure 1 describe the two essential components of the musical experience: creation and reception. In their most common form, the two elements are performing and listening. Each of the circles can also represent the agents—the people—engaged in these activities. Whether we define the person(s) acting on the left side of the diagram as performers, composers, or teachers, and the person(s) on the right as listeners, patrons, or students, the relationship between them always consists of an exchange of something: a "this" for "that" transaction (or quid pro quo) represented by the arrows that connect the circles.

There is an immense utility in recognizing patterns and their recurrence, because the music business is nothing if not cyclical. Even though

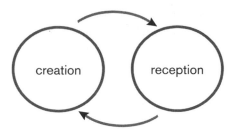

FIGURE 1. Music transaction diagram.

(as noted in the introduction) musical styles, social behaviors, and the tools of production, distribution, and consumption were all quite different in 1899, the practical concerns of music content providers at the turn of that century were quite similar to those in 1999: piracy, new media, and changing consumer attitudes and patterns of consumption.

A practical understanding of past patterns and their relevance today, requires—in addition to awareness of them—the ability to distinguish between the elements and relationships that remain relatively stable over time and those that change more often. As we consider consistency and change, we will examine the forces that both drive and resist change, as well as the larger economic, cultural, and social frameworks in which those forces act.

TRANSACTIONS: COMPOSING, TEACHING, AND PERFORMING

In addition to the performing-listening transaction, two other musical activities have traditionally supported value creation in music. Both composing and teaching music have long been integral to the professional lives of performing musicians, and both remain relevant to the performance enterprise of many musicians today.

Composing

Some musical cultures are based on learning traditional music aurally, while others emphasize improvising music in the moment. In the classical European tradition, by contrast, music is normally composed in advance of a performance, sometimes on demand for specific occasions. As a result, the role of the composer is prominent in the classical music tradition, as is the songwriter in the realm of popular, commercial music.

But regardless of the stylistic framework, in situations where there are a large number of performers or a limited amount of time to prepare a performance, being able to pre-arrange music via written notation (or other "instructions") has practical and economic value. For much of history, to the present day, many performers also compose and even more create written arrangements of compositions to customize their performances.

In earlier centuries, music writing and arranging were typically compensated with one-time, event-specific payment, or were unpaid yet necessary for a paid performance to occur. It was not until music publishing emerged in the mid to late 1800s and subsequently functional copyright laws were written to support the rights of musical content producers that the ongoing revenue potential of music composition was fully realized by composers. The development of music publishing and copyright laws affecting it is discussed in more detail chapter 2.

Teaching

Music education—teaching people how to play music—also has a long history of integration into the work lives of professional performers. As part of the European patronage model, providing music lessons for the children of the patron's household was a standard duty for a court composer/performer. It was not, however, until the emergence of a true "middle class" in the 1800s (people with leisure time and discretionary income) that expanding the scale of music lessons to a larger segment of the population—and selling printed instructional and student-level performance music—became practical. The musico-economic implications of the rising middle class in Europe are also discussed in the next chapter.

Music composition, music lessons, and music performance in various combinations remain relevant and continue to produce revenue streams for the majority of professional musicians in the twenty-first century. At the heart of the musical experience and the musical enterprise, however, is performance.

Performing

The foundational relationship for realizing musical experience has been (and remains) performing music live for an in-person audience. This practice dates as far back as there is history and occurs across virtually every place on the planet. There are few if any cultural or historical settings where people do or did not appreciate listening to music or incorporating music (and, therefore, musicians) into life's important, celebratory, and solemn moments. We know, for example, that in the 1700s musicians in northern Europe often made money by playing for dances, weddings, church services, and important civic events. Those activities and events would also describe the professional schedule of many musical performers so far in the 2000s and all the decades in between.

It is important to observe that many of the foundational historic models discussed in this text—particularly in the early chapters—are drawn from European traditions in music and music commerce. These models are relevant to us today for two reasons. First, European practice in music performance, composition, education, publishing, and copyright law directly informed the emergence and development of those practices in North America. Second, even when non-European musicians, musical styles, and audiences emerged and developed—blues, jazz, rhythm and blues, and so on—they were supported, constrained, and in some cases exploited via those same cultural values and practical frameworks.

While specifics change, the fundamental process models that support transactional music relationships between performers and audiences have remained remarkably constant over time. One feature common to all such models is the importance of recurrence; that is, of ensuring ongoing opportunities for performers and audiences to connect and reconnect.

PERFORMER-LISTENER TRANSACTION MODELS

One way to look at the performer-listener connection is to consider it from an economic perspective: how much money a performer needs to make within a given time frame and how to connect with the listener(s) willing to provide it. Consider a musician who needs to earn $1 million per year. Factoring that amount against the number of listeners/consumers necessary to provide it yields possibilities ranging from one person who will pay $1 million for a single performance to 1 million people who will pay a dollar each—either collectively (an audience of a million people) or individually (a million one-to-one performances).

Obviously there are additional variables. You could find someone willing to pay $100,000 for ten performances or a thousand people to pay a $1,000 at a single performance. The abstract permutations are nearly endless, but in reality, there are constraining factors that limit the number of practical options.

The primary constraints to this kind of music endeavor are the logistics of delivery and the economic conditions and divisions in society. Doing a million individual performances in a year would mean performing over twenty-seven hundred times per day, which is obviously impossible. Performing one time for 1 million people is possible today, thanks to massive sound systems (not to mention, recordings, broadcast media, and the Internet). But, before electrical amplification was invented (around 1909) and applied to musical performance (around 1925), playing "live" for more than a few hundred (or, under ideal conditions, a few thousand) listeners at one time was impractical simply because the performance could not be heard by everyone in attendance.

Further, even if the maximum number of people heard (and paid for) the maximum number of performances per day, there are still limitations to consider. How far could a performer travel in a year to reach the requisite number of listeners? How many people in each location's potential audience pool would be willing—and financially able—to buy the musical experience being sold on a given day?

One way to view the significance of later technological developments such as recording, broadcasting, and so on, is in terms of how they have affected or, in the case of emerging technologies, have the potential to affect the constraints on performer-to-listener delivery models. But, regardless of whatever performance-enhancing technology is available, sustaining economic models in music (supporting a musical career) always depends upon "repeat sales"—audiences who are willing to pay for multiple experiences over time.

In practice, three models defined performer-listener relationships and supported ongoing transactional musical ventures in the prerecording and prebroadcasting era. These structures have been in use for centuries and remain, to varying degrees, relevant today. In their most basic configuration, they are as follows:

1. *Touring model*—performer travels frequently, finding new audiences at each new location.

2. *Tourism model*—performer stays in place, new audiences cycle through.

3. *Patronage model*—performer and audience relationship is relatively stable, but performance content changes as per the expectations of the patron—the primary (or exclusive) financial sponsor.

The *touring model* has been in use since minstrels and troubadours wandered across tenth-century Europe and has been integral to the business of music making in every century since. As the nineteenth century progressed, however, tours became more elaborate and more lucrative both in Europe and the United States. National and international tours were foundational to the music business in the twentieth century.

The *tourism model,* at least in the form of street musicians playing for passersby, has been around at least as long, if not longer than, touring. Today tourism-based performing can be seen in situations as diverse as the levee in New Orleans, musicals on Broadway, and the music performed at theme parks and other tourist-oriented destinations around the world.

The European *patronage model* is discussed in more detail below, but examples of patronage can also be found in the history of musicians serving the nobility in ancient China, Greece, and Egypt. Contemporary patronage tends to be institutional rather than individually supported. Casinos and civic institutions (symphonies and opera companies), as well as colleges and universities, all continue provide (to some extent) long-term employment opportunities for musicians.

As these examples suggest, each of these performance models is scalable from the small and low-cost to the immense and expensive. An example indicating the upper end of the scale is U2's 360° Tour (2009–2011). That tour presented 110 shows around the globe and produced revenue of over $700 million.[2] The costs to launch and operate the tour, produced by Live Nation, were estimated to have been approximately $150 million, including roughly $750,000 per day to keep the show on the road.[3]

The success of either touring or tourism approaches, as measured by cost-benefit comparison, depends upon a number of interrelated factors:

Price of each ticket sold

Number of tickets sold per event

Number of events

Startup costs—to have a single event

Ongoing costs—to present additional events

Additional considerations include the following:

Venue—how many people will it hold?

Acoustics—can everyone with a ticket hear the performer?

Market—what is current cost of comparable events, number of competing events, and the larger economic context?

Community or neighborhood factors—is the area safe or dangerous, a recognized or unfamiliar location for performance, the site of previous successes/failures?

As with any business venture, leveraging cost of production against revenue generated is the critical management challenge in the business of live musical performance. Increasing the number of tickets sold is an obvious means to increase revenue. In the modern era—post-1964 British invasion—sports stadiums have become preferred locations to maximize tickets sold per event. The Beatles, for example, performed for fifty-five thousand fans in a single concert at Shea Stadium in August 1965, grossing $304,000—worth nearly $2.3 million in 2015 dollars.

By contrast, classical performances in the patronage era (pre-1800s) tended to be for small, select audiences, funded by a single payer. Although this type of patronage is uncommon today, there are still opportunities for single, small-scale events that produce significant revenue. Elton John, for example, earned $1 million for performing at radio personality Rush Limbaugh's August 2010 wedding. Much more typically—both historically and today—performers must seek to sell more tickets per event at a more reasonable cost to listeners, leveraged across additional concerts in multiple locations (see chapter 7, "Scaling and Selling Live Performance").

Even well-planned and competitively priced events can fail due to economic conditions in society at large. Summer tours, for example, can be particularly vulnerable to this economic "halo effect." Numerous tours scheduled during the summer of 2010, for example, were downsized as a result of poor advance sales that were likely a reflection of widespread economic anxiety. Even the consistently "bankable" Eagles canceled dates, Christina Aguilera canceled her entire tour before it began, and numerous promoters waived service fees and offered steep discounts to entice buyers.[4]

During the period of history we are about to consider—the seventeenth, eighteenth, and part of the nineteenth century—the technology and distribution/delivery logistics for mass-market music were not yet in place. The alternative to a then-impossible large-scale delivery was to find a smaller number of listeners willing to pay significantly more. Until the nineteenth century, the most effective model for doing this was the patronage system.

PATRONAGE: ARTIST/EMPLOYEE

Consider the graph shown in figure 2. It is a symbolic representation of the distribution of funds available for music across society in the baroque and classical eras of music in Europe—from roughly 1600 to 1800. Note that while there are many with few resources on the left and a (naturally) much smaller number of very wealthy people on the right, the middle of the graph is empty. This distribution represents the socioeconomic structure of European society for centuries: many lower-class "commoners" and a very few wealthy, aristocratic elites. During this period, there was no group of people in the "middle," who, though perhaps not wealthy or noble by birth, might have had sufficient discretionary income to support art or entertainment ventures.

Obviously, there are only two places in the socioeconomic structure represented by this graph in which musicians could make money. From the "common" man, there were many potential sources, but each with extremely limited funds. Working with this population would require many, many performances with a very low return on each one. Alternatively, working for the aristocratic class, where there was money available, meant developing longer term relationships with one or more of a much smaller pool of potential musical customers.

Most often, opportunities to make music for the aristocratic classes took the form of an employee-employer relationship. In this era of the artist/employee, so-called household musicians had the economic and social status of domestic servants. This arrangement could and did provide stable income, clothing, and housing, but the trade-off for musicians was a loss of autonomy, mobility, and control over their creative productivity. This trade-off often applies to more contemporary patronage models as well.

As the patronage system came to an end--for large-scale social and economic reasons beyond the scope of this discussion--professional performers and composers came to rely more and more on paid public performances as their primary source of revenue and opportunity to promote their reputations. The era of the artist/employee consequently evolved into that of the *artist/entrepreneur.*

The viability of the artist/entrepreneur model depended upon an emerging middle class able and willing to spend money on public concerts and enough venues willing to present concert events. London became one of the first loci of public concerts supported by a public eager for musical experience. According to Villanova professor of

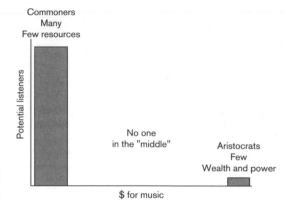

FIGURE 2. Audiences and
resources during the
baroque and classical eras

law and music copyright historian Michael Carroll, "By the early eighteenth century, the concert series had become a central part of the aristocratic social season in London. Performance spaces included two theaters operating under patent, Covent Garden and Drury Lane, as well as pleasure gardens (i.e., public parks), such as Vauxhall and Ranelagh."[5]

As the eighteenth century came to a close, public concert opportunities continued to expand even as economic conditions negatively impacted the aristocracy. As a result, patronage opportunities for musicians began to diminish, while public ones continued to increase. But not every composer responded effectively to the decline of one model and the rise of another. A comparison of the career strategies of four prominent composers in the European tradition both before and during this time of social and economic transition follows.

From Artist/Employee to Artist/Entrepreneur:
A Tale of Four Composers

The greatest name of the baroque music era was Bach. Johann Sebastian Bach was a success in every aspect of music enterprise then available. His work spanned multiple long-term positions in both noble households and church institutions. He wrote both religious and secular music, was a respected music teacher and renowned keyboard performer, and produced a body of work over a long lifetime (1685–1750) that remains influential today. His income was substantial and he was able to sustain a full family life; he was married twice and raised twenty children, several of whom came to prominence in musical careers of their own. J. S. Bach is the model of the musician perfectly positioned for artistic and economic success in his time.

Musical Patrons

DUKE WILHELM ERNST—WEIMAR, GERMANY

Bach's productivity always paralleled the interests of his employers, and Duke Wilhelm supported the composer in his creation of many secular cantatas as well as vocal and instrumental works. The duke so valued Bach's contribution to his household that he raised the composer's salary to discourage him from accepting offers from other noblemen.

PRINCE NIKOLAS ESTERHAZY—EISENSTADT, AUSTRIA

Members of the Esterhazy family were Franz Josef Haydn's most important and enduring patrons. The family continued to pay him a salary even during his later trips to London and afterward. This suggests the importance and "status value" attached by the family to being the patrons of an increasingly famous composer.

JOSEPH II, HOLY ROMAN EMPEROR—AUSTRIA

Known as a patron of the arts and the "Musical King," Emperor Joseph was an occasional, short-term patron of Wolfgang Amadeus Mozart, commissioning the opera *Abduction from the Seraglio.*

Unfortunately for Mozart, the emperor did not fully understand or appreciate the composer's musical style and consequently their relationship did not flourish. Despite this, Mozart continued to hope for a more permanent position in the imperial court while pursuing his own creative vision.

Beethoven was also commissioned by the emperor to compose a funeral cantata, which was never performed at the court due to the music's technical difficulty. In contrast to Mozart, however, Beethoven never pursued a permanent patronage relationship, preferring to maintain his creative and economic independence.

Franz Josef Haydn was eighteen years old when Bach died in 1750 and only beginning to make a career for himself in the new classical style of music. Initially, Haydn attempted a freelance approach to his work as a composer and performer, but ultimately he obtained a position in a noble household and remained there for nearly forty years, working much as Bach had and achieving similar results professionally and personally. With the passing of his patron in 1790, however, Haydn journeyed to

London to once again explore presenting his music directly to the public. His public concerts there were an immense critical and financial success.

Why did this happen? In addition to his talent, Haydn's timing was excellent.

Haydn's career spanned the ending of patronage and the beginning of the paid public concert era. This was particularly important because his work exemplified the taste and symbolized the elite social status of the aristocracy. Many of the arts, goods, and services supported by the members of the emerging middle class in the late 1700s reflected their aspirations to elevated social standing. By the time Haydn traveled to London following the death of Prince Esterhazy, his music embodied those aspirations perfectly.

By recognizing the status attendant upon his specific patronage position and the change in the broader social circumstances around him, Haydn successfully made the transition from an established yet declining business model to the beginnings of a new one. Haydn's career is an excellent example of adaptability, going from success in an existing socioeconomic model to success in an emerging one.

A younger contemporary of Haydn's, Wolfgang Amadeus Mozart, entered the marketplace at an even more challenging time. By 1785, when Mozart met Haydn, the patronage system had deteriorated significantly. Mozart struggled for years—long after Haydn's success in London had suggested an alternative path—to obtain a permanent position in a noble household or a wealthy church.

After Haydn's return from Europe, he specifically advised Mozart to abandon the pursuit of patronage and to take his music directly to the public. The younger man was reluctant to relinquish his dream of working among the elite in his native Austria. Ultimately, despite producing some of the most indisputably brilliant music of the classical era, Mozart died deeply in debt. Though he had the example of Haydn's transition from patronage to entrepreneurship in front of him, Mozart was unwilling to embrace the changing social and economic context in which he produced his own work.

Finally, there is Ludwig van Beethoven, one of the most influential and continuously marketable composers in the history of European art music. Beethoven was fourteen years younger than Mozart and was also acquainted with Haydn. Unlike Mozart, however, Beethoven rejected the patronage model early and completely, preferring to make his own way financially in order to avoid the compromises inherent in being the employee of a single patron.

Beethoven was aided in this enterprise by the continuing expansion of the middle class in Europe and the growth of public concert opportunities. He was also actively engaged in the relatively new business of music publishing. We will examine the history of music printing and publishing in more detail in the next chapter, but it is important to note here that by selling his printed music, Beethoven added a new revenue stream to his work in the traditional fields of performance, composition, and teaching. Though he struggled with publishers and as a result became an early advocate of legal protection for composers, Beethoven was a creatively and financially successful pioneer whose musical genius and professional acumen were recognized by his contemporaries and later generations.

Beethoven: Iconic Brand

Beethoven was extremely well known to his professional contemporaries and the Austrian public at large. His signature mane of hair made him an immediately recognizable and admired figure on the streets of Vienna.

Beethoven's music is widely appreciated today and considered the definitive body of work in the transition from the classical to romantic style periods in western European music. It is also among the most "bankable" body of classical music and among the most frequently programmed of the modern era. Beethoven's music was, for example, ranked first for symphony orchestra programming in the 1980s, 1990s, and the early 2000s.

Beyond the specific value generated by live performances, recordings, and published editions of his music, Beethoven provides considerable symbolic and cultural value as well. Themes from his compositions, such as the "Ode to Joy" from his ninth symphony, have been used films ranging from the Beatles's *Help* to *A Clockwork Orange*.

Beethoven's name and image are often synonymous with classical music and a refined (if now old-fashioned) sensibility. His image is almost ubiquitous in this context, used for stores, coffee shops, T-shirts, and so on. His image has penetrated deeply into popular culture. Charles Schulz's *Charlie Brown* comic strip, a staple of newspaper and animated television specials for over fifty years, featured one character, Schroeder, who performed Beethoven's music on a toy piano, sometimes with the composer's frowning bust sitting on top.

Today, in an era permeated by marketing, we would consider Beethoven's brand to be iconic. Iconic brand status is in many ways the epitome of brand value. Beethoven's name, music, and image represent a very early example—predating by a century the concepts of marketing and branding—of the power and longevity of iconic brand status.

In this text, the primary reason for studying historical musicians and practices is to understand the processes then in play and, more critically, the patterns they potentially represent. Comparing Mozart to Beethoven is an excellent example of how this works. Both were immensely talented musicians who were creative geniuses. Mozart clung to an outdated music business model, perhaps for emotional or sentimental reasons, long after it was evident that it was not working for him. He died young, leaving his family deeply in debt. Beethoven, in contrast, embraced the newest technology (high-volume music printing), the business opportunity it represented, and the socioeconomic realities of his time, using all of it to his advantage.

The decisions of those two composers and the results they produced have implications that go far beyond the classical music scene in Europe around 1800 (see the "Further Consideration" section at the end of this chapter for a more in-depth discussion). Both composers show how larger social and economic conditions can affect musicians and their creative productivity. The following section introduces three socioeconomic concepts that have an ongoing impact on music transactions of all kinds.

OWNERSHIP, ACCESS, AND CAPITAL

Larger socioeconomic realities, like those that Beethoven exploited so successfully, change over time as social, political, and creative trends interact with emerging technologies and business opportunities. There are, however, certain concepts that—regardless of the details associated with them in particular times and places—remain consistently valid for music and musical commerce in general.

These are *ownership, access,* and *capital*. All three are foundational to Western civilization and market-driven societies in general and, as such, to the music business as well. But in addition, because they are all integral to the tensions and synergies among economic reward, public good, and exchange of value across society, they are specifically relevant to the social and economic enterprise of music.

The following overview of the first two—ownership and access—is a brief introduction. These concepts will be explored later in this text in different historical contexts and in reference to various developments in technology, law, and business.

The multiple kinds of capital, however, including their interrelationship and issues of convertibility, are discussed here in more detail.

Though theoretical in nature, the forms of capital framework is extremely useful for "unpacking" the complex, interlocking value-creating structures that define enterprise—especially modern enterprise—in music.

Ownership

Who owns a musical performance? The answer determines who has the right to benefit from presenting it to the public. Once we determine ownership, how do we balance the interests of those who create/perform with those of the audience? As we examine the evolution of copyright and performance rights laws in later chapters, we will see that the answer to "who owns music?" has changed frequently, driven not only by new technologies but also by social change, and through both business and political influence. There is, however, no concept more foundational to value production in music or that cuts across all means of creation, production, distribution, and consumption.

Access

In practice, the issue of ownership is closely related to the concept of access. How access to a given "property" is managed, in terms of both availability and restriction, is critical in every instance in which a musical experience is monetized. Too much access can lead to loss of ownership. Too little access restricts the amount of value—of all kinds—produced.

An English tradition dating from the 1700s provides an illustrative example of the importance of the relationship between ownership and access. The term *commons* refers to jointly owned public lands or natural resources (forests, fisheries, etc.) that are considered to be for the common good. Such land was available for any individual to use (by grazing sheep, or fishing in a river, for example). A critical restriction on common land use was that no one had the right to erect an "enclosure"—that is, a wall or a fence—to restrict the access of others. The act of erecting a fence in and of itself turned common land into private property.

A contrasting perspective comes from the idea of a "market." A traditional market is a place where people with goods to sell and people looking for goods to buy come together. In a market, you can only sell what you already own, that is, something that you have a right to "put a fence around" or otherwise to limit access in exchange for payment or some other consideration.

In music, the concept of the commons has historically been expressed through folk music and family musical traditions such as the lullaby someone sang to you when you were little or the songs people in a given society all know how to sing, such as (in the US) the "Star-Spangled Banner" at sporting events. Accessing these musical commons is, as with the traditional physical commons, normally free of cost.

The majority of musical productivity is, however, market based. In the years preceding print music and records, what musicians "owned" was the musical service they could provide. The only way to "put a fence around" that was to control access by establishing a "pay for play" model. A patron did not acquire the musical skills of a performer or literally own the musician's person. What the patron purchased was access by paying for services. If they wanted those services on a 24/7 basis, they hired the musician as a live-in household servant.

As in any market, there was competition among performers for the better-paying patronage positions, and patrons paid top dollar for the best musicians. Less affluent patrons engaged musical services for shorter terms and, when paid public concerts began to replace patronage entirely, audiences purchased even shorter term access. Managing the relationship and the tensions between ownership and access is foundational to every aspect of music enterprise. Most of the organizational structures, legal frameworks, and mediating technologies that developed over the course of the late nineteenth, twentieth, and so far in the twenty-first centuries developed in the context (and contributed to the evolution) of the ownership-access relationship.

Having considered the basics of how ownership and access are interrelated in a system of value exchange, we need to understand the actual mechanism of exchange. Musicians have performed for beer, food, lodging, and recognition, as well as—naturally—money. While any and all of the above may be involved in a given transaction, by far the most convenient and efficient medium of exchange for sustaining musical enterprise over time is money, or to be more economically precise, capital.

Capital

In any market-based economic system, *capital* is a foundational concept. Informally, we think of capital as money or cash. From an economic perspective, capital refers to the accumulated resources available for one's use. That can of course include money, but also refers to other assets and their value—particularly the usefulness of those assets for producing more capital. For example, a high-quality guitar is an asset with a cash value. But, in addition, for a professional guitarist, the guitar is a capital asset that, through use in paid public performances, can produce more capital.

Certainly monetary capital is relevant to music-based transactions. Professional musicians invest their time and effort in producing music in the hopes of receiving money in return. That money can be used for the benefit of their music, their families, and themselves. Even great musicians have to pay for housing, food, clothing, and so on. Time and energy spent preparing for and performing music is time that cannot be spent making money in other ways. So, in a very real sense, unless independently wealthy, the professional musician must be concerned with establishing and sustaining a business. Put another way, professional music making is, with very few exceptions, a capitalistic endeavor.

There is more to understanding the music enterprise, however, than appreciating the monetary aspect of capital. According to cultural theorist Pierre Bourdieu, fully understanding how the social world works (and, remember, the social realm is the only place where music enterprise can exist) depends on understanding not only economic but also social and cultural forms of capital, as well as the interrelationships among them.[6]

Economic Capital

Economic capital refers to money or assets that are directly convertible to money, or property rights that have a measurable monetary value. In music enterprise this can be measured by sales figures for tickets, recordings, or merchandise, as well as (in the modern era) the value of copyrights held and the back catalog of previously released music. The material resources that support the production of these things (instruments, recording equipment, studios, etc.) are also capital.

Social Capital

Social capital is based on the number of people in your social network and the resources they are willing to place at your disposal—in short, the "who you know" phenomenon. Any social network can be measured by both the number of connections and the value of the interconnected resources.

One example of a large-scale utilization of social capital would be the We Are the World project. In 1985, celebrity performers Michael Jackson and Lionel Ritchie, along with prominent producers Quincy Jones and Michael Omartian, brought together dozens of musical artists to donate their talent and celebrity in support of famine relief in Africa.[7] Appeals for participation were made using social connections and, while there was some recognition value in participating, no one received monetary compensation for the recording session (and video), as all the proceeds from the sale of the CDs were earmarked for charity.

Social capital is thus convertible into economic capital, both directly in the form of mass sales to fans who are "in the network" of the artist and indirectly in the form of influence and access to noncash resources.

An additional form of social capital that has emerged since 2005 is found in social media such as Facebook. On that platform, "Friends" and "Likes" have become a symbolic currency that can contribute to both social and professional success. As we will see in chapters 10 and 11, newer social media platforms offer even more explicit ways to connect and convert social to economic forms of capital.

Cultural Capital

Cultural capital exists, according to Bourdieu, in three forms: enduring attitudes or feelings (the way fans relate to favorite performers over time); physical artifacts and the values we attach to them ("classic" albums like *Dark Side of the Moon* or *OK Computer,* for example); and objective forms of recognition (such as Grammy awards, gold or platinum records, honorary degrees, and so on).

Like social capital, cultural capital is convertible into economic capital. A performer can, for example, use a song or name/image to endorse a product. In 2010, country singer Martina McBride joined with Sunny Delight Beverages in their Time to Shine marketing campaign, which was coordinated with the artist's Shine All Night tour.

According to the news release announcing the marketing partnership: "'SunnyD is delighted to be partnering with Martina McBride for the Time to Shine promotion,' says Mark Ozimek, assistant brand manager for SunnyD. 'This partnership is a great fit as it brings together two enduring, spirited brands that encourage children to achieve their best.'"[8] The company used McBride's cultural capital to enhance its own brand and increase sales. McBride was compensated for her appearance (economic capital) and received additional public exposure by appearing in the commercials (cultural and social capital).

Another example of capital conversion is performance artist Amanda Palmer's leveraging of her "hipster" cachet (cultural capital) into social capital (fans connecting with fans to promote and attend her performances) and economic capital (voluntary donations for concerts and records as well as feeding and housing the artist on tour).

Celebrity Capital

As noted in the McBride and Palmer examples, having celebrity status— being a celebrity—can generate value on its own. It might be argued that because it is related to status, celebrity is a form of cultural capital. But celebrity status also has an effect on the social network comprising the celebrity's fans. Most fundamentally, the greater the degree of celebrity, the larger the fan base becomes. Beyond that, being a fan and being a consumer of celebrity-branded products—including knowing about them and being known as a person who knows—can also confer status on the consumer.

Obviously, there is a difference between being a consumer of prestige products and embodying that prestige oneself. In 2012, for example, the "cool kids" knew about Troye Sivan's YouTube channel, but that didn't make them Troye Sivan or afford them his resources.[9]

Sivan's fans are a resource that belongs to him, just as Martina McBride's fans are a resource she contributed to her partnership with Sunny D. But without the secondary, "shared" celebrity experience of consumers, it is unlikely that being famous could be used to produce the same amount of value. And that is a value that cannot be expressed exclusively in terms of either social or cultural capital; it is a hybrid of both.

Whether one considers celebrity capital as a subset of cultural capital or a separate form, it is clear that celebrity significantly impacts the music marketplace, and—as later chapters will discuss—has done so for centuries. If nothing else, celebrity is an expression of the relationship between performer and audience—another product of the transactional music experience.

Limits to Convertibility

While cultural, social, and celebrity capital are convertible to economic capital, it does not necessarily work the other way around. Even established musical artists with heavy economic support from their labels do not necessarily get popular or critical support for a given album or tour. For example, both Madonna's *MDNA* and Lady Gaga's *Artpop* albums logged precipitous sales declines after the first week— 86.7 percent for Madonna and 82 percent for Gaga—as well as many negative reviews. Critical reactions to *Artpop,* for example, ranged from "it's a decent, if flawed, pop album" and "it's hard not to feel under-whelmed by *Artpop*—but then, that's the danger of hype," to "a bizarre album of squelchy disco."[10]

The reasons for the relative "failure" of *Artpop* are complex, includ-ing the evolution of music delivery systems since Lady Gaga's previous release, as well as changes in her creative approach. But the results them-selves are hard to dispute. Despite a $25 million promotional budget, sales of only 258,000 in the first week, though decent, were significantly less than sales of her previous album. That number, plus the sharp decline in the second week, were discussed at the time as a disaster and even rumored to be the cause of layoffs at her label, Interscope.

Lady Gaga publicly dismissed that rumor, stating there was "no truth" to it, nor to the rumored $25 million losses.[11] But by mid-2014, even though it was apparent that the poor financial performance of *Artpop* had been exaggerated, the album still represented a financial disappointment for Interscope and a public relations disaster for all involved.

Sharp declines in album sales in the second week are typically consid-ered an indication of bad word of mouth among fans and thus a possible measure of declining social capital. From a similar perspective, negative or even mixed critical response is an indicator of diminishing cultural status. Not only did Lady Gaga and her label Interscope fail to get a reasonable return on their material capital investment, but *Artpop* also damaged her social and cultural capital portfolios.

Today, new technologies and social media platforms offer novel ways to connect artists with audiences. As we will see in later chapters, the principle of using music to generate social and cultural capital and then converting them to economic capital remains valid, despite changing technological tools.

Another possible exception to the convertibility principle is the celeb-rity capital that accrues from being well known and frequently "hit" on digital social media. This type of capital appears more difficult to convert to the economic variety than earlier, nonmediated types. There are undoubtedly a variety of reasons for this, but one we must consider is that, at least in music, people are demonstrating real reluctance to change from "liking" an artist to "paying for" access to an artist's work.

An example of this phenomenon (from the summer of 2014) is found in the YouTube posting of OneRepublic's "Counting Stars" (2013). As of June 11, 2014, the official video, uploaded to the YouTube channel, VEVO, had been viewed 314,933,885 times, with 1,443,689 likes and 40,148 dislikes. Obviously, if nearly 315 million viewer/listeners had paid ninety-nine cents at the iTunes or Amazon music stores for the chance to hear the song, sales would have been astonishing (platinum times 300+).

In fact, however, as of the end 2014, the song had "only" 5.3 million sales in the US and a million or so more internationally. Those are significant sales and far outpace the YouTube "likes," but fall far short of the "hits" for this one posting on a single site. While not everyone who checks out a song on YouTube can be expected to buy a copy, the fact that roughly 95 percent of the YouTube viewer/listeners did not go on to buy this song seems like a significant number.

The type of cultural capital defined by "hits" on social media, therefore, appears to have less potential to directly attract economic capital than winning a Grammy or VMA award, or even the opportunity to perform "live" on such an award show. That said, the aggregate recognition of chart placements, international gold/platinum albums, and social media popularity can be seen as having an impact on live touring. Certainly OneRepublic thought so, citing the popularity of the "Counting Stars" video as the reason they expanded their summer 2014 tour from sixteen to twenty-seven dates.[12]

To summarize this discussion of capital, *economic* capital includes money and other tangible assets. This is "real" capital, while all other forms are "symbolic." *Social* capital is embodied in the resources of the people in a social network that are available for the use of others. *Cultural* capital is embodied in a person (social status, celebrity), an object (Rolls-Royce, Rolex, Louboutin, etc.), or an institution (a Grammy award, a degree from Harvard, etc.). *Celebrity* capital is a hybrid of the social and cultural forms and is threaded throughout music production and reception in most eras, as well as across the majority of musical genres.

Most forms of enterprise in music are hybrid in terms of the capital that they generate. This is the result of both the complexity of human motivation ("I want to make music that is meaningful to me, that other people like, and pay me for") and the convertibility of capital—within the constraints discussed here—from one form to another.

FORMS OF VALUE AND SYNERGY

Comparable to the forms of capital, the value created by music comes in various forms: artistic, social, and economic. Like capital, musical value is also convertible from one form to another. But even more than conversion, musical value is synergistic. Without the presence of all three forms—artistic, social, economic—a musical venture rarely succeeds and is never sustainable. With powerful artistry, social impact, and economic stability, the art lasts longer, more people enjoy and benefit from it, and more economic value is created for the artist and the larger economy.

As we go forward, you are encouraged to look not only for all the forms of value being created in a particular context, but also for the synergistic relationships among them. In its most fundamental form, the musical experience is a transaction between performer and listener. But the value it is capable of producing is both widely varied and incredibly complex.

CORE PRINCIPLES

Music enterprise becomes possible when musical experience is an exchange between people.

OPERATIVE DYNAMICS

Musical experience as transaction

KEY CONCEPTS

Forms of value: artistic, social, economic

Transactional frameworks: performance, composition, education

Performance transaction models: touring, tourism, patronage

Cost-benefit factors in performance models

Patronage

Artist/employee

Artist/entrepreneur

Middle class: social and economic implications for music

Socioeconomic concepts: ownership, access, capital

Forms of capital: economic, social, cultural, celebrity

Convertibility and synergy: capital and value

FURTHER CONSIDERATION

Multiple Forms of Value and Synergy

Called the "face of fusion philanthropy" by the *New York Times,* Bono and his band, U2, have used their celebrity status to support a number of humanitarian causes, including global hunger, human rights, and debt relief. Of the three forms of capital—economic, social, and cultural—which is most important to a social/political enterprise like this? Could similar results be achieved without any of the three? Why or why not?

See Tom Zeller Jr., "Trying to Throw His Arms around the World," *New York Times* 11-13–2006), http://www.nytimes.com/2006/11/13/us/13bono.html?_r = o.

Learning from Mozart and Beethoven

What lessons can the careers of Mozart and Beethoven teach us? Students sometimes wonder about what it would take to start a record label today. If you are thinking of starting a record label or other music-based enterprise, consider the following:

Are you clinging to a familiar but outdated conception of music business, perhaps for sentimental reasons?

Or are you thinking: "Record labels are dead. I need to engage the newest technology and align my enterprise with current socioeconomic realities and apply my creativity accordingly"?

Are you being Mozart or Beethoven in your approach? Which do you want to be?

CHAPTER 2

Transience to Permanence

Once music ceases to be ephemeral—always disappearing—
and becomes instead material . . . it leaves the condition of
traditional music and enters the condition of painting. It
becomes a painting, existing as material in space, not
immaterial in time.

—Brian Eno

As a time-bound art form, for centuries music could only exist in the moment, as it was being performed and heard. In order to have a musical experience, it was necessary to be present while someone was making music. This reality fostered both musical amateurism (as a matter of, if nothing else, convenience) and professionalism—performers, composers, and teachers—to provide the services necessary to create musical experiences for the nonmusician.

Most if not all forms of human productivity—including music—can be divided into two broad categories: *goods* and *services*. Goods are physical things. Goods can be touched. Goods can be transferred in an instant, from one person to another. Services are intangible. Services are provided through the actions of people. Services are typically not transferred, but rather provided over time. For example, scissors are a good, while a haircut is a service.

The musical activities of performing, composing, and teaching are services. Their revenue-generating potential can be realized only through the actions of musicians providing services over time to listeners, other musicians, and students. There have been music-related goods—musical instruments, for example—for many centuries, but because musical experience depended upon performance, it was primarily service based. The musical experience facilitated by that service was transient and ephemeral. A musical experience in the context of live performance does not last forever. Once it is over, it is gone.

CATCHING THE EPHEMERAL

The earliest attempts to capture the fleeting experience of music and render it more permanent were based on creating a written record of what was (or was about to be) performed. Music notation systems made it possible for music—or at least some of the elements of music (pitch, rhythm, and pacing, for example)—to be transcribed onto paper or other physical media to facilitate later performance.

Not every culture developed notational methods for music; many were primarily improvisational or relied upon memorization. But where notation did develop, copies of written music became musical goods, facilitative of, yet separate from, performance.

An economic principle applicable to all goods and services, including music notation, is the assumption that the consumer receives some utility from using them. In this sense, "utility" is associated with human wants and needs and the things or people that can fulfill them. Performers, for example, fulfilled the needs of listeners in search of musical experience by providing the service of performing.

For copies of notated music to become economically viable goods, two conditions had to be met:

· A system of musical notation widely enough adopted by musicians to provide a sufficient customer base
· A practical, cost-effective means to produce enough copies to satisfy customer demand

It took centuries for these two elements to develop and align. Initially, most musicians could not read or interpret musical notation. Further, multiple locally based systems of notation developed for those who could. Handwritten music copies were time-consuming to produce.

Ultimately, music printing provided part of the solution and helped to transform the music business, just as text printing transformed the business of the written word. Beyond facilitating the establishment of the publishing business, however, Gutenberg's invention of the printing press is often said to have "changed history," "changed society," or "changed the world."[1] Understanding what "changing the world" means and, more specifically, what it might mean as applied to music printing, requires more than acknowledging the technological innovation involved.

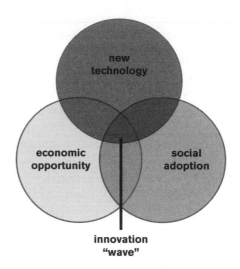

FIGURE 3. Innovation synergy model.

INNOVATION SYNERGY: "WAVES"

For technology to truly matter—to be able to "change the world"—it is necessary for there to be an appropriate synergy of technology with social and economic conditions, all present at the same time and on an appropriate scale.

One way to understand this synergistic relationship comes from the Media Laboratory at MIT. In 2003, Andrew Lippman and David Reed (Media Lab researchers), writing about viral (rapidly spreading, Internet-based) communications, stated: "Innovation often comes in waves when the social and economic environments synchronize around a technologically primed opportunity."[2]

That observation came as part of an analysis of "game-changing" technologies, specifically, the capacity of Internet-based media to make information "go viral." But it is clear that the analysis could apply to anything that fundamentally affects the way people understand and interact with the world. One way to look at this concept is with a Venn diagram (see figure 3).

What happens when the innovation "wave" concept is applied to the music business models prevalent in Europe during the eighteenth century? The 1700s marked the end of the absolute power of the European aristocracy and the rise of a merchant class. That group—comprising people with money, but without a noble name—became the class "in the middle" between the aristocrats and peasants.

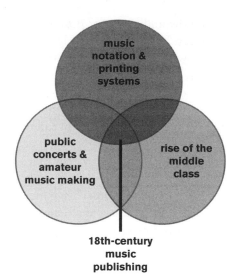

18th-century music publishing

FIGURE 4. Innovation synergy: music publishing.

For musicians, this new group represented economic opportunities: they did not hire household staff musicians, but they did buy tickets to concerts, take music lessons, and would become the customers for printed music. Without the emergence of a class of people with money and the desire to "elevate" their status socially, the invention of mass-production technology for music printing would not have spawned a music publishing industry. This, then, is a social environment synchronized with an economic condition creating a "primed" environment for a new technology: music printing.

Consequently, mapping eighteenth-century developments onto the MIT model to explain the "explosion" of music publishing during that century produces the following: music notational systems and printing achieved viability (*emerging technology*) as middle-class desires for music education and experience rose (*social adoption*), and coincided with increased public demand for professional and amateur concerts and music lessons (*economic opportunity*). It was, in effect, a "perfect storm" of opportunity, a "wave" of innovation that changed the world for music makers and consumers (see figure 4).

This innovation synergy also aligns with the three forms of value necessary for a sustainable music enterprise: artistic value, social benefit, and economic viability (see chapter 1). In terms of artistic productivity, music printing increased opportunities for the creative work of composers to reach performers and thus the public more broadly. Socially, music students, amateur performers, and the audiences for professional performances benefited from greater access to the work of highly talented composers. Economically, the growth of amateur performance supported by professional music lessons, along with paid public concerts, dramatically expanded the market for musical experience.

The congruence of large-scale innovation synergies with the internal processes of music enterprise is a critical predictor of success or failure. Over the past two centuries, as social and economic conditions aligned and re-aligned with emerging technologies, the complex system that is the music business adapted internally. The adaptation strategies that optimize good music, social value, and economic resources have inevitably been the most successful. Both the larger scale alignment—the innovation "wave" itself—and the internal optimization are processes. Some process elements happen by design (the invention of movable type for music), some are coincidental (the decline of patronage around the time musical type is perfected), and some are the "organic" results of complex intentional and situational factors (the intersecting circles of the innovation diagram shown in figure 4).

Recognizing that a complex process is in play—not historically, but in real time—is an essential entrepreneurial skill. Understanding that intentional actions can align with or even direct that process is even more critical. At the highest level of entrepreneurial expertise comes the ability to determine how and when to act to produce a specific outcome.

For example, in late 1999 and for several years thereafter, the recording industry was in crisis. The appearance of the online file-sharing service Napster appeared to threaten the economic framework for music production, distribution, and consumption. Napster was an innovation that involved a huge selection of popular music, available at no cost, to an eager global audience. It was indisputably an innovation wave.

In order to align internally with this external wave, the record industry would have needed to find a way to respond to the artistic value (huge selection of popular music), social value (individual songs, on demand, accessible anywhere with an Internet connection), and economic incentive (free). That solution was forthcoming, but it was not provided by the labels themselves. It came from Apple in the form of the iTunes store.

The file-sharing era and the impact of the iTunes store are discussed in more detail in chapter 10, "Digitization." Here, it is important to understand that despite the organic nature of innovation synergies and the inherent adaptive qualities of the complex music production and distribution system, that system can be affected by intelligent action.

The process elements that led to the establishment of the music publishing industry in the eighteenth century and some of the entrepreneurs who "gamed the system" to make that happen are discussed below.

MUSIC ECONOMICS: PRINTING, PUBLISHING, PIRACY, AND PROTECTION

The practice of music notation, which was foundational to the development of music printing, was motivated by practical goals: to reduce dependence on memorization, to facilitate more efficient performance preparation, and to improve consistency from performance to performance. In addition, notated music made it easier to deal with issues arising from progressively larger performing ensembles and the more complex music characteristics of patronage-supported situations.

The elite few musicians supported by the patronage system were the most literate and technically sophisticated professionals in Europe. For centuries, these were the performers who found the greatest utility in written or printed music. In contrast, the majority of professional musicians played and sang traditional and less formal music that was not notated, nor could the performers typically read such notation.

Given the narrow distribution of music notation literacy across the population of professional musicians, there was, for a long time, very little incentive to produce printed music on a large scale. In fact, even by the late 1400s, when the printing press was already the primary means of producing and distributing literary and educational texts, music was still primarily handwritten for a select clientele of performers.

The slow adoption of printed music was not just the result of low demand. There were many incompatible systems of music notation, often locally developed and used, each of which would have required a specialized process to print, adding to cost and reducing market size. Further, while there are only twenty-six letters in the alphabet and some dozens more special symbols, there are hundreds and hundreds of musical symbols, and most of them are variable. It was not until the 1700s, some 250 years after movable type was established for text printing, that music font sets became widely available.

By then, as the technology reached a point of practical efficiency and a single notational system had been widely adopted, the professional music world was changing in other ways as well. The conditions were primed for the emergence of a new technology-driven model for music production and consumption.

Printing: Technology and Business

The critical technology for music printing to become a viable business was musical type. Due to the complexity of musical notation compared to alphanumeric text, a comparably practical movable type for music took much longer to develop. Earlier attempts to create alternatives to handwritten music included woodcut techniques that could produce both visually appealing and easily replicable product. Woodcuts were, however, a skill-intensive technology.[3] Engraving came next, using metal rather than wood as a medium, but it was also skill and time intensive to produce.[4]

A practical solution for movable music type was provided by printers Breitkopf in Germany and Caslon in Great Britain in the late 1700s. It was the Breitkopf movable type system that became the industry standard and, because that system made large-scale production possible, the Breitkopf company was positioned to become one of the first and most successful publishers of music.[5]

But even as musical type was increasingly adopted in the late 1700s and refined in the 1800s, engraving remained important because it could be used to add graphic and decorative elements to printed music. Regardless of the technology for producing the music itself—woodcuts, engraving, or movable type—it was consistently observed that having artistic elements, including drawings and decoration, added value to printed music and increased sales.[6]

The final music printing technology to consider is lithography. Lithography, which uses stone as a printing medium, made multi-color printing practical. The development of photolithography was the final technological piece necessary to support the mass production of musical copies. With the photographic system, instead of needing to engrave a stone by hand, a photo could be taken of a previously engraved image and transferred to a light-sensitive stone or metal plate.[7] Photolithography thus became the basis for the high-speed mass production necessary for the growth of a music publishing industry. By the late nineteenth century, music publishing in Europe and North America was generating annual revenues in the millions of dollars.

Publishing: Aggregating Creativity and Commerce

Because of the primacy of the Breitkopf type fonts for music, music publishing was established first in Germany. Bernard Christoph Breitkopf was a printer who founded his printing and publishing company in Leipzig in 1719. His son, Johann Gottlob Breitkopf, was responsible for the improvements to music typesetting noted previously. By the second half of the 1700s, Breitkopf was the publisher for most major European composers and the most sought after by aspiring ones.[8]

In 1795, the firm was sold to Gottfried Christoph Härtel, who added his name to the company masthead. Breitkopf and Härtel are among the most prominent names in music publishing even today. Härtel was the first to envision putting out "complete works" of composers and under his guidance, Breitkopf and Härtel published many artistically and historically significant collections. In addition, Härtel directed the company to begin manufacturing pianos, as he correctly understood the rapidly increasing importance of that instrument to middle-class consumers. The particular genius of this decision was that the company was positioned to sell both the "hardware" (the piano) and the "apps" (the music to be played on it).

It was also Härtel who worked with Beethoven—often frustrating the composer—as he established his career as a performer, conductor, and composer independent of the patronage system. The correspondence between the two men is illustrative of the time, but also of the enduring possibilities and constraints inherent in music publishing. Beethoven constantly sought to place more works with the publisher at a higher royalty rate. Härtel countered by declining to publish works for which he perceived lesser public demand and negotiated fees downward whenever possible. The only aspect of their negotiations that could not equally apply to composer-publisher communications in the late twentieth and early twenty-first centuries is the fact that they were using the physical postal service to communicate.[9]

Competing publishers soon challenged the primacy of Breitkopf and Härtel. Their early advantages were quickly erased by new publishing technologies and the willingness (and technology-facilitated capability) of some publishing houses to replicate already published editions. As publishing houses appeared in greater numbers not only in Germany but also in France and England, music publishing became one of the most competitive business sectors of the nineteenth century.

The expansion and profitability of music publishing reveal the power of *aggregation*. For example, while individual composers could and did benefit from their work being widely distributed, their ability to generate revenue through publishing was constrained by their own capacity to produce compositions (and support them by public performances, an essential element of publishing success). Publishers, by contrast, could make contractual agreements with dozens, if not hundreds, of individual composers and profit from all of them, leaving the time-consuming business of creation and performance to the composer and associated performers.

> A capacity to aggregate the productivity of many music creators confers a competitive advantage. Aggregating listeners/consumers increases that advantage.

The aggregation of creative productivity is a core principle of music enterprise. Aggregation remains a key strategic advantage for music publishers today, but it is also applicable to record labels, concert promoters, and all broadcast and Internet-based media, as well as digital download and streaming music services. When institutions have the capacity to aggregate listeners and consumers as well as music, a dominant competitive advantage tends to emerge. Breitkopf and Härtel held this advantage in the early 1800s but, as in every era, this advantage dissipated as a result of competition, emerging technologies, and changing social behaviors.

Over the course of the 1800s, music publishing became the first music industry worthy of the name, with massive international sales, hundreds of publishers, and publishing houses in every European country and North America. In the first twenty-five years of that century, American music publishers alone printed over ten thousand individual pieces of music. By the 1890s that number was over twenty thousand songs annually. The first million-selling piece of sheet music, "After the Ball," by Charles K. Harris, was published by the Oliver Ditson Company in Boston in 1893. Business was booming, but a serious threat to nineteenth-century music publishers—not only those in Germany, but everywhere—loomed: piracy.

Publishing and Piracy

If we informally define *piracy* as the appropriation of things that don't belong to you and *pirate* as a person who commits the act, it becomes apparent that these terms are broadly synonymous with *stealing* and *thief.* One can speculate as to the reason theft of intellectual property came to be labeled "piracy," but what we know is that it has been used in this way since the 1700s and dates from a period of debate in England in which control of the publishing industry was hotly contested.

In his book *Piracy*, Adrian Johns observes that "the contest came at a turning point in European history. It was a time in which medieval forms of politics and culture were being confronted by newer, potentially revolutionary alternatives." Among these alternatives, Johns lists changes to public life that resulted from the wide adoption of print and the growth of the commercial economy.

"Not least—and not coincidentally," Johns continues, "the golden age of Caribbean buccaneering was about to begin: the era of Blackbeard . . . and Captain Kidd." Taken together, these forces not only sparked a debate about the ownership and control of intellectual property but also "ignited a furious and fundamental conflict about politics, property, and print. Its consequences are still with us. The concept of piracy was one of them."[10]

By the late 1800s, the damage from piracy to the music publishing industry was considerable. In 1881, for example, the Music Publishers Association in Britain "estimated that 90 percent of printed sheet music coming into England from America consisted of pirated reprints of English copyrights."[11] Australian and Canadian "pirates" were also active in the appropriation of music published in England. Lawsuits initiated by individual publishers were often based on the discovery of hundreds of thousands, and in some cases millions, of illegal copies of printed music.[12]

The response of publishers to the vast scale of print music piracy was both collective and individual. One of the first British publishing firms to act against piracy was Francis, Day, and Hunter. According to Johns, one of the owners, David Day, "hired the services of a detective agency and raided a piratical warehouse himself, seizing 500 copies of pirated sheet music."[13] Subsequent raids by Day and his agents yielded thousands more. The success of these raids inspired Day to establish the Musical Copyright Association, an organization that launched an "offensive that would skirt the fringes of illegality, that would pursue tactics soon disowned even by the MCA's own lawyers, and that would depend for its success on the reluctance of the pirates to have recourse to the courts."[14]

The raids soon turned into violent conflicts; one result was a growing disapproval among the public of what were seen as overly aggressive tactics by music publishers. Even within the music business, there were those who saw the pirates as a potential blessing for music retailers and the public in that their copies were much less expensive than the authorized ones. In addition, the public was made aware of the disproportionately small share of revenues received by composers for their published work. "The *Evening Standard,* for example, recalled how, at a time when 'pirated craft cruise through the main and other thoroughfares of the metropolis,' Strauss's Blue Danube had made £100,000 for its publisher in just one year but, Strauss had pocketed only £40."[15]

As a consequence, at the end of the 1800s the print music industry had even greater problems than piracy: collaborators who found their share of revenue inadequate and a public view of publishers as greedy, overly aggressive, and unconcerned about either the art of music or the public good. The parallels with record labels and the Recording Industry Association of America (RIAA) in the late 1900s are striking and, unsurprisingly, industry responses to piracy then and now came to include both public relations campaigns and legal action.

Foundations and Early Development of Music Copyright Law

Much as the technologies for printing music lagged behind those for printing text, so did legal protection for composers as compared to authors. Some of the reasons for the delay are based on differing legal structures from country to country. And, much as conditions in Germany favored the development of music publishing, so copyright law began in England.

The history of English copyright begins with royal licenses granted to printers. Under this system, only certain printers had permission to print official documents. In 1557, the crown granted the Worshipful Company of Stationers of London a monopoly on printing.[16] The monopoly and thus that company's prominent position among printers remained intact through several reigns.

In the early years of the 1700s, Parliament undertook a series of revisions to the laws pertaining to publishing and directly relating to the royal license for printing. The main thrust of this work was to consider, for the first time, the rights of authors as opposed to those of printers. One aspect of this consideration was to reduce the term for which printers held exclusive publishing rights of a given work. The resulting law, the "Statute of Anne," enacted in 1710, vested all rights of ownership in the authors themselves. It was not until 1777, however, that the courts ruled that musical works specifically fell under the provisions of the statute.[17]

The Statute of Anne was foundational to the development of copyright law in the US, and several key provisions of the original statute were incorporated by American lawmakers. The Copyright Act of 1790 referred to "useful" works being eligible for copyright protection, but not music specifically. It was not until the Copyright Act Revision of 1831 that music compositions were specifically added to the law. Understanding the evolution of copyright as applied to music—specifically, why music was protected so much later than text—involves looking more deeply into the intellectual and practical history of copyright law in general.

The first laws concerning "intellectual property" were, as you might expect, based on tangible property law. A basic principle for understanding the legal history of physical property is that the emergence and increasing complexity of property law followed the increased value (and perception of value) for that property. In other words, the more value property has and the greater economic resource it represents, the more laws are created around it.

As stated by Carroll in "The Struggle for Music Copyright":

> From this . . . perspective, copyright would apply to music at the point in time when music's value as a resource had risen sufficiently to make the administrative costs of copyright socially worthwhile. The reader may well ask how music functions as a resource. Most people experience music either by listening to or playing it, and music's value increases when people, on average, value more highly these experiences.[18]

Thus, for the period under consideration in this chapter—the late eighteenth and early nineteenth centuries—the value of printed music would have been seen as limited as long as the market for printed music was confined to a relatively small population of professional musicians serving an elite clientele under the patronage system. But, as the demand for the consumption of musical experiences increased significantly—facilitated in part by printed music—the perceived value of musical experience also rose, leading to the emergence of copyright laws that specifically included music.

Pursuing this line of thought about valuation, Carroll continues:

> To measure such an increase in value, economists look for data showing a willingness and ability to pay higher prices or a larger share of one's financial resources for musical experiences. An economist looks not only at prices of direct musical experience, such as the price of concert tickets, but also at the prices of all inputs into musical experience, including musical instruments, musical education, and, most importantly for our purposes, new musical compositions to play or to hear.[19]

From this perspective, it should not be surprising that the music publishing business was already well established before copyright protections for music were enacted. If Carroll's analysis is correct, it was only after measurable evidence of the economic value of music was established over the course of the eighteenth century that music copyright laws *could* appear. This is an ongoing phenomenon that in explains, at least in part, why copyright laws evolve slowly as new technologies appear, changing music production and consumption patterns.

Looking back to the eighteenth century, we must note that in terms of value-producing potential, performance was considered integral to the music publishing business. In part, this was based on the practical value of public performance to promote interest in printed music. Beyond that, it was also based on patterns established during the patronage era, when virtually all composers were also professional performers, with performances generating a significant part of their revenue.

The perspective that performance drove value creation led composers to view early copyright law differently from text authors, who depended on book sales rather than public readings. Increasing numbers of paid public concerts in the eighteenth century further complicated the issue. Increased performance opportunities and the income they produced further obscured—at least for performers—the value of publishing and the importance of copyright law to their own professional productivity.

In contrast, for music publishers, professional performance served little purpose other than to advertise printed music. The widely held view of the time was that novelty was what sold printed music to the general public, based on the reasonable assumption that no one needed multiple copies of the same piece of music. As noted by Carroll: "Consequently, success in the music publishing business required speed, an acute sense for changing tastes, and little regard for proprietary claims of rivals or composers."[20]

Thus, though as a practical matter it was clear that publishing, composition, and performance were interconnected, an adversarial relationship between composers and publishers was a foundational characteristic of the music business of the late eighteenth century and throughout the nineteenth century.

Professional Protective Organizations

Ongoing conflicts of interest between publishers and composers were a widely recognized phenomenon in the late nineteenth and early twentieth centuries, not least because of the potential negative effect on the public interest. In the US, for example, the 1909 revision of US copyright law (see below) specifically addressed the issue of balance among the rights of publishers, composers, and the public. As later chapters will reveal, this balance would need to be adjusted and readjusted a number of times up to and including the present day.[21]

In addition to much needed changes to copyright law, professional protective organizations for both publishers and composers were established during the decades after and prior to 1900. The Music Publisher Association in Britain was established in 1881. Unlike David Day's somewhat renegade MCA, the MPA employed legal means to protect its member companies' interests.

Tin Pan Alley publishers formed the Music Publishers Association of the United States in 1895, unsuccessfully lobbying the US Congress to extend the term of copyright for published music from twenty-four to forty years and to be renewable for twenty-eight instead of fourteen years. The MPA remains today an influential voice for the interests of music publishers.

In 1914, several highly successful and influential American popular music composers, including Victor Herbert, Irving Berlin, and John Philip Sousa, founded the first performing rights organization (PRO), the American Society for Composers, Authors, and Publishers (ASCAP). Its purpose was to create a professional association to "assure that music creators are fairly compensated for the public performance of their works, and that their rights are properly protected." ASCAP and its counterpart, the British Performing Rights Society (also founded in 1914), had an immediate impact by improving the collection of music royalties for composers; both organizations remain active and important in the music industry today.

MUSIC PUBLISHING IN THE UNITED STATES
US Copyright Law

The 1909 revision to US copyright law broadened the scope of what could be copyrighted to all works of original authorship (including musical compositions) and extended the renewal term from fourteen to twenty-eight years.[22] Congress specifically responded to concerns about musical authorship and the need to balance public access with the rights of composers:

> The main object to be desired in expanding copyright protection accorded to music has been to give the composer an adequate return for the value of his

composition, and it has been a serious and difficult task to combine the protection of the composer with the protection of the public, and to so frame an
act that it would accomplish the double purpose of securing to the composer
an adequate return for all use made of his composition and at the same time
prevent the formation of oppressive monopolies, which might be founded
upon the very rights granted to the composer for the purpose of protecting
his interests.[23]

The 1909 law was foundational to the concept of ownership in the music
business in the early twentieth century. Note particularly the expression
"all use made of his composition." The flexibility of this language allowed
for any use created by emerging technologies to be covered by this law.
One result was that there were no changes to US copyright law until
adjustments in 1961–1962 and then major overhauls in 1973 and 1976
(see chapter 6, "Massification"). Consequently, the 1909 law governed
copyright issues throughout the first half of the twentieth century, during
a period explosive growth in both the recorded and broadcast music
industries.

Since expansions to copyright law are typically preceded by a rise in
the value and perception of value for the intellectual property in question, it should be no surprise that the years immediately preceding the
1909 copyright revision were a time of remarkable productivity and
rising profits for music publishers in the US. This was the era when New
York became the center of music publishing, particularly in the district
that came to be known as Tin Pan Alley.

Tin Pan Alley and the Sheet Music Industry

The place where the business of composers and publishers intersected in
the United States was called Tin Pan Alley, a nickname for the music
publishing district in New York, located on West Twenty-Eighth Street
between Fifth and Sixth Avenues. The area was established, unofficially,
in 1885 when a number of music publishers opened offices to follow the
movement of theatrical productions to that part of the city.

The origins of the district's name are attributed to the discordant
sound made by the many pianos in various offices and buildings all
playing different tunes. While there were publishing companies elsewhere, those in Tin Pan Alley became so powerful that they would (for
a percentage of royalties) produce and distribute music for regional
publishing firms, and their approach to creating and marketing popular
songs became the standard for the music industry.

The Tin Pan Alley process began with songwriters hired by publishers to be "on staff." Staff writers gave the publisher exclusive rights to publish their works—an example of what is called "work for hire" under copyright law.[24] Because publishers carefully tracked sales figures for popular songs, they directed their songwriters to either work in a general style or even imitate a specific, highly successful song. Next, songs would be "tested" with performers and listeners and their reactions noted. Only songs that tested well were published

Once published, sheet music was distributed to music shops in cities around the country. New sheet music songs were performed live in many shops by "song pluggers" in order to let potential customers hear the music and serve as a friendly, encouraging sales force. These techniques, including market research and "focus group" testing (before the term was invented), make it apparent that the music publishing models of the 1800s were being replaced by a highly organized mass-production business system.

Not everyone was pleased with the sophistication of this business model. William Fisher, for example, stated in 1933:

> The Alley's strident songs and nervous dance tunes, its blurbs and ballads and banalities are as evanescent as the encircling smoke in which they are ground out in accordance with constantly changing recipes. In one essential however, there is no change, for this frankly commercial pursuit involves a ceaseless and eager following of the taste of the crowd—the indiscriminate and undiscriminating crowd—an inseparable part of the American scene.[25]

Tin Pan Alley publishers were eager and effective at "following the taste" of the American public, including the rising demand for amateur music performance in the home. The song "After the Ball," written by Charles K. Harris and published by the Oliver Ditson Company in 1892, is an early example of the economic power of Tin Pan Alley. Harris paid a popular performer of the day $500 to perform the song in a touring production of the musical *A Trip to Chinatown,* by Charles Hoyt. Even though it was not part of the original Broadway production of the show, "After the Ball" sold 2 million copies during the year it was published and an additional 3 million copies over the next few years, making it the biggest selling title of the 1890s. At the height of its popularity, the song was earning Harris over $25,000 per week.

Those results demonstrate Harris's own entrepreneurial acumen and the effectiveness of Tin Pan Alley methods. It was a lesson followed by many other composers and publishers. But in addition to adeptly following public tastes, Tin Pan Alley became capable of shaping those tastes as well.

The Culture Business: "Oh, You Kid"

The business of Tin Pan Alley was based on the production and distribution of popular music in sheet music form. When all of the component elements of production, marketing, and distribution processes worked as intended, a hit song was produced. Millions of copies were sold and sometimes the words and music were on the lips of millions—at least for a while, until the next hit came along. Consequently, although Tin Pan Alley was nominally a popular song business, it was also—by producing songs that "everyone" came to know—in the culture business.

One example of the cultural impact and reach of Tin Pan Alley began in the spring of 1909 with the publication of "I Love, I Love, I Love My Wife, But Oh! You Kid!" with words and music by Jimmy Lucas and Harry von Tilzer. Jody Rosen tells the story of the song this way:

> The saga of "I Love, I Love, I Love My Wife—But Oh! You Kid!" began like many on Tin Pan Alley: with theft. In 1908, the Shapiro Music Company published "Oh, You Kid!," by the songwriters Edgar Selden and Melville J. Gideon. "Oh, You Kid!" was standard fare, a typical comic-courtship song: a catchy trifle, carrying a whiff of sex, but moderate in temperature and tempo.
>
> The appeal of "Oh, You Kid!" lay mainly in that slangy endearment, "kid." Like another novel usage of the period, "baby," "kid" held a hint of pillow-talk intimacy—a frisson that was enhanced by the threat to "scold" the kid who fails to deliver a quick kiss.[26]

Early in 1909, the the *New York Star* reported, "'Oh, You Kid!' has passed the one hundred-thousand mark," indicating that the song was reasonably successful by the standards of the day. Later that year, another songwriting team (Armstrong and Clark) took the "oh, you kid" refrain and used it for a song called "I Love My Wife, But Oh, You Kid!"

This "reworking" was hardly unusual. As Rosen observes, "A pilfered song was, in the language of the trade, 'a steal'—a fact of life in a cutthroat industry that thrived on trendiness and topicality, and held as an article of faith the belief that every hit could and should serve as a launching pad for dozens of light rewrites." Armstrong and Clark's version did not sell as well as the original, but it did inspire a third song.

Nine days after Armstrong and Clark released their song, Lucas and von Tilzer released their own version. "It was a heist and an upgrade, improving on the Armstrong & Clark original with a more winning melody, with sharper and racier lyrics, and with not one but three 'I Loves' in the title." As Rosen observes, the success of this third version was in part based on the fact that it was better written and more melodically memorable than its predecessors. The tone of the von Tilzer version and specifically the "relish with which extramarital shenanigans were depicted" seemed to strike a chord with the public, both titillating and offending.[27]

Whatever the reason, or combination of reasons, the von Tilzer "Oh! You Kid!" was a massive hit. By the beginning of summer of that same year, the song's title was being used in newspaper articles and headlines across the country. It was parodied by comedians and intellectuals. Clothing and novelty items were sold with "Oh! You Kid!" emblazoned on them. The phrase quickly became ubiquitous, appearing everywhere from newspaper ads to church hymnals (a joke, presumably) to even the White House, when guests at a gala sang "We love, we love, we love Roosevelt—but oh, you Taft!" to the president. Dozens of "We Love . . . But Oh! You . . ." songs were pumped out. Ministers preached and newspaper editorials railed against it. Ultimately, when people got bored, around the beginning of 1910, the craze became a cliché and finally faded away.

Selling a million copies of a given song facilitated countless performances by many performers, professional and amateur, in public venues and private residences. By building a sheet music industry, Tin Pan Alley publishers were able to extend the impact of individual songs beyond anything previously known. Part of that impact was due to the mass scale of distribution. But the fact that what was distributed was printed copies—permanent musical goods—gave the songs a staying power in the public consciousness that individual live performances could not produce. Sound recordings and broadcast media intensified this effect, but the first musical goods—sheet music—and the publishing industry that produced them clearly suggest how much the shift from transience to permanence could reshape the musical experience for producers and consumers.

The success and specific impact of "Oh! You Kid!" suggests another, even broader shift that could be driven by commercialization in popular music and entertainment. The song's impact was disturbing to people who, perhaps not even fully understanding why, saw the song as a social danger. But the larger implication was that business sectors that were ostensibly making casual commercial entertainment, like Tin Pan Alley, might be capable of shaping or reshaping culture on a very large scale.

CORE PRINCIPLES

Innovation synergies: technology, social adoption, economic opportunity

Alignment of large-scale synergies and enterprise-specific processes

Aggregation: creativity and listeners

KEY CONCEPTS

Musical services and goods

Synergy of technological, economic, and social forces

Alignment of external innovation waves with essential elements of music enterprise: art, social good, and economic sustainability

Aggregation

Piracy

Statute of Anne

Protective organizations: MPA and ASCAP

Tin Pan Alley

Culture Business

FURTHER CONSIDERATION

Early Music Publishing

Scan the communications between Beethoven and Härtel in "Beethoven's Correspondence with Gottfried Christoph Härtel and the Publishing House Breitkopf and Härtel (1808—1812)," http://www.raptusas sociation.org/haertelbriefe_e.html. Does anything in their communication seem relevant to current struggles between content creators and content distributors? If yes, consider what that is and, more importantly, why that is.

Bach v. Longman

Consider the following account, excerpted from Carroll's "The Struggle for Music Copyright":

Johann Christian Bach and Karl Friedrich Abel were immigrant entrepreneurs drawn to London's growing markets for music. Bach was the youngest son and eighteenth child of Johann Sebastian Bach. Among their entrepreneurial activities, Bach and Abel launched in 1765 what became the most popular concert series of the day at Vauxhall Gardens.

Initially, they enjoyed economic and social success. With respect to music publishing, each composer had obtained a printing privilege from the English Crown for his respective music. Both men had come into conflict with the publishing firm Longman and Lukey. This conflict occurred during a period when both men were enjoying financial success. By agreement, Bach filed suit against Longman, seeking injunctive relief.

Bach's royal privilege was the legal basis for his suit, but he understood that this foundation was eroding. One would have expected Bach to hedge his legal risk by adding claims under the Statute of Anne and common-law copyright. However, Bach's lawyer filed two bills of complaint, both of which relied principally on Bach's printing privilege and possibly on a claim of common-law copyright but made no mention of the Statute of Anne.

Why do you think Bach and his attorney chose to file under the existing license provision, nearing the end of its practical utility, and not the relatively new and much more composer-oriented Statute of Anne?

Do you think perceptions of social class and the traditions of nobility were a factor in this decision?

Was it the most practical choice as basis for the legal claim? Why or why not?

What was the ultimate outcome of the decision?

Carroll's research is available at http://www.floridalawreview.com /wp-content/uploads/2010/01/Carroll-BOOK.pdf.

CHAPTER 3

The Rise of Commercial Markets

Every crowd has a silver lining.

—P. T. Barnum

Over the course of the nineteenth century, changing social and economic conditions in the larger cities of Europe and the United States created new commercial opportunities for musicians. This led to a fundamental transformation of the relationship between artist and audience. Pleasing a single, relatively sophisticated patron over an extended period of time was the benchmark of success in the patronage era. In contrast, economic viability in the public concert marketplace required selling music with immediate appeal to many casual listeners, over and over again. The necessity of selling tickets every night to a changing and relatively unsophisticated audience affected every aspect of music creation and reception.

Even "classical" composers began to write music in response to the trends of the day. The incidental music of Mendelssohn, the operettas of Gilbert and Sullivan, and Johann Strauss's waltzes, as well as many more compositions, were created for popular concert and theatrical events. Performers in the classical tradition changed the way they presented themselves to the public. The 1800s thus marked not only the rise of commercial markets for music but also the beginnings of increasingly commercialized music intended for an expanding "mass" audience.

The rapid proliferation of popular music, according to Derek Scott, also "resulted in a polarization between the style of musical entertainment ('commercial' music) and that of 'serious' art."[1] That distinction— entertainment versus art—led to increasing condemnation of popular music by the cultural intelligentsia and social elite.[2] That dichotic view of music—"serious" meaning "good" and "popular" meaning "bad" (or at least "lesser than")—persisted throughout the nineteenth century. In fact, that perspective helped to shape everything from music education to concert hall etiquette and more, well into the twentieth century.

Despite the critiques of some, the growing public appetite for popular music affected not only the concert hall but also the "parlor." Amateur musical performance in the home—especially of popular and "light" classics—became a major source of revenue for composers, publishers, and music teachers. It was a golden age for amateur music making and the entrepreneurs who supported them. Amateurs also tended to be avid consumers of professional performance and public concerts.

Concerts were, however, only one part of the public entertainment spectrum in the nineteenth century. Theatrical performances in Britain and the US were more commercially successful than concerts and tended to have more influence on music publishing. In addition, once it became clear how much theatrical presentation could drive ticket sales, dramatic techniques began to be incorporated into the production of concerts, including even those in the classical tradition. Much of what we understand today about the concert experience—especially how they are staged—is based on techniques developed in the commercial music markets of the nineteenth century.

LONDON: PUBLIC CONCERTS AND MUSICAL ENTERTAINMENTS

In the nineteenth century, London offered listeners an amazing range of concerts and theatrical entertainments—perhaps more than any other city. The first public concerts in London occurred long before the end of the patronage era, and music had had an important role in other forms of public entertainment throughout the seventeenth and eighteenth centuries.[3] It should be no surprise, then, that when socioeconomic conditions in the nineteenth century became more favorable for paid public entertainment events, London became the epicenter of a large-scale shift toward market-driven music performance.

Attempts to take advantage of this shift took a variety of forms. Some composers, performers, and presenters embraced popular music forms. Others—such as composer and violin virtuoso Nicolo Paganini—continued to perform "serious" music but reframed it for public consumption by emphasizing personal charisma and adopting a flamboyant performance style. Still others—conductors in particular—found ways to enhance concert music presentation by combining specially composed "light" classical music programming with spectacular visual elements, including costumes, sound effects, and other theatrical devices. Thus, even in the "golden age" of late classical and romantic music in the 1800s, high artistic purpose was often paired with basic—and in the opinion of some, base—showmanship in public performance.[4]

Artist/Employee to Artist/Entrepreneur

As noted in the previous chapter, the decline of patronage drastically reduced opportunities for composer/performer/teachers to be the employees of aristocratic patrons. As the artist/employee of that system adapted to new public performance opportunities, the role of the artist/entrepreneur became much more important. Despite that fundamental shift, the underlying services that created revenue for musicians—performing, composing, and teaching—remained important. The marketplace for those services, however, did change substantially.

As a result, the emerging commercial markets for music of the nineteenth century mark the first time that musician/entrepreneurs had to develop their existing skill sets into multiple revenue streams for different segments of the public. Where a musical patron was the "consumer" of all of a court musician's services, public concerts, music publishing, and music lessons appealed to different, though interrelated, types of consumers. It was one thing to adjust one's composing or performing style to have more popular appeal. But it was entirely another—and far more complicated—to develop these skills into multiple revenue streams involving hundreds if not thousands of customers in search of a musical experience. All of this unfolded in an increasingly competitive marketplace.

Not every composer/performer had a skill set or temperament that was well suited to this new commercial environment. But those that did were able not only to succeed but also to help shape how the music business worked in the early twentieth century. The evolution of the classical concert business from market based to grant funded will be discussed in more detail in chapter 7, "Scaling and Selling Live Performance."

Impresario: The Director/Entrepreneur

Because not every composer/performer was an effective entrepreneur and because an increasingly competitive marketplace demanded new, nonmusical skills, a new role developed in the music business: the professional manager. These were the people who developed strategies for both what was performed and how it was presented to the public.

In part because of the importance of showmanship in London concert life, these managers came to be called impresarios. From the Italian, *impresa,* or "undertaking," an impresario is an entrepreneur or manager of any enterprise. Though the term was originally used to describe the managing directors of Italian opera companies, it came to be used to describe anyone who presented large-scale, visually spectacular productions with mass audience appeal. Impresari typically operate in competitive market-driven entertainment environments and consequently must consistently create events that are both remarkable and commercially viable.

While the artist/entrepreneur largely replaced the artist/employee of the patronage era, the impresario—or director/entrepreneur—coexisted with and often exploited the artist/entrepreneur. For the individual artist/entrepreneur the primary challenge of the era was to find enough performance opportunities for large enough audiences to maintain sufficient income—and to do so using only the resources of his own individual creativity. The director/entrepreneur, in contrast, was in a position to draw on the creativity of many musicians. This—like music publishing—is another early example of the advantage derived from being able to aggregate the creative productivity of others.

Much as publishers could contract with dozens or hundreds of individual composers, director/entrepreneurs were able to diversify their concert offerings using the services of many individual performers, composers, and theatrically enhanced productions. Some of the key impresari who defined the role of director/entrepreneur and shaped the future of concert production, content, and business practices are discussed below.

Frederick Gye was the manager of the Royal Italian Opera at Covent Garden from 1848 to 1878, and in that role he was often referred to in the press as an impresario. Opera was a competitive business across Europe, and Gye's was not the only opera house in London. He believed that local competition kept him just "out of the red" in terms of profits and that "popular sentiment and enthusiasm for its aesthetics aside . . . he regarded opera as a business about money, a 'speculation.'"[5]

Gye was not an outlier in holding this opinion. The role of the director/entrepreneur, the manager who balanced artistry with money, had become widely accepted as essential in public entertainment by the mid-nineteenth century. Gye worked to achieve preeminence in that capacity in the London market using a variety of aggressive strategies, including engaging the most popular opera singers of the day and securing financial backing to completely rebuild the opera house.

At the height of his success and influence in 1869, an artist roster of outstanding soloists, a state-of-the-art venue, and the lack of viable competition "produced the best results of Gye's career: subscription and box-office sales of £70,000, receipts from concerts of £10,000, and a gross profit of £36,000."[6] Frederick Gye's business acumen and aesthetic judgment helped him dominate the London music scene and made him one of the most influential opera impresari in Europe.

Specific management expertise aside, opera performances have several inherent advantages over classical music concerts, particularly from the perspective of the more casual music consumer. Unlike classical instrumental music—symphonies and chamber music, for example—opera includes words and thus sustains a literal narrative. Opera is intrinsically theatrical and incorporates costumes, lighting, and scenic design. In addition, the classical music concert, particularly the instrumental concert, had developed for a clientele more accustomed to having such music integrated into their lives and who, thus, had developed more sophisticated listening habits.

While there were middle-class music patrons willing to attend and support classical concerts, those events did not attract large audiences in comparison to opera. Though the audiences who did buy tickets to classical concerts tended to appreciate the musical complexity and refined sensibilities of the music—or saw supporting such music as a chance to increase their own cultural capital and social standing—there were (and are) limits to how many people would buy a ticket on a given night.

The inherent characteristics and popular appeal of the operatic form, taken together with Gye's particular acumen as a presenter, made it inevitable that London concert presenters would begin to emulate his approach and incorporate celebrated soloists and theatrical elements into classical music concerts.

Among the first concert presenters to implement a more accessible style of presentation was Parisian conductor and promoter Philippe Musard. Musard's "promenade concerts" were imported from Paris to London specifically to appeal to the "one shilling public."[7] These concerts emphasized famous soloists and "lighter" programming intended to attract a more casual music listener. The Promenades Concerts à la Musard were introduced in 1838 and became both popular and profitable.

Another conductor, Adolphe Jullien, blended theatrical spectacle with classical music in his concerts. Audiences responded enthusiastically to the special effects and dramatic productions, as well as to Jullien's personal style as a conductor. Many attended both the Jullien and Musard events to see the men conduct. As such, they were among the first to establish the "brand" of an ensemble from the conductor's podium, something that became a standard approach for symphonic orchestra performances over the course of the next century.

Other presenters recognized that no single event format, regardless of its appeal to the public, could generate sufficient revenue to keep an individual artist—let alone an organization or a venue—solvent. This led to changes in the way the performer-listener transaction models (see chapter 1) were applied. For the artist/entrepreneur, it became increasingly evident that only the *touring model* would provide sufficient opportunity to perform for paying audiences. For venue-based presenters—the director/entrepreneurs—the *tourism model* worked best, drawing people in night after night with a varied menu of spectacular entertainments over the course of a concert season. The relationship between touring artists and venue-based presenters remained foundational to concert production throughout the twentieth century as well (see chapter 7).

In the nineteenth century, venue-based variety programming was successfully pioneered by Robert Newman at the Queen's Hall in London. Newman was also a proponent of the idea that concert programming and presentation should be designed to attract casual music listeners, those who might not otherwise seek out classical music.[8] Newman said, "I am going to run nightly concerts and train the public by easy stages. Popular at first, gradually raising the standard until I have created a public for classical and modern music."[9]

Promenade concerts were already a London tradition, even before Musard introduced his own version in the late 1830s. They were typically outdoor concerts, presented in parks and "pleasure gardens." Audiences were able to stroll the grounds ("promenade"), talk, eat, and drink while listening to lighter musical fare. Another of Newman's ideas was to bring the promenade concert indoors, into the newly constructed and acoustically appealing Queen's Hall, while retaining the casual amenities of the outdoor version.

Newman shared his idea for an indoor "prom concert" series with young conductor Henry Wood. Wood was taken with the idea and thrilled when Newman offered to hire him to organize and conduct the orchestra for the concert series. Newman assured the younger man that "given the right orchestra, you will become a great conductor. Anyhow, I mean to run you and make you. The public will support us. The time is ripe for an English conductor . . . and now . . . Can you put up a little capital . . . say two or three thousand pounds?"[10]

Wood could not do so himself, but he did put Newman together with a financial backer who was willing to underwrite the series. As a result, the Henry Wood Promenade Concerts—commonly known as "the Proms," began in August of 1895. In addition to initiating the concept and attaching a young, charismatic conductor to it, Newman also developed a season ticket pricing strategy that was a remarkable value for the time and that proved appealing to consumers.

The first season was a financial success and the Proms went on to become one of the most beloved concert traditions in the world, enduring to the present, some 120 years after the inception of the series. Henry Wood remained conductor of the Proms through 1944, leading the ensemble as it became a staple of BBC radio programming, and made roughly one hundred recordings with Columbia and Decca.

Newman is not as well remembered today as Wood, but his programming ideas continue to be the basis for modern classical programming. For many symphony orchestras, other classical music presenters, and academic music programs, the idea that popular music is best used to coax listeners toward "better" music remains a relevant, even if unspoken, motivation and justification.

From Director/Entrepreneur to Owner/Producer

At the level on which Newman and Gye operated, in highly successful concert and opera enterprises, the interests of individual composers and performers were necessarily marginalized. The success of concert seasons at significant venues depended on the overall series of offerings more than on any individual event. One well-attended concert by a classical "star" of the era, such as violinist Nicolo Paganini, for example, would not keep a hall running any more than it kept Paganini's individual enterprise solvent.

As the monetary potential of year-round variety programming and theatrical, spectacle-infused music events became more apparent, individual and corporate owners of concert venues began to replace director/entrepreneurs in the management and promotion of public concerts. Newman led the way in this trend as well, by hiring a charismatic conductor as the "face" of his concert programming. In addition, Newman was astute enough to lease the appealing Queen's Hall as the perfect venue for his indoor "promenade concert" experiment.

Progressively, having the right venue in which to present a varied array of artists became the definitive criterion for success. As Weber notes, "Even Jullien's enterprise was subsumed in 1856 in the Surrey Garden Company, launched with a capital of £40,000 to build an immense concert hall for 10,000 people."[11] Thus, the most important role in public musical performance shifted again from director/entrepreneur to the venue-based owner/producer.

The lesson is not only that it takes capital to launch and maintain an entertainment venue of sufficient grandeur and scale to draw the public. This example also delineates the primary challenge of managing a concert hall: keeping it full of paying audience members year round. No single artist, or even charismatic conductor like Jullien or Musard, could hope to provide the quantity and variety of content to be competitive for an entire year in a single venue. As a result, the director/entrepreneur increasingly became an employee of well-capitalized presenting organizations and their owner/producers.

Powerful corporations and the managers they employed, along with a handful of musical "stars," came to dominate a business in which a middle ground was increasingly difficult to find. Increasingly, artists, conductors, and ensembles were aggregated and exploited by presenting organizations in both concert and theatrical traditions. It was not until near the end of the nineteenth century, when popular music and theatrical forms entirely dominated public programming, that talent agents and business managers representing individual artists (primarily theatrical and vaudeville performers) became a staple of the entertainment industry.[12] For further discussion of artist management in music see chapter 6, "Massification"; chapter 7, "Scaling and Selling Live Performance"; and chapter 11, "State of the Art."

Popular Music and Entertainment in London

In addition to classical and light classical concerts and opera, nineteenth-century London public entertainments included ballet, pantomime, puppet shows, and non-operatic musical theater. Although music in, or influenced by, the classical tradition was a prominent feature of some of these forms, popular music (traditional and newly created) had been a feature of English musical life for hundreds of years, and the public amusements of the 1800s were no exception.

Music Halls

One form of entertainment devoted to popular music that grew to great popularity in the nineteenth-century was the *music hall*. Music halls began as public houses (taverns) that catered primarily to people who had come to the city from rural areas in search of industrial employment. These were the places where people who were far from the comforts and culture of their homes gathered for drink, socialization, and familiar music.[13]

As social migration to the urban industrial centers continued, the popularity of such places grew and, by the 1850s, venues specifically built to be music halls began to appear. As the number of such venues increased, the demand for new popular songs grew as well, attracting professional songwriters to provide music for a growing group of increasingly celebrated music hall performers.[14]

The development of the music hall business and its impact on performance, songwriting, the food and beverage industry, and the audiences of the day is an example of how a city can become the locus of creative, social, and economic energy surrounding music. London is an early example of what would later be called a "music scene." Scenes and musical geography in general are discussed in more detail in chapter 5, "Convergence and Crossover."

Much as Tin Pan Alley publishing was closely associated with musical theatre in New York (another early music scene), the sheet music for music hall songs was an important part of British music publishing. While the separation of popular and "serious" music—especially judgments about their relative artistic and social values—continued in Britain and the US, the economic and cultural impact of popular styles continued to grow on both sides of the Atlantic.

UNITED STATES: PUBLISHING, PIANOS, AND PROMOTION

The first American music, both classical and popular, was primarily imported from Europe, and Britain in particular. Early concert and opera presenters brought performers from across the Atlantic or else engaged artists who emulated European musical programming and style. Over the course of the nineteenth century, however, distinctly American musical styles, modes of presentation, and publishing also developed. The resulting cross-pollination of music and musicians led to an expansion of markets both in the US and Britain.

As noted in chapter 2, the music publishing business centered in the Tin Pan Alley district of New York was immensely successful and influential—and not only in the US. Tin Pan Alley hits became familiar to music hall audiences, and popular music hall songs were often published or republished in New York. By the end of the 1800s, music publishing was an international industry generating millions in revenue annually, both reflecting and shaping popular musical taste in the US and abroad.

Sales of sheet music were fueled to a large extent by the demands of amateur musical performers, and in the second half of the 1800s, popular music represented an increasingly large percentage of printed music sold. For a variety of reasons—tradition, cost of printing, and typical use by music purchasers—sheet music editions of a popular song were usually arranged for vocal performance (melody and words) with a piano accompaniment.

The piano had increasingly become the instrument of choice for "parlor music" performance in the home, and piano sales increased exponentially in the second half of the century. From the 1860s onward, US piano manufacturing began to dominate the world market, and by 1900, half of all pianos were built in the United States.[15] The symbiotic relationship of home piano sales and popular music publishing was further amplified by a growth in music education, particularly of piano lessons. Owning a piano and being able to play it became important measures of social and cultural capital for Americans.

In addition to taking a leading role in popular music publishing and piano manufacturing, the United States differentiated itself in its transformation of the European impresario into the American "showman." While the terms *impresario* and *showman* share common definitional elements—both refer to "a person who produces or presents shows as a profession"—the words have different connotations.[16] Just as "serious" music was considered of greater value than popular music, so an impresario, by being associated with opera, was considered of higher status than a showman, who would have been associated with circuses, carnivals, and other amusements of the common rather than elite social classes.

The history of promoting commercial music in the United States is closely tied to the many showmen who popularized carnivals, medicine shows, and similar entertainments. No individual, however, defined and embodied American showmanship more than entertainment entrepreneur Phineas Taylor Barnum.

P. T. Barnum: "Every Crowd Has a Silver Lining"

In his day, P. T. Barnum (1810–1891) was the most recognizable show-man in the world. He was then, and continues to be, an exemplar of the entertainment promoter whose relationship with audiences is considered predatory. Though there is no evidence that he actually ever said it, the statement most often attributed to Barnum is "There's a sucker born every minute."

Barnum's name is also associated with one of the most famous entertainment companies of the nineteenth and early twentieth centuries, the Barnum & Bailey Circus. His career did not, however, begin with the circus. He came to that work in his sixties, after he had already established his expertise in other entertainment ventures, including Barnum's American Museum (established 1841). The museum featured oddities and curiosities (such as the "Feejee Mermaid") as well as musical performances (for example, "child prodigy" Tony Pastor). In 1846, the museum was drawing over forty thousand visitors per year.[17] It could be argued that the combination of museum "lectures" and the variety of performances was a direct inspiration to Pastor and others who would later be involved in developing vaudeville.[18]

Barnum also arranged tours by popular performers from the museum. On one such tour in England, Barnum became aware of Jenny Lind. A soprano known as the "Swedish Nightingale," Lind was then at the height of her popularity in Europe. Though Barnum himself never heard her sing (!), he determined to bring her to the US and present her on a major concert tour.[19]

It was a bold and risky move for Barnum. He was already known as a purveyor of "low" entertainments of questionable authenticity. His initial offer to Lind was for $1,000 per night for 150 performances, with Barnum covering all expenses. This was an enormous amount of money in 1850—over $4.5 million in 2014 dollars—and a very large financial commitment with little certainty of success. At the time he noted, "The public is a very strange animal, and although a good knowledge of human nature will generally lead a caterer of amusement to hit the people right, they are fickle and ofttimes perverse."[20]

In addition, Lind insisted on the services of a German conductor and pianist as well as an Italian baritone to join her on the tour. This brought the fees to which Barnum was committed to over $187,000 in 1850 dollars. Further, Lind insisted on payment in full, in advance. Although

Lind was not then at all well known in the US, Barnum was convinced that he could use her European reputation as a singer and philanthropist in his promotional campaign. Barnum's press release announcing the tour stated: "A visit from such a woman who regards her artistic powers as a gift from Heaven and who helps the afflicted and distressed will be a blessing to America."[21]

Barnum heavily promoted her history of giving benefit concerts for hospitals and orphanages, and before Lind even left England, Barnum had made her a household name in America. In a statement to the *New York Herald*, Barnum spoke of the huge sums he had committed, but assured the paper, "If I knew I should not raise a farthing profit I would yet ratify the engagement, so anxious I am that the United States should be visited by a lady whose vocal powers have never been approached by any other human being, and whose character is charity, simplicity and goodness personified."[22]

Before Lind left Britain, Barnum arranged for two "farewell" concerts that were heavily attended. He made sure that the concerts were reviewed and that the reviews would be reprinted in papers in the US. As a result of this and his other calculated press releases, Lind was reportedly met in New York at the docks by between thirty and forty thousand people.[23]

The tour itself was a critical, popular, and financial success on an unprecedented scale. Once Lind recognized how much money Barnum stood to make, she renegotiated her contract with him so that she was not only paid her $1,000 artistic fee per concert but also received the remainder of the ticket proceeds after Barnum got his $5,500 per concert management fee.

Lind's tour was a big payday for everyone, though true to her reputation (and Barnum's promotional strategy), the tour included charity concerts, and Lind insisted that Barnum make a certain number of tickets at each concert available at a drastically reduced price.

The scale of the tour's success inspired others to imitate this kind of touring approach for "classical" artists, particularly those from Europe. Barnum also established a number of core practices for how to promote performing artists in the United States. In fact, if we consider the thousands of fans waiting at the airport in anticipation of the Beatles' arrival for their first appearance on American television in 1964, we can see a similar media and public appearance strategy at work, some 114 years after Barnum invented it.[24]

Stephen Foster: Minstrel Shows and Parlor Songs

Stephen Foster was an American composer, born on the Fourth of July in 1826. As the child of a middle-class family, Foster received a private education, including musical training in the German tradition. Despite his early affinity for music and active participation in amateur musical groups, at age twenty Foster went to work as a bookkeeper at his brother's steamship company in Cincinnati. He continued to pursue his musical interests, however, and published some songs, including what would be his first hit, "Oh! Susanna."[25]

That song reflected the importance of the *minstrel show* to the music business in the United States in the mid-1800s. Though an in-depth study of the form is beyond the scope of this text, it is important to note that this theatrical genre, incorporating comedy, dance, and music and based on ethnic stereotypes of African Americans, was by 1850 the dominant form of popular music entertainment in the US. As such, it not only shaped cultural attitudes—in ways that would be considered profoundly insulting and racist today—but also, like all successful forms of theatrical entertainment, it had a major impact on the music publishing.

Part of Foster's genius was his recognition that there were two distinct markets for his music, and to tailor it accordingly. His primary source of revenue was licensing his songs to specific minstrel show companies for their exclusive performance. Theoretically this exposure should have stimulated strong sales of his printed music. For a variety of reasons involving both legitimate publishing practices of the day and publishing piracy, it did not.

Unlike many professional musicians in the nineteenth century, who disparaged amateur music making and, in particular, the proliferation of pianos as "an evil influence on home music," Foster embraced amateurism.[26] Anticipating the trends that were to develop later in the century, when pianos became a standard fixture in one out of ten American homes, songs like "I Dream of Jeannie with the Light Brown Hair" and "Old Folks at Home" became—by design—sentimental favorites. In the first three years after publication, "Jeannie" sold 10,890 copies, but only earned Foster $217.80. Foster's financial difficulties, from this and other publishing-related issues, led him to sell "Jeannie" and "Old Folks at Home" outright.[27]

One modern view of Stephen Foster—and one that reflects the commonplace idea that musicians in general have no "head for business"—

is that he was creative but not pragmatic. According to one source, however, Foster "kept his own account books, documenting down to the penny how much his publishers paid him for each song, and he calculated his probable future earnings on each one. His contracts were written out in his own hand; they are the earliest ones we know of between American music publishers and individual songwriters."[28]

Foster's problem was not his business sense. It was structural. In his day the music business was based entirely upon the synergy between presenting live performances and publishing printed music. Publishers and agents acted independently, often reprinting music published by others without regard to copyright. There were no "performing rights" fees from concerts or other theatrical performances. For Foster, who was not a performer, the only ways to earn money were through royalties on sheet music sales (ranging from 2 to 10 percent), or though the outright sale of a song to a publisher or theatrical producer.

Because he did not perform music professionally, unlike many composers in the nineteenth century, Foster himself was not well known to the public. Even during his lifetime, his songs were often referred to as "folk songs." In total he earned just over $15,000 in royalties and almost nothing in performing rights (the yearly average was less than $1,400 for his eleven most productive years). His heirs later earned approximately $4,000 in royalties, so that the total known royalties produced by Foster's music amount to less than $20,000. Although that sum would be worth over $300,000 dollars today, Foster's true creative output should have been worth millions.

In the 1850s and '60s there was no practical way for Foster to know all the locations where his music was being performed or that he was being paid for all the copies his publisher sold. Of course pirated editions of his songs—and there were many—paid him nothing. On January 13, 1864, he died at age thirty-seven, with only thirty-eight cents in his coin purse.[29] Despite his best efforts both as an artist and an entrepreneur, Foster was hindered by the prevailing business practices and primitive state of music copyright laws of his time. His career exemplifies what happens when the relationship between creators and the aggregators of creativity is out of balance.

Scott Joplin: Ragtime and Opera

Scott Joplin's musical career provides both comparison and contrast with Stephen Foster's experience. Though Joplin in many ways had a profoundly different upbringing, there was one crucial commonality between the two men. Both were exposed to the piano and the classical music world while young, and both also developed a fascination with the popular music of their time. More critically, both Foster and Joplin exemplify the power generated when previously disjunct styles of music converge—a pattern that has recurred many times in American music.

In 1898, Joplin published his first composition, "Original Rags," a medley of ragtime dances. Carl Hoffman of Kansas City published the music as "arranged by" Charles N. Daniels and sometimes as "written by" Daniels. It is possible that Joplin had not yet mastered formal music notation, so the credit was due to whoever transcribed his performed music into printable notation. More likely, though, it was a fraudulent practice—then quite common—for the publisher to cheat Joplin of some of the royalties due him as the sole composer.

The lesson was not lost on the young Joplin, and before publishing his next work he contracted with a local attorney to negotiate a better deal with Sedalia publisher John Stark. Joplin made only one cent per copy of the "Maple Leaf Rag," but its sales produced a modest income that lasted his lifetime, generating over $420,000 over the next twenty-five years or so.[30]

In 1901, Joplin relocated to St. Louis, as did publisher John Stark, and together they became the hub of the "classical" ragtime scene. Joplin's creativity was recognized by many in the formal musical establishment (i.e., the classical music world), and he was hailed by many as a genius of ragtime music. Joplin, however, aspired to do more than write even high-quality popular music. The remaining years of his life were devoted to writing, seeking funding, and getting performances for his two operas, *Guest of Honor* and *Treemonisha*.

Unlike his popular rags, Joplin's operas were not considered to have any commercial potential by publishers, including Stark. In addition, as an African American in the early 1900s, Joplin had limited access to funding sources. As a result, his operas were never performed during his lifetime (Joplin died in 1917), and it was not until decades after his death that his opera *Treemonisha* was given a public performance, and not until the 1970s that his piano works were revived. He was awarded the Pulitzer Prize posthumously in 1976.[31]

Like Foster, Joplin is both an exemplar of the synergy between live performance and publishing and a cautionary tale for creatives. Joplin, though much more financially successful than Foster (both due to advances in copyright law and his own advocacy for his rights as a composer), was marginalized from the work that he most valued—opera. This was, in part, a consequence of his race and then-current social attitudes, but also a result of the difficulty inherent in securing funds to produce theatrical performances, which were far more expensive. Had Joplin wished to remain focused on ragtime, there is little question that he would have made more money. But Joplin, like Foster, was creatively ahead of his time and suffered the consequences.

Both Foster and Joplin exemplify creative artists whose opportunities were constrained by misalignment with technology, economic opportunity, and/or social adoption. Ironically, Foster was fully in line with everything except the publishing system, which at the time favored fast, unscrupulous practices with few legal constraints. A generation later, he would have become a millionaire. Joplin, though his later-career shift to writing opera reduced his earning opportunities, was initially perfectly aligned with the growing public fascination with the piano and its music. But due to social attitudes about race, the public recognition of Joplin's entire body of work would take nearly a century to be realized.

The Piano Business

One feature of ragtime music that contributed greatly to its popular and commercial impact was that it was primarily performed on the piano. It came along in the later 1800s at exactly the right time to intersect with the rapid growth of piano sales and manufacturing in the US and the growing appetite for music to play on pianos in the home. In this case, the music—ragtime—was the innovation that coincided with existing social and economic conditions.

By the end of the century, both ragtime and pianos were legitimate "crazes" in the US. "By 1890, Americans [already] fed half the world market for pianos. Between 1890 and 1928, sales ranged from 172,000 to 364,000 per year."[32] The piano represents a manufacturing segment that had an immense impact on music production, consumption, and the economy at large.

The upright instrument, in particular, was produced and sold in large quantities and available anywhere in the US, including by mail order from Sears, Roebuck and Company. An advertisement from the 1902 Sears catalog, for example, shows the "New American Home Upright Parlor Grand Piano" with "Our Factory to Consumer Price" of $98.50. Shipping was extra, but purchase included a twenty-five-year guarantee "as binding as a government bond."[33] Because pianos were, for most

Americans, the single largest purchase following their homes, they are sometimes cited as the product that established the concept of consumer credit, or "buying on time."[34]

People without the time or inclination to learn how to play the piano—and ragtime was technically very difficult—created a demand for an instrument that could produce music without years of expensive lessons and painful practice. Business responded and the pianola, or "player piano," was brought to the marketplace. Early versions were operated by foot pedals, but soon electric motors were added.

The rolls of paper that ran through pianolas to make them play were created by musicians who performed the music in real time on special pianos designed to punch holes in the paper for "playback" on home instruments. This also generated an additional economic opportunity for pianists, and it is of particular interest to note that Scott Joplin created a piano roll for his most popular composition, "Maple Leaf Rag." Since he was never recorded, this roll remains the only indication of how Joplin interpreted his most popular creation.

Player pianos were not fully replaced by phonographs until the early 1920s, and they represent a bridge from traditional amateurism to the "playback" culture of the recording era. The player piano—specifically the piano rolls—also prompted changes to US copyright law, inspiring the first "mechanical license."

Mechanical Licenses

Music publishers, interested in protecting sales of printed sheet music, were resistant to the production of piano rolls. The fundamental issue was one of control. Publishers wanted to have the exclusive right to produce the rolls of their music for use in player pianos and to be able to refuse licensing to any other entity.

This issue was specifically addressed by the Copyright Act of 1909. Concerned that granting the exclusive license sought by the publishing industry could lead to a monopolistic control of music—potentially by a single company—Congress created a "compulsory" license for the production of piano rolls in order to protect public access. Section 1(e) of the 1909 act includes a provision whereby anyone could make a "mechanical reproduction" of a musical work providing that the individual had (a) secured authorization from the copyright owner for the first mechanical reproduction of the work, (b) notified the copyright owner and the US Copyright Office of the intention to make a mechanical reproduction, and (c) paid a royalty of two cents per reproduction to the copyright owner.

Although the focus in 1909 was on piano rolls, the law was also applied to the emerging recording industry. The two-cent rate set in 1909 remained in effect until January 1, 1978 (see chapter 6, "Massification," for subsequent developments in mechanical licensing).[35]

SUMMARY: MASS CONSUMPTION

Pianos were not the only instruments popularized by mail-order catalogs. The Montgomery Ward catalog was the first to sell (and the most widely associated with) guitars. The availability of inexpensive acoustic guitars produced an impact similar to that of the piano, but primarily among less affluent and more rural customers, the company's original consumer base. These were the people who created guitar-based music such as country and the blues, and mail-order guitars were indisputably facilitative of that creation.

The sales history of the piano and the acoustic guitar exemplifies how the synergy among innovation (mass production of instruments, consumer credit, and mail order/delivery), social demand (middle-class desire for music in the home, especially for ragtime and other popular music), and economic opportunity (middle-class resources and, for less affluent buyers, consumer credit) can produce sweeping change—enhancing business opportunities, amplifying social trends, and supporting the emergence of new styles of music.

Or, put another way, this synergy of business initiatives, creativity, and social adoption illustrates the potential of commercialized music to shape and ultimately transform life and culture. At the dawn of the twentieth century, all of that was about to happen on an unimaginable scale.

KEY CONCEPTS

Commercial concerts and musical entertainments

Director/entrepreneur

Owner/producer

Blending "serious" music and showmanship

P. T. Barnum

Publishing and live performance

Stephen Foster

Scott Joplin

Convergence of previously disparate musical styles and audiences

Piano manufacturing, retailing, consumer credit

Performance, publishing, and pianos

Mechanical licenses

FURTHER CONSIDERATION

Engineering and Selling Music and Musical Life

The wide availability of the piano and the acoustic guitar made them essential components of the creation and popularization of emerging styles of music and informal music making. Consider what musical device today is both sufficiently available and widely enough adopted to produce a comparable impact. The computer? The "tablet"? The smartphone?

For whatever you choose, consider the following:

Has this tool changed musical styles, fostered the creation of new musical genres, or changed the way people listen to music at home?

Is it possible for the availability of a "mechanical" or otherwise technological device to have that kind of impact now?

If so, what would the subsidiary, peripheral, or interlocking businesses be?

Sex, Music, and Queen Victoria

See Anton Cebalo, "The Victorian Era: Sexuality and the Family," in *Into the Rose-Garden* (blog), https://antoncebalo.wordpress.com/2013/02/10 /the-victorian-era-sexuality-and-the-family/. Based on the author's perspective and your own insights into the contemporary music marketplace, consider the following questions:

Do Victorian values about sexuality and the family continue to impact popular and "official" attitudes about musical performance and performers today?

Do people talk about certain music and performers being "good" or "bad," not only in the sense that they make or don't make good music, but as role models for young people?

If you think they do, is there also any value to be derived from transgressing such social and moral values? In other words, can a performer generate value by being overtly sexual or not family-friendly enough?

If you believe that there is a "value matrix" that includes an axis for Victorian concepts of good/bad and one for successful/unsuccessful, where would you locate performers such as the following on that matrix?

Justin Bieber

Miley Cyrus

Robin Thicke

Pharrell

Beyoncé

Kanye West

Thom Yorke

Others?

CHAPTER 4

Media Revolutions

The menace of mechanical music.

—John Philip Sousa

In 2007, one hundred years after many of the events discussed in this chapter occurred, the *Freakonomics* blog asked "five smart people" to answer this question: what is the future of the music industry? One of the respondents was Fredric Dannen, author of *Hit Men: Power Brokers and Fast Money inside the Music Business,* who stated,

> I believed I had discerned something about the consumption of recorded music—something startlingly obvious that has somehow eluded the record industry throughout its history, and led to the industry's irreversible decline.
>
> My epiphany, if you want to call it that, was simply this: consumers of recorded music will always embrace the format that provides the greatest convenience. No other factor—certainly not high fidelity—will move consumers substantially to change their listening and buying habits.[1]

Dannen's response makes a point that is critical to understanding music consumption patterns, whether in the nineteenth, twentieth, or twenty-first century. Throughout those eras, the legalities of music ownership have received and (continue to receive) massive attention. Though understanding and maintaining ownership is vital, it is not the *most* important determinant of what works and what doesn't in the music business. What matters most is *access.*

Protection of ownership without public access has little value. In practice, music consumers in the 1800s, much like music consumers today, embraced whatever mechanism of music delivery provided them the greatest convenience. Providing access—especially convenient access—is the key component of every successful music enterprise.

MUSIC ON DEMAND

For many centuries, having a musical experience depended upon access to performing musicians. In the patronage model, larger noble houses and church institutions often paid for the services of musicians on a 24/7 basis, while smaller establishments would contract musical services for more limited periods of time. On the lowest levels of earning power and prestige, itinerant musicians came and went, typically for brief stays, and were only infrequently accessible to the average person. In terms of access, then, if you wanted to hear music whenever you wished—on demand—the only ways to do that were to have a household musician or to perform the music yourself.

One might argue that "playing it yourself" would have been the most convenient method of hearing music on demand. In fact, musical amateurism *was* much more common before the advent of recordings and broadcast media.[2] The amateur solution, however, raises the issues of the talent, time, and energy necessary to develop the requisite musicianship, as well as costs associated with musical instruments. Learning how to play the piano well enough to be able to hear "Maple Leaf Rag" whenever you wish to, for example, turns out to be not all that practical or convenient.

Together, the challenges and inconveniences of musical amateurism created demand for expert performance. As a result, musical amateurism notwithstanding, for hundreds of years the primary mechanism for monetizing musical experience was by controlling and providing access to live, in-person performance. Thus, the decline of patronage and with it opportunities for live-in household musical employment in the early 1800s marked the end of the first era of what we might call *music on demand*.

While middle-class music consumers, music publishing, and the increasing popularity of paid public concerts fundamentally changed the music marketplace, they did not replicate the easy availability of household musicians. Even in the largest European and American cities, with multiple public concerts in numerous public venues, a music aficionado was still constrained on any given day to hearing only the concert programs at the times and locations they were offered.

Desire for convenient access to musical experience impacted both creation and production of music. Music suitable for amateur performers needed to be less difficult technically and require fewer resources in terms of players and instruments. At the same time, to justify the greater expense and inconvenience of going out and paying to hear music in concert halls, professional repertoire and programming became larger and increasingly spectacular as the nineteenth century advanced.

Those changes were minor, however, compared to the revolutionary impact of sound-recording technology. The emergence of that technology and its diffusion across society created entirely new patterns of consumption. For the first time in history it was possible to hear a string quartet via a recorded cylinder or disc and a playback device without musicians being present or even nearby. A previously recorded performance could be replayed whenever and wherever desired. Sound recording thus marked the end of the exclusivity of live performance and the beginning of the "playback" era—an era that entirely redefined both access and music on demand.

Nothing—for musicians or listeners—would ever be the same.

Within a few years this revolutionary development was amplified and extended via the invention of the first wireless broadcast medium. Radio was capable of sending either live or prerecorded sounds thousands of miles to be heard on radio receivers in businesses and homes across entire hemispheres. While the record player facilitated the ultimate personal, on-demand access to music, radio rendered geography and location completely irrelevant. Millions of listeners from Canada to Mexico could and did hear radio broadcasts such as the *Grand Ole Opry* at the moment the musicians were performing, thousands of miles away.

In the first decades of the twentieth century, recordings and radio completely eliminated the constraints of time and place that had for centuries defined and supported a profitability model based on physical access to musicians. It was no longer necessary to leave home— providing one had a radio or playback device—to experience live or recorded music from distant cities. Even if you didn't have the devices in your home, a short drive to a local business near your farm in Iowa could provide access to a musical performance at Carnegie Hall in New York.

Both radio and record technologies and their widespread social adoption revolutionized music production and reception. Because this new, mediated music on demand was so powerful, it virtually destroyed the models of production and reception that preceded it. The synergy between recording and broadcasting—combined with a no longer dominant, but still valuable, live performance model—would come to define the music business in the twentieth century. Below, we look at the emergence and adoption of sound recording and broadcast technologies, the businesses they made possible, and their revolutionary impact—both singly and collectively—on music and society.

SOUND RECORDING

It takes a thousand men to invent a telegraph, or a steam engine, or a phonograph, or a photograph, or a telephone, or any other important thing—and the last man gets the credit and we forget the others. He added his little mite—that is all he did.

—Samuel Clemens

Invention, Optimization, Aggregation, Diffusion

There was an incredible proliferation of inventions and new technologies during the nineteenth century. A number of these—electricity, telecommunication, radio, and sound recording—not only changed music production and consumption but also fundamentally altered the character of everyday life.

Obviously, sound recording and commercial radio broadcasting are of primary interest in the study of music enterprise. But in addition to examining the development of those technologies, along with associated business models and their impact on social behaviors, there were processes in play that were even more foundational.

These processes can be defined as the *operative dynamics* that both facilitated and constrained the actions of the main stakeholders in the development of entertainment technologies. As defined in this text, an operative dynamic not only describes what happened with a specific technology at a given time and place, but also applies to different eras and other technological developments.

The process most relevant to this discussion moves through the following phases: *invention, optimization,* the *aggregation* of invention(s), and cultural *diffusion.* Applying the "waves of innovation" concept discussed in chapter 2, we can situate these processes as indicated in figure 5.

The cultural transformation "wave" at the center of the diagram could be occupied by the phonograph, or by recorded music generally. But what if we consider agency? In other words, who did the most to

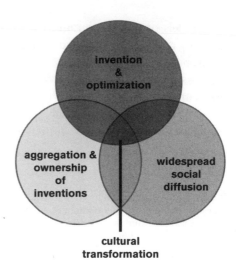

FIGURE 5. Innovation synergy: culture.

create that "wave"? This question is based on the premise that game-changing innovation waves don't "just happen," but are instead the result of intentional design. If this premise is correct, it suggests that successful entrepreneurship—whether technological, cultural, or both—is not just a "right time, right place" phenomenon.

As we will see in the next section, the invention of sound recording and its optimization resulted from the work of a number of people. Likewise, the development of the businesses to build and promote the playback devices and create the recorded content to maximize the social demand for those products was both a collective and competitive effort. But there was one person whose work across all of these domains was uniquely opportunistic and effective.

As a result of a multifaceted initiative that included invention, optimization, aggregation, and promoting his products to encourage cultural diffusion, Thomas Edison gets credit for the invention of sound recording even though, as Samuel Clemens pointed out, others came before him and contributed significantly to the success he realized. Edison was not the sole inventor of the relevant technology, but he *was* the most effective engineer of the technological, economic, and cultural wave that followed.

Innovation waves can be engineered through a process of invention, optimization, aggregation, and cultural diffusion.

The Four Goals

This idea of engineered—or intentional—technological/cultural/economic innovation is closely tied to a concept more often applied to scientific than cultural endeavors. But the four goals of science—*describe, understand, predict,* and *control*—are entirely applicable to music enterprise in both study and practice.

For example, mapping the evolution of sound recording onto the "wave" diagram shown in figure 5 is useful for both describing what happened and understanding the technological, social, and economic elements whose intersection made it all possible—goals 1 and 2.

More usefully, understanding the interplay among these forces and the actions of the primary participants can also be used predictively—goal 3. As applied, for example, to the contemporary "churn" between streaming and downloading music providers, determining which of them is the most effective optimizer and aggregator of these technologies would be predictive of competitive advantage. What business is most effectively encouraging cultural diffusion and adoption? Once identified, wouldn't that business and those actors be better positioned to rise to the top in the coming months and years?

The greatest value of this (or any) analytical model would be produced not just from its power to predict, but from its potential to guide the development of a strategy to influence and *control* outcomes—goal 4. That is exactly what Thomas Edison did with Edison Records, despite early misjudgments and intense competition. What might a critical analysis and application of the four goals to the early history of recorded sound reveal about how to design and encourage widespread social adoption and cultural acceptance of new technologies, new products, new behaviors, and even a "new normal" in daily life today?

Who has done that in recent years? Steve Jobs. Jeff Bezos. It is no accident that both Apple and Google (including YouTube) have become immensely influential in twenty-first-century music production, distribution, and consumption. They have done so via invention, optimization, aggregation, ownership—and by changing the culture.

The popularly accepted truth is that the sound-recording era began in 1877 at the New Jersey laboratories of Thomas Edison, the "Wizard of Menlo Park." That is only a partial description of what happened, but the popularity of that narrative clearly shows that Edison was not only an inventor but also an optimizer and aggregator of inventions (buying outright or adapting the work of other inventors) and a sophisticated promoter of his own brand. Edison not only recognized possibilities inherent in technology, the marketplace, and society, but also manipulated and engineered circumstances to control the results he wanted. Edison was an unusually good inventor and business manager, but he was also a genius at cultural entrepreneurship.

To be able to apply this historical model to contemporary conditions, it is necessary to understand the technological, commercial, and social contexts that served as the backdrop and springboard for Edison's enterprise.

Sound-Recording Technology: A Brief History

Sound-recording technology was invented in Paris in 1857 by Leon Scott. His Phonautograph used a stylus attached to a membrane that moved with sound vibrations traveling through the air and etched patterns on a turning cylinder.[3] This recording technology anticipated Edison's work by twenty years, but with one critical difference: Scott's device could not play back the sound it recorded. Despite the undisputable significance of being able to make a permanent record of sound and the potential marketplace advantage of being a "first mover," the inability to hear the sounds recorded was—to say the least—a major drawback to sparking public enthusiasm or making any sales.[4] As a result, the Phonautograph did not produce a wave.

In April 1877, the year that marked the birth of both recording and playback technologies, the initial description of a practical process was not made in New Jersey, but again in Paris. Charles Cros—who had already optimized telegraph printing technology—proposed an improvement of the Scott recording technology using a photoengraving process to etch sound waves on metal cylinders. Cros also proposed a playback device using the same cylinders as a source. Cros did not, however, get past the design stage with his Paleophone.[5]

In July of the same year, Thomas Edison produced a working prototype of a recording and playback device using tin foil cylinders and a hand-cranked machine. The sound quality was extremely poor by modern standards but was revolutionary at the time.[6] As had the French inventors before him, Edison considered the primary function of his device to be recording human speech, hence the famous recording of the inventor reciting "Mary Had a Little Lamb" on his first successful attempt to use the device.[7] Though Edison recorded music as part of his early efforts, as did others, entertainment content was considered a novelty, while speech-based applications were considered the practical commercial application for the devices.

Unlike Cros, Edison not only produced a working prototype but also acted immediately to secure patents for the device, cylinders, and processes in Britain and the US.[8] In 1878 he established the Edison Speaking Phonograph Company by selling the tin foil cylinder patents in exchange for 20 percent of future profits.

The next significant sound-recording technology developer, Emile Berliner, began to experiment with the Edison cylinder machine with an eye to optimization, much as he had done with the Alexander Graham Bell laboratory's telephone. Berliner considered the sound quality of the cylinders to be too poor, and in 1884 began to develop a disc-recording medium. In 1886 he completed that process along with an adjunct technology critical to commercial applications: the capacity to mass-produce copies of the recorded discs. In the meantime, in 1885 Bell and his associates established the Volta Graphophone Company to promote that device to the public and in 1886 created the American Graphophone Company to retail the Graphophone in the US and Canada.

In 1886 Edison—undoubtedly aware of Berliner's work, as well as that of Bell and other competitors—secured the patent for his improved wax cylinder. This not only effectively ended the era of the tin foil cylinder but also marked the beginning of a "format war" between cylinders and discs, along with the companies that produced them. In 1887, Edison bought back the intellectual property of the Edison Speaking Phonograph Company and established the Edison Phonograph Company.

The next major stakeholder in the development and popularization of recording technology was not an inventor. In 1888, Jesse Lippincott became the principal stockholder in the American Graphophone Company. He established the North American Phonograph Company to lease the phonographs and dictation machines manufactured by Volta. He also bought control of the patent and exclusive sales rights for the Edison phonograph, which was still manufactured by Edison. As a result of these acquisitions, Lippincott became the first aggregator of recording technology devices and recorded media created by different inventors.

In 1889, Edward Easton and a group of investors established the Columbia Phonograph Company in Washington, DC, and acquired the local sales and service rights from both Edison and Lippincott for their devices. In addition, as did many regional companies, Columbia produced its own cylinder recordings. Following the demise of Lippincott's company in 1894, Columbia sold only its own recordings and players.

While the early inventors, optimizers, and promoters like Bell and Edison considered entertainment discs and cylinders to be novelties whose main purpose was to promote their machines for business purposes, later companies like Columbia increasingly made and sold music and comedy recordings. The confirmation of the commercial potential of entertainment recordings and the impetus for an industry-wide shift toward that kind of content came with the introduction of coin-operated music players.

In 1890, Louis Glass and William Arnold invented a coin-operated attachment for the Edison phonograph. Customers listened through tubes—a kind of acoustic headphones—so that multiple players could be used in public arcades and saloons. Coin-operated phonographs were typically loaded with entertainment recordings, with an emphasis on comic monologues. The success of these early versions of the jukebox made it plain that there was a significant public appetite for entertainment discs and cylinders, which intensified the competition and litigation among manufacturers and retailers.[9]

On the technology front, design improvements continued to fuel competition among record player companies. In 1896 Eldridge Johnson patented a wind-up spring motor record player that established his device as a major rival to the Phonograph and Graphophone. In 1900, Johnson first used the now-familiar image of a dog looking into the cone of an early Gramophone accompanied by the words "His Master's Voice," taken from the painting of that name created by James Francis Barraud (of his dog, Nipper) in 1884. The image (and Nipper) were immortalized by the Victrola Record Company and later, RCA Victor.

In 1901, Berliner and Johnson merged to form the Victor Talking Machine Company, and in 1906 Victor introduced the Gramophone. The discs played by that device, considered by many to be acoustically superior to the wax cylinder, began to seriously erode the market advantage held by Edison and his cylinder.

Early Recording Studios: Technology in Practice

When the shift from business-oriented applications to entertainment recordings began in the late 1890s and early 1900s, recording techniques were typically improvised in the field by engineers. Due to the technical constraints of acoustic recording, which depended upon the singers and instrumentalists performing into a cone that transferred sound vibrations directly to a cylinder, musicians had to be physically arranged with the most important sound source closest to the cone. In practice, this meant that the balance among the sounds was heavily weighted toward the voice or other soloist, with accompanying instruments acoustically and literally in the background.[10] This practice was also encouraged by the perceived importance inside the business of having the soloist be by far the most prominent sound, as that person was presumably the reason the consumer would buy the record in the first place.

This somewhat primitive approach did not fundamentally change until 1925, when the Westinghouse Company introduced the electric microphone. Microphones made it possible—hypothetically at least—to record in larger, resonant spaces more comfortable for performers and conducive to better recordings. Practical considerations, however, such as the limited frequency range of early microphones and the need to eliminate or reduce environmental noise, meant that most commercial recordings were made in small, relatively sound-deadened rooms.

The electric microphone is also an example of how the equipment and techniques used in early twentieth-century recording studios were adapted from radio broadcasting. In fact, as a matter of convenience—and setting the stage for the media mergers to come—many of the early recording studios that adopted electric sound-recording technology were built by radio stations.[11]

The majority of the early recording studios, however, were owned and controlled by record labels. The labels themselves were often side businesses for recording technology inventors, intended to promote the sale of the hardware devices they produced. Later, as the production of prerecorded discs and cylinders became a significant revenue stream, labels began to separate from hardware manufacturers. Three of the most influential and adaptive of the early labels were Edison, Columbia, and RCA.

Early Record Labels

Edison Records

Although historically Edison Records was the first record label, its emphasis on hardware reflected the inventor's belief that his primary value was in building playback and recording devices. In that capacity, Edison's influence on the recording business of the day was significant. Though limited in terms of their potential to be mass copied, Edison cylinder blanks were used by most record companies of the era.

While others labels were quicker to recognize the market potential of prerecorded content beyond the value of blank cylinders or discs, Edison remained committed to the machines and blank discs (early phonographs could also make recordings) as business-oriented devices. Edison believed this so strongly, seeing prerecorded records purely as promotional tools, that for quite some time Edison Records recordings always had Edison's name on the label, sometimes that of the composer, and rarely that of the performer.

But by 1910, Edison had begun to put artists' names on his labels in response to prevailing and more successful business practices—though he kept his name and his image on the label, too. As the 1910s progressed, Edison continued to release new recordings on cylinders—even as he lost market share—while secretly exploring disc technology. Despite the undisputed advantages of the disc format, Edison persisted in selling his blank and prerecorded cylinders through 1917. In fact, that year he released one of the first jazz recordings, Collins and Harlan's "That Funny Jas Band from Dixieland" on his then state-of-the-art Blue Amberol cylinder.[12]

Edison also released the recording on his own newly developed disc format a few months later, but sales of the song helped to keep the cylinder format alive. Edison Records continued selling cylinders until the company went out of business in 1929. After the closing of the label, Edison shifted many of his employees and resources to radio technology, belatedly recognizing the technological shift of the 1920s. Ultimately, despite the initial competitive advantage that his innovation, optimization, aggregation, and diffusion strategy brought him, Edison was surpassed by disruptive changes in technology and patterns of social adoption.

Columbia Records

Founded in 1889, the Columbia Phonograph Company was the successor to the American Gramophone Company.[13] It was originally a local retail store run by Edward Easton, distributing and selling Edison phonographs and phonograph cylinders in Washington, DC, Maryland,

and Delaware. It derived its name from the District of Columbia, which was the company's headquarters.

As was the custom of many regional phonograph companies, Columbia also produced commercial cylinder recordings of its own. Columbia's ties to Edison and the North American Phonograph Company were severed in 1894 with the North American Phonograph Company's breakup, and Columbia thereafter sold only records and phonographs of its own manufacture.

In 1927, adapting to changing technologies and business structures that Edison was still resisting, the Columbia Phonograph Company purchased United Independent Broadcasters. With that purchase, the Columbia Broadcasting System—the media conglomerate known as CBS today— was established. Throughout the 1920s, Columbia Records continued to make groundbreaking recordings, acquired Okey Records, a leading independent label specializing in blues artists and music, and compiled an impressive catalog of early blues and jazz artists.

Columbia Records remains a premiere subsidiary label of Sony Music Entertainment. In 2009, during the reconsolidation of Sony Music, Columbia was partnered with Epic Records to form the Columbia/Epic Label Group, under which it currently operates as an imprint. Today, Columbia is headed by chairman and CEO Rob Stringer, recognized as one of Billboard's "Power 100" and recipient of the Clive Davis Visionary award in 2016.[14]

Columbia, in contrast to Edison Records, was an effective optimizer not so much of the hardware, but of the entertainment "software"—the entertainment recordings. In addition, by positioning itself on the intersection of recordings and radio broadcasting, Columbia laid the groundwork for a broader impact on the culture of music consumption. On that basis, it should be no surprise that Columbia long outlasted its senior rival, Edison.

RCA Records

In another radio and record label merger, the Radio Corporation of America (RCA) purchased the Victor Talking Machine Company in 1929. Victor was a well-established manufacturer of phonographs (the Victrola) and recordings. In this case, as with the Columbia Records and United Broadcasting System merger, the resulting media conglomerate experienced both immediate and long-term success.

In the 1950s, RCA Records constructed a then state-of-the-art recording studio in Nashville to facilitate its country music operations there. Studio B was where the "Nashville sound" was first created and where artists from Elvis Presley to Carrie Underwood have recorded.[15] In 1983, RCA joined with the Bertelsmann Music Group, and in 2004 Bertelsmann merged with Sony to form Sony-BMG. In 2006 Sony acquired BMG to become Sony Music Entertainment, and today the RCA Music Group is an important subsidiary of Sony.

Jukeboxes

Coin-operated attachments for early phonographs were first patented in 1888 and 1889.[16] The devices were quickly adopted for use in public places, particularly bars, where live music was an impractical expense. In the first decade of the twentieth century, these machines, known as jukeboxes, were improved to allow for multiple song selections and even pre-electric amplification systems.[17]

By 1927, the modern jukebox appeared. Using a business plan developed for the coin-operated player piano business, various vendors had put some eighty-five hundred jukeboxes into public operation by the end of 1927.[18] By the end of the 1920s and well into the 1930s, the jukebox was a popular feature in many public spaces all over the country because it provided musical entertainment at a nominal cost—typically five cents per song—paid for by customers, not management.

Much as performing musicians began to be marginalized by the convenience of using records and radio broadcasts to bring music into homes and places of business, record labels (and publishers) struggled with the increasing popularity of coin-operated record players. Since the 1909 copyright law had been amended to specifically exclude coin-operated music machines as public performances, regardless of how many thousand times a record was played on a jukebox, the publisher received royalties only on the original sale of the record.[19]

Radio broadcast networks were required to pay for a performance license for the music they broadcast, which did benefit publishers, but not for the use of the record. So for record labels, neither jukebox nor radio plays produced any revenue beyond the initial purchase of the recording being used. Compensation for the public performance of recordings to the owner of the original recording was not made part of copyright law until the 1976 revision of the US code, which provided for ownership rights in sound recordings for performers and producers.[20]

Pressure from jukebox sales and the capacity of radio to broadcast records to an enormous national audience without paying royalties of any kind to the record producers was considered the death knell for the sale of home record players and discs. This created a strong incentive for mergers between radio and record labels such as Columbia and RCA. Additional acquisitions of record labels by radio companies soon followed. In fewer than fifty years of technological and commercial development, the recording business moved through invention, optimization, aggregation, and cultural diffusion to marginalization and being aggregated themselves by the next wave: radio.

BROADCASTING
Wired and Wireless Communication

The history of communication technology is one of continuous and accelerating innovation with the goal of overcoming the constraints of time and distance. For most of human history, the primary means of communicating has been in person, whether one to one (as in conversation) or one to many (as in public speaking or the theatre). When communication was not possible face to face, the available methods using written language and the postal service involved significant time delays that were proportional to the distance a written message had to travel. It was not until the 1800s that experiments using electricity began to open the door for instantaneous long-distance communication.

The first widely adopted result of that experimentation was the *telegraph*, which enabled the sending of simple coded messages in the form of electrical pulses across vast distances—between any two points connected with a telegraph wire. The patent issued to American inventor Samuel Morse in 1837 opened a new era in communications, and the telegraph played a significant role in the social and economic development of the United States.

The telegraph, while improving the speed, efficiency, and cost-effectiveness of long-distance communication, was not a viable medium for music. Consequently, it had no impact on the business of live performance or music publishing during the nineteenth century. It was the development of the first wireless communication system that extended the communication revolution to the realm of music and entertainment.

Marconi and Radio: Invention, Aggregation, Implementation

In the late 1800s, a number of inventors, including Thomas Edison, were working on ways to send telegraph signals without wires. From a logistical standpoint the advantages of this would be enormous. Wires took time and money to run, and the longer the distance and more difficult the geography, the more expensive the process. But it was the invention of Guglielmo Marconi that transformed telegraphy from a system that could only send a simple code to one that could transmit sounds of all kinds over vast distances.

In 1896 Marconi was awarded a patent for his radio. As with all new technologies there was the initial expectation that this would revolutionize basic communication, which it actually did by removing the necessity of wiring a physical connection between nodes of communication. It also provided the basis for a much more far-reaching revolution. Fairly quickly, the invention went beyond transmitting the simple electrical impulses of the telegraph to transmitting the sound of the human voice. Paired with the possibility of speaking person to person via the relatively new telephone, radio communications began to supersede the once essential telegram as a regular means of communication.

Moreover, radio was recognized as having enormous potential for transmitting not only speech but also music and other sounds. In addition, radio represented the first true *broadcast* system of communication in that one source could be received by many radios—as many as existed in the space reachable by the broadcast transmitter.

While the telephone was a simple extension—using the actual voice of the communicating individual in real time—of systems like the telegram, it was still a one-to-one communications medium. Radio was fundamentally different: instead of one-to-one communication, it was one to many. It was an extension of public speaking and performing, but on a scale so broad that a voice could be heard across a continent. This broadness of scale led to the term *broadcasting*. As such it became a foundational element of twentieth-century mass media, as well as the mass production and mass consumption of culture.

Commercial radio stations began broadcasting in the first decades of the twentieth century; the first license was issued by the US government in 1920 to KDKA in Pittsburgh, Pennsylvania. KDKA, like other early stations, did not operate by selling airtime for advertising, but rather was owned outright by a department store that used the station's programming to promote the sale of its radios. Other stations were owned by newspapers that used broadcasting to sell papers and extend the reach of their editorial point of view. It was not until 1922 that the first paid radio advertisements were put on the air, establishing the model of advertising-based broadcasting that dominated twentieth-century media.

NETWORKS, "FREE" CONTENT, AND MEDIA CONGLOMERATES

The impact of radio networks on the production and reception of music was revolutionary. By 1934, 60 percent of American households had a radio, as did 1.5 million family cars. Radio networks sent daily programming across the US with an ever-expanding schedule of drama, comedy, music, news, and advertising. This content was entirely free to the audience—once they had purchased a radio—and represented the beginning of the end for many businesses based on selling tickets for live entertainment or selling music on recordings.

This so-called Golden Age of radio is very different from radio in the second half of the twentieth century, with its emphasis on records, news, weather, sports, and "talk." In the Golden Age, radio took everything that was currently on the popular stage and concert hall and broadcast it. It is typical of new media to begin by using the content of previously existing forms and only later developing content types specifically suited to the new medium. So initially, radio content was drawn from the theatre just as television content a few decades later was initially drawn from radio.

By the 1930s it was obvious that a new business paradigm for music and entertainment had been established. Performers needed to be on the radio to enhance their recognition by the public and increase their opportunities to perform live and sell recordings. For example, the *Grand Ole Opry* was not only an important live performance venue in Nashville but was also a weekly radio program heard nationally. The *Grand Ole Opry* radio broadcast made national success and celebrity possible for artists in genres like country, bluegrass, and old-time, which had previously been considered regional at best.

These relationships established the value of a widely broadcast public performance that could produce a large impact on live performance ticket and record sales even though direct compensation was minimal. That economic impact was also the justification for the exemption of broadcast radio from the requirement to pay for the use of sound recordings on the air. The idea was that the value of "free" promotion of playing records on radio was more than enough to compensate performers and the producers who made the recordings. That situation does not apply to streaming or to Internet-based radio, but to date, it still applies to terrestrial radio.[21]

Musicians' Advocacy Organizations

It is no coincidence that the rise of the professional, collective bargaining musicians' union parallels the rise of mass production and industrialization of music in Europe and North America. The American Federation of Musicians (AFM), founded in 1896, became an influential stakeholder in the music business in the US during the twentieth century. The union's policies and political activities often attempted to prevent or delay the impact of social and technological change on the working musician. As we will see, this kind of advocacy was not always successful. But regardless of individual triumphs and defeats, the AFM remains the primary professional organization for instrumental musicians in the US today. Vocalists are represented by the American Guild of Musical Artists (AGM), as well as the American Federation of Television and Radio Actors and the Screen Actors Guild, combined as SAG-AFTRA. Comparable organizations exist in many nations around the world.

RISE OF CONSUMERISM

For a variety of technological, economic, and social reasons, the nineteenth century brought a remarkable expansion of musical amateurism. Public performances of amateur groups such as town bands, choral societies, and the like became increasingly popular. In many places, especially towns and smaller cities, amateur performances of this nature became a substantial part of a community's publicly available music (see chapter 6, "Massification").

But as the phonograph fundamentally shifted the calculus of music consumption, musical amateurism began to decline. This phenomenon was widely identified as an issue of concern early in the twentieth century. It was not just that this decline was bad for musical instrument makers and music teachers. Some social observers considered it bad for professional music making, for the musical discrimination of the average person, and even for the national character.

One of the leading American musical figures who sounded a warning about such dangers was the immensely successful composer and bandleader John Philip Sousa. Sousa predicted in his 1906 article "The Menace of Mechanical Music" that "music producing machines" would lead to a "marked deterioration in American music and musical taste."[22]

Sousa, according to one observer, predicted that

> recordings would lead to the demise of music. The phonograph, he warned, would erode the finer instincts of the ear, end amateur playing and singing, and put professional musicians out of work. "The time is coming when no one will be ready to submit himself to the ennobling discipline of learning music," he wrote. "Everyone will have their ready-made or ready-pirated music in their cupboards." Something is irretrievably lost when we are no longer in the presence of bodies making music, Sousa said. "The nightingale's song is delightful because the nightingale herself gives it forth."[23]

While his words are poetic and, as a professional composer and performer, Sousa was admittedly not without an economic interest in the matter, he was also articulating a concern shared by many. Certainly the popularization of recordings had an impact on amateur music participation because it made listening to professionally performed music so much more convenient than doing it yourself. In addition, as Sousa also noted, recordings reduced opportunities for professional musicians, particularly the local opportunities that the majority of professionals depended (and still depend) on for their livelihood.

It is difficult to assess the degree to which phonographs damaged the "finer instincts of the ear" or led to other musical aspects of society being "irretrievably lost." But by the end of the twentieth century, there were indisputably far more musical consumers than producers, and expectations of outstanding musicianship had unquestionably changed.

One thing to consider about Sousa's predictions is how times of technological "churn"—periods when technologies and their social adoption rapidly evolve—generate stress. This is particularly true for anyone invested in the status quo, whether professionally or as a matter of personal familiarity.

Alvin Toffler, in his 1970 book *Future Shock,* described this as the feeling that there has been "too much change in too short a period of time." Toffler considered this a fundamental characteristic of twentieth-century life—what he called the "post-industrial age." Sousa's remarks, considered from this perspective, show him to be a kind of "canary in the coal mine" regarding the stress arising from ongoing rapid cultural and social change.

As the twentieth century advanced, the rate of technological change and social adoption accelerated. Such "compressive effects of technology" drive production, reception, and utility of entertainment content. Moreoever, they move forward at an ever-increasing rate, destabilizing business models—and daily life—faster and faster. Arguably, "future shock" has become a "normal" condition of life in the twenty-first century.[24]

One can only imagine what Sousa might have written a century later, in 2006. Thankfully, he was spared the ordeal of confronting the long-term results of the dramatic shifts he observed, though perhaps he would have felt vindicated. As we move forward through the history of music enterprise, it is important to acknowledge how much the compressive effects of technological development and social adoption change the playing field for creativity and commerce. At the same time, we should also recognize that certain operative dynamics and principles—the importance of convenient access, for example—continue to shape the behavior of consumers and are, therefore, reliable maps even for a changing market landscape for music.

CORE PRINCIPLES

Convenience of access trumps all other factors

The four goals: describe, understand, predict, control

OPERATIVE DYNAMICS

Engineering an innovation wave: invention, optimization, aggregation, diffusion

KEY CONCEPTS

Music on demand

Recording and playback devices

Thomas Edison

Edison Records

Jukeboxes

Wired and wireless communications

Guglielmo Marconi

Early media conglomerates

Rise of consumerism and the end of amateurism

Compressive effects of technology

FURTHER CONSIDERATION

The Menace of Mechanical Music

John Philip Sousa's remarkably prescient essay from *Appleton's Magazine* (1906) is available at http://www.mbsi.org/journal/MBSI-1968–15–2/MBSI -1968–15-2-04.pdf.

After reading it consider the following:

Does the essay explain Sousa's early advocacy for the first performing-rights organization, ASCAP? Why?

Does his professional interest completely explain his position, or does he seem genuinely concerned about social as well as economic issues? Why do you think so?

Can you find examples of similar essays, blogs, or interviews in the past fifteen years that express comparable sentiments for the modern era? What technologies and social behaviors are the sources of such concerns?

Be sure you explore the following:

Steven Van Zandt, "A Crisis of Craft," *Little Steven's Underground Garage* (2–2–2010), http://undergroundgarage.com/essays-and-speeches/a-crisis-of-craft.html.

Stuart Dredge, "Thom Yorke Calls Spotify 'the Last Desperate Fart of a Dying Corpse," *Guardian,* http://www.theguardian.com /technology/2013/oct/07/spotify-thom-yorke-dying-corpse.

James, Grebey, "Dave Grohl—Not an 'American Idol' Fan," *Spin* (10–29–2014), http://www.spin.com/articles/dave-grohl-american-idol-the-voice-music-talent-shows/.

Brad Paisley, "Start a Band" (song).

Exploration

Thomas Edison

"Where Modern America Was Invented," National Park Service, http://www.nps.gov/edis/index.htm.

National Park Service (Edison sound recordings), http://www.nps .gov/edis/photosmultimedia/the-recording-archives.htm.

Volta Labs Playlist

"Listening to the Past, Recorded on Tin Foil and Glass, for the First Time in over a Century," *MetaFilter* (blog) (2–10–2012), http://www.metafilter.com/112641/Listening-to-the-past-recorded-on-tin-foil-and-glass-for-the-first-time-in-over-a-century.

Music Technology Timeline

Callie Taintor, "Chronology: Technology and the Music Industry," *Frontline,* NPR (5–27–2004), http://www.pbs.org/wgbh/pages/frontline/shows/music/inside/cron.html.

CHAPTER 5

Convergence and Crossover

Bright lights, big city.

—Jimmy Reed

The years between the end of World War I in 1919 and the beginning of World War II in 1939 were a period of sweeping social and economic change in the United States. Due to the progressive and large-scale shift from an agricultural to a manufacturing economy, people—numbering in the millions—left rural areas in the South and Appalachia and migrated to large northern cities in search of industrial employment, better wages, and social opportunity.

During the same period, newly formed alliances between the recording and radio industries began to lift the business of making and selling music to unprecedented levels of financial success and cultural influence. The seemingly unlimited potential of the popular record business inspired the launch of new record labels and motivated all labels—both startup and established—to seek out new music and new audiences.

At the beginning of the 1920s, the recording industry had sales in excess of $100 million, but by 1925, pressure from radio had driven sales downward to $59 million. By 1929, new synergies and corporate partnerships had helped sales to rebound to $75 million. That same year the sale of record players reached 1 million units.

The arrival of the Great Depression in October of 1929 changed everything.

During the worst years of the depression (1929–1933), both sheet music and record sales were devastated. The sheet music sector had already been in decline since the late 1910s due to competition from records. When the depression hit, music publishers had to significantly reduce both prices (from an average of thirty cents per copy to twenty-five cents or less) and sales expectations (from "success" defined as five hundred thousand–plus copies sold to two hundred thousand sold). By 1933 record sales had fallen to an annual total of $5 million from a peak of $75 million prior to 1929.[1]

Radio was also affected, although the rising popularity of the medium and the fact that radio content—once you had the receiver—was free to consumers provided a bit more insulation from the worst economic effects of the depression as compared to music publishers and record labels. Jukebox operators also did reasonably well even during the worst years of the depression since profitability increased with each coin-operated play after the initial purchase of the recording.

The record industry developed a number of responses to the depression. Some followed the example of the sheet music industry, reducing prices and number of titles, and dropping artist contracts. Others, like the American Record Company (ARC) and American Decca, used the economic instability of the period to sign up artists—some very well established—who had been dropped or were dissatisfied with struggling labels. These adaptive strategies were effective enough for ARC and American Decca to come out of the depression years in a much stronger competitive position. Still others sought new audiences and new music to appeal to them.

The impact of socioeconomic conditions on recording and broadcasting industry business models can be summarized by three processes: *commercialization* of folk and traditional music and marketing to consumers previously untapped by the commercial music industry; *convergence* of previously distinct musical styles to create new commercial forms; and *crossover* buying patterns.

The third process is particularly important. Understanding the demography of consumers (who they were and where they lived) and correlating that with music preference made it possible to recognize when purchasing and listening behaviors transcended conventional expectations. When the popularity of a record was a result of consumers shifting from their predicted musical preference to that of a different group, the record came to be called a "crossover hit." While the phenomenon was initially surprising to industry professionals, soon deliberately creating crossover hits became a driving force in music production and a critical component of success in the record business.

COMMERCIALIZATION OF TRADITIONAL MUSIC

In addition to the "folk" musical styles that grew out of American regional traditions in the early twentieth century, there was also music produced by commercial entertainment businesses located in large cities like New York, Boston, Philadelphia, and Chicago. Minstrel shows, as well as other forms of public musical entertainment had, as noted previously, been immensely popular and profitable since the mid-1800s and toured widely across many regions of the country. Music publishing was based in New York, but produced sheet music that was sold all over the country.

As successful as this music industry was in the aggregate, it did not reflect every musical tradition or taste in the country, nor did it aspire to—at least not initially. There was a distinction between professionally produced music and folk styles, which were considered by music professionals to be more primitive and less valuable. But like any commercial enterprise, the music business was then (as now) driven by the desire not only to produce and popularize music but also to make money. As the music business developed the capacity to produce products on a mass scale and sell them to the largest possible number of consumers, issues of music supply and customer demand became ever more pivotal to success and failure.

By the later 1920s it had become apparent that continuing to expand the market for both sheet music and records depended upon finding both new sources for music and new audiences. One approach was to "collect" music, via field recordings, from regions outside the Northeast. The theory behind this was that music recorded in Appalachia, for example, could be sold to audiences in that region who might not buy "mainstream" music produced in one of the larger northern cities, like New York. This was the basis for many regional recordings being made and independent record labels being established.

Song Hunters: Collecting Regional Music

As music moved from one region of the country to another following social migration patterns, it began to change and adapt to new circumstances. As a result, even a decade or so into the twentieth century, those in search of "authentic" regional music were required to travel to its region of origin and find performers who remembered and could still perform the old music in the original way. At first this was motivated by an academic desire to catalog cultural history and practice. But even within that context, it became apparent that there was an audience far larger than scholars and folk song collectors to be tapped.

Alan Lomax and the Magnecord Tape Recorder

The Lomax family were song hunters. In the 1920s, John Lomax carried his wind-up mechanical phonograph and a supply of black discs all over the American South to make recordings of local musicians. According to the documentary *Lomax, the Songhunter:* "In 1933, the first time that Alan Lomax accompanied his father on a collecting trip, John was still using a wax cylinder phonograph, and other folklorists continued to use cylinder recorders throughout the 1930s. But the 1930s began the era of disc recorders, which was the equipment of choice for the younger generation of collectors."[2]

During the 1930s and 1940s, the Lomaxes carried disc-cutting machines on their trips, visiting farms, prisons, bars, and back porches. They recorded cowboy ballads, work songs, and blues. As noted by the American Folklife Center, "They were tireless collectors with an uncanny knack for finding traditional singers with large repertoires, and convincing them to sing and play for the cumbersome disc-cutting machine they carried with them."[3]

By the end of the 1940s, magnetic tape was becoming the preferred medium for audio recording. It was highly portable and produced a better-quality recording than disc-cutting machines. Alan Lomax was an early adopter of this technology, and it helped him to make better and more informal field recordings. Many of Lomax's most famous recordings, including Ray Charles, Woody Guthrie, and Leadbelly, were made using a Magnecord tape machine, manufactured in Chicago.[4]

John and Alan Lomax were by no means the first to make field recordings of regional music, although they were uniquely talented at finding people willing to record who also knew a great deal of traditional music. Where Alan distinguished himself as a song hunter was in the transition from his work for the US Library of Congress to the commercial recording world.

After recording thousands of songs and interviews for the Library of Congress, in 1942 Alan shifted his efforts to commercial recordings, primarily for Decca Records, and to concert promotion, including a number of historic "folk music" concerts at Carnegie Hall. Prior to that he had overseen the RCA release of Woody Guthrie's *Dust Bowl Ballads* in 1940 as well as Leadbelly's *Midnight Special and Other Southern Prison Songs*. Not only were these two albums successful commercially but they also helped to spark popular revivals of folk music and traditional blues. It is not an exaggeration to say that the explosion of commercially recorded regional music releases in the 1930s and 1940s were inspired by the work of John and Alan Lomax.

Commercial Field Recordings and Independent Labels

While the earliest song collectors, like the Lomaxes, typically worked for educational or governmental institutions—though not necessarily without economic motivation—the next wave of traveling recordists were directly seeking commercial product. A number of early record labels specializing in regional music styles began with a trip to the place where the music was born. In addition, once it became apparent that there was money to be made from regional music, other labels outside those regions began to entice performers to come to their studios, typically in or near Chicago and in the Northeast.

Three foundational twentieth-century musical styles that were discovered and adapted in this way were country, blues, and gospel. All three genres remain relevant on the record charts today—particularly if we include rhythm and blues, the direct, Chicago-based descendant of southern rural blues. The origins and commercial development of these genres are summarized below.

Country: The Bristol Sessions

The recording sessions produced in 1927–1928 in Bristol, Tennessee, by Ralph Peer for the Victor Company became the first important springboard for regional musicians to reach national audiences and launched the style that became known as country music. Several of the performers Peer recorded did not just sell records; they became the first country music celebrities.

The Carter family arguably became the first stars of country music, and Maybelle Carter inspired a generation to imitate her guitar playing on the record "Wildwood Flower." Jimmie Rodgers "probably sold more records for Victor than any artist before Elvis Presley." It is not an exaggeration to say, as Johnny Cash famously did, "These recordings in Bristol in 1927 are the single most important event in the history of Country music."[5]

The modern billion-dollar country music industry is rooted in those sessions recorded in a room at the Taylor-Christian Hat Company in Bristol, Tennessee. Ralph Peer and Victor had begun what was to become one of the most successful and far-reaching aggregations of talent ever undertaken—one that would help to define the modern music industry, the sound of American music, and American identity.

The Blues: Robert Johnson and H. C. Speir

Robert Johnson was born in Hazlehurst, Mississippi, in 1911 and spent much of his childhood living on plantations in the northern part of the Delta region. After a typical informal apprenticeship as a young musician, Johnson achieved a level of competence sufficient to be able to make some money and begin to establish a reputation. Johnson began to tour, visiting all of the major blues centers of the South, including Helena, Arkansas, as well as bars all over the Midwest and even into Canada.

For most blues musicians in the Delta, the path to wider recognition and financial success was making records. Johnson recorded twice in his lifetime, first in San Antonio, Texas, an important blues city, in 1936, and then in Dallas, Texas, in 1937. "The twenty-nine songs he recorded during those two sessions display an appreciation for the medium by being tight, thematically coherent, and short enough for one side of a 78 disc. Johnson's performances were unequalled. Bottleneck leads alternating with driving rhythms and lyrics sung in a high tense voice create masterpieces of the genre."[6] Critical recognition for the quality of Johnson's recorded work came only later, long after his violent death, when his recordings were rediscovered by famed artist and repertoire (A&R) man John Hammond, who convinced Columbia Records to release them as *King of the Delta Blues* in 1961. As a result of that record, Johnson finally achieved the commercial success and artistic influence he did not see during his lifetime.[7]

There were a number of record labels located in the South (as well as further north) that specialized in blues recordings—both those that came directly from the Delta and commercialized styles created for theatres and recording studies in the industrial North.

One of the most important figures in regional blues recording was H. C. Speir. Speir was a blues fan and music storeowner in Mississippi. Around 1926 he began describing himself as a "talent broker" because he would refer local blues musicians directly to record labels as well as make test recordings to forward on their behalf to his connections, for example, Ralph Peer at Victor. Speir became widely recognized as a reliable source for talent referrals and thus became one of the earliest A&R men in the record business.

Located in Wisconsin, Paramount Records was an important label for the blues, and numerous blues greats from Mississippi traveled to record in Paramount studios between 1929 and 1932—many of them as referrals from H.C. Speir. In 1930, Paramount management offered the company to Speir for $25,000, including the cost to relocate everything to Mississippi. Speir, however, did not have the cash, nor was he able to raise it.

Despite this roadblock—and Paramount in Mississippi would have undoubtedly been a "game-changer" for blues recordings—Speir remained active and influential. He did the original demo for Robert Johnson in Jacksonville. Impressed with the young, unknown artist's talent, Speir forwarded the demo to the American Record Company (ARC), where the arrangements for the San Antonio and Dallas sessions were made. Eventually, ARC released Johnson's recordings on one of their imprints, Vocalion.[8]

Gayle Wardlow, noted blues historian, observed that "Speir was the godfather of Delta Blues. H.C. Speir was to the Twenties and Thirties country blues what Sam Phillips was to Fifties rock & roll—a musical visionary. If it hadn't been for Speir, Mississippi's greatest natural resource might have gone untapped."[9]

Gospel: "Turn Your Radio On"

Though radio was indisputably critical to the popularization of both blues and country, no regional music was more fully integrated with radio than was southern gospel. Many performers, record label owners, engineers, and other music business professionals (of all ethnicities) cited listening to live gospel music on Sunday morning radio as a formative force in their lives.

Southern gospel music was advanced by live radio, but also by publishing. Although publishing became a subsidiary revenue source for all styles of music in the twentieth century—as well as the mechanism, under copyright law, for collecting all monies—a number of publishers played a particular role in the emergence of gospel as a cultural staple in the US.

One of the earliest and most often cited as a formative influence was Charles Davis Tillman, who was a pioneer in the composition and publishing of gospel music in the late nineteenth century. According to Wayne W. Daniel, country and gospel music historian, "During the almost 60 years that he was involved in the music business, he wrote some 100 songs, published 22 songbooks, and toured extensively as a song director with several evangelists, one of whom was his father."[10]

As the child of parents who were professionally involved with the evangelism movement in the South, Tillman grew up hearing the music sung in both white and African American communities. Daniel recounts one of Tillman's most inspirational moments: "Attending an African American camp meeting in South Carolina, Tillman heard the congregation singing a song called 'My Old Time Religion.' He quickly wrote down the words and music, revised them later at home, introduced the song to white audiences, and published it in 1891 in one of his songbooks. 'Gimme That Old Time Religion' soon became a standard in the canon of spiritual music."[11] Tillman repeated this process of inspiration, sometimes through direct appropriation, sometimes through collaboration, from the African American gospel tradition. Through successful publishing and regular radio appearances performing on WSB in Atlanta, Tillman became a powerful influence on the genre that came to be known as southern gospel music. The National Broadcasting Company broadcast an hour of his music nationally, and he recorded for Columbia Records.

Tillman business model incorporated personal performance, composition, and publishing, the three cornerstones of all professional music ventures in the nineteenth century. In addition, he was an early and effective adopter of the emerging technologies of radio and recording.

The next formative figure in the popularization and commercialization of gospel music was James D. Vaughn. Citing the inspiration of Tillman's early and innovative approach, Vaughn established the James D. Vaughn Music Publishing Company in Lawrenceburg, Tennessee, in 1902. Vaughn's innovation on the Tillman model was to sponsor a traveling gospel quartet to perform the music his company published, thus advertising and selling it at the same time. If Tillman was the originator of commercial gospel music, Vaughn was the man who created an industry based on it.[12]

In addition, recognizing the critical importance of education to establishing a complete commercial platform for southern gospel, Vaughn established a school of music in 1911 and held an annual event hosting gospel's most outstanding performers and composers. Vaughn also broadcast regularly on the radio, beginning with one of Tennessee's earliest radio stations, WOAN, "a station he founded in 1922 and continued to operate until 1930."[13] In addition, he launched one of the earliest record labels based in the South, Vaughn Phonograph Records, in 1921.

Vaughn can be seen as an optimizer of Tillman's approach, making several critical improvements. First, both men used performance, both live and on the radio, to improve their publishing opportunities. Vaughn established his own radio station to control this critical component. Vaughn also created his own regional record label, while Tillman depended on an established label with few regional ties. Having his own label also allowed Vaughn to aggregate other southern gospel artists by releasing and profiting from their creative efforts. Finally, by establishing a music school, Vaughn was able to encourage more gospel singing and provide the instructional materials for it, expanding both his potential audience and the amateur market for his published music.

The final step in moving gospel from the South and loosening its connection to the southern church came as the result of the misfortune that befell prominent commercial blues composer and performer Thomas Dorsey. Following severe illness in the mid-1920s, Dorsey changed his thinking about how he was making music and making a living, and sought to combine the spirituality of traditional gospel with the commercial appeal of the blues.

At the first meeting of the National Convention of Gospel Choirs and Choruses in Chicago in 1932, Dorsey's innovative and somewhat commercialized musical approach to gospel was enthusiastically received by an overwhelming majority of Baptist preachers and others. The result of those accolades not only validated Dorsey's individual strategy but also established the basis for all modern gospel music and gospel-influenced performance. The convergence of spirituality and physical exuberance, of the church and the marketplace, proved powerful and transformative. It is no exaggeration to say that without Dorsey's innovations, modern popular music—not just gospel but also rhythm and blues, rock and roll, and everything after—would not be the same.

CONVERGENCE OF ARTISTS AND AUDIENCES

One of the most powerful forces pulling Americans together across regional, economic, and racial divisions has been music. In the early years of the twentieth century, sound recordings and broadcast technologies dramatically expanded the diffusion of music, and in so doing, increased the integration of music and culture across geographic and social barriers. In addition, as patterns of social migration led to large numbers of people moving from rural to urban areas, artists and audiences who otherwise would never have crossed paths came together in newly shared spaces. As the middle years of the twentieth century approached, new music, new markets, and new audiences appeared as a result of both kinds of convergence—mediated and physical—and the interrelationships between them.

Barn Dances, Biscuits, and Border Blasters

Radio was a powerful aggregator of all regional styles and artists as well as an unprecedented distributor of music. In the process, the new medium began to exert an influence on content, moving from being a relatively passive conduit to shaping what was presented and the manner in which listeners experienced it.

Radio programs began to become venues, "places" where people "went" to have a musical experience. One of the features of this kind of mediated experience was that radio programs began to adopt aspects of the live performance experience, having masters of ceremony, stage banter among performers, and the sounds of an audience reacting to the performances. In aggregate, these audible details were intended to give the impression of "being there" at the event, wherever one might actually be while listening to the radio.

National Barn Dance

One of the most striking and influential platforms of this kind was the radio "barn dance." Though rarely, if ever, broadcast from or listened to in a barn, this format became astonishingly popular and an important platform for the national popularization of early country music.

The radio program *National Barn Dance* debuted on April 19, 1924, the first Saturday night after station WLS signed on the air from its Chicago studio. According to Edgar Bill, the first WLS station manager, "We had so much highbrow music the first week that we thought it would be a good idea to get on some of the old time music. After we had been going about an hour, we received about 25 telegrams of enthusiastic approval. It was this response that pushed the Barn Dance!"[14]

It was a good thing they received those telegrams. The station's owner and primary advertiser, Sears-Roebuck, was aghast by this "disgraceful low-brow music" being broadcast on its new station. When Bill was confronted by angry Sears-Roebuck executives, he was able to document the audience's overwhelming approval.[15] The show continued.

National Barn Dance was a success because it reached both rural audiences and Chicagoans who had come there from the South and other agriculture-based regions. Many recent arrivals to the city were still emotionally connected to the music of their homes, and the barn dance show provided an invaluable sense of connection for them. WLS became an important platform for country musicians as well as comedians. A regular spot on *National Barn Dance* often led to an invitation to perform on a national radio network.

The success of the program and the popularity of its emcee, George D. Hay, in particular, led to a series of "defections" as performers were recruited by other companies with radio stations looking to produce a similar impact. Not surprisingly, one of the biggest competitors for *National Barn Dance* and for the country music market generally was based in Nashville. Thus it was that the most important media platform for country music, the *Grand Ole Opry*, was appropriated from Chicago, the heart of the industrial North.

> The Grand Ole Opry began just five years after commercial radio was born in the United States. In 1925, the National Life and Accident Insurance Company built a radio station as a public service to the local community and with the hope that the new medium could advertise insurance policies. The station's call letters, WSM, stood for the company's motto: "We Shield Millions."
>
> Soon after going on the air, National Life hired one of the nation's most popular announcers, George D. Hay, as WSM's first program director. Hay, a former Memphis newspaper reporter who'd most recently started a barn dance show on Chicago radio powerhouse WLS, along with championship fiddler, Uncle Jimmy Thompson, created the WSM Barn Dance.
>
> Hay's weekly broadcasts continued and proved enormously popular, and he renamed the show the Grand Ole Opry in 1927. Crowds soon clogged hallways as they gathered to observe the performers, prompting the National Life Company to build an acoustically designed auditorium capable of holding 500 fans. When WSM radio increased broadcasting power to 50,000 watts in 1932, most of the United States and parts of Canada could tune into the Opry on Saturday nights, broadening the show's outreach.[16]

In a very real sense, the history of the *Grand Ole Opry* radio broadcast is the history of commercial country music. Everything we know today about the Nashville sound (and regional variants), Nashville publishing, record labels, celebrities, and so forth, is the result of the opportunism and reach of this amazing show. As of 2015, it was in its ninety-first year (first as *WSM Barn Dance,* then as *Grand Ole Opry*) of continuous broadcasting.

King Biscuit Time

Though never achieving the same geographic scope or audience size, the *King Biscuit Time* radio show was to the blues what the *Grand Ole Opry* was to country music. *King Biscuit Time* was first broadcast on November 21, 1941, by station KFFA in Helena, Arkansas, an important city for touring blues musicians. The radio station took advantage of that status by airing some of the finest blues musicians in North America as they passed through.

The show was named after its sponsor, King Biscuit Flour, as a result of a deal in which the local distributor agreed to pay for a short daily show if blues giants Sonny Boy Williams and Robert J. Lockwood would play live in the studio and if the show would mention King Biscuit Flour.

Guests varied, but there was a relatively stable group of studio musicians that regularly performed. The impact of this short daily show includes inspiring a syndicated rock show, the *King Biscuit Flower Hour,* as well as several southern blues festivals, including the King Biscuit Blues Festival in Helena.[17]

Border Blasters

The final radio-based convergence from this era was driven by so-called border blaster radio stations. The term *border radio* generically describes American-owned radio stations established inside Mexico near its border with the US, many of which were established during the 1930s. Because FCC limitations were not enforceable in Mexico, these stations could blanket North America with powerful radio transmitters (which would have been illegal inside the US) that reached from Mexico to Canada.

In the early years, the programming that proved most popular was so-called hillbilly music. The 1930s was a crucial time for that genre's commercial development, and the "border blaster" stations played an important role in its popularization. These stations "also familiarized American listeners with Mexican and Mexican-American artists.[18]

New agreements between the US and Mexico that allowed for shared use of high-powered frequency ranges essentially ended the era of the border blaster, or, as they were sometimes called, "clear channel" stations. But while they lasted, those powerful stations were a significant component of the widespread, continental dispersion of regional music whose original performers rarely traveled or performed more than a few miles from home.[19]

Music Scenes: The Geography of Musical Creativity

In addition to the mediated "spaces" created by radio broadcasts, there is another kind of place—a physical one—that can bring artists and audiences together: crossroads cities. Traditional crossroads cities tend to be large and situated on one or more means of transportation that facilitate the movement of people and goods, and support a robust economic and social infrastructure. They attract people from diverse locations, drawing them with work opportunities as well as quality-of-life resources, including material goods, health care, education, and social opportunities.

Richard Florida describes cities that provide an environment that nurtures musicians and musical creativity as "music scenes," a term he states "was originally used to describe the geographic concentrations of specific kinds of musical genres that evolved in mid-20th century musical centers like New Orleans jazz, Nashville country, Memphis soul, Detroit Motown, or Chicago blues."[20]

The Tin Pan Alley publishing district and the New York music theatre district can also be viewed as "music scenes" using this definition. London in the nineteenth century met the same criteria and was, as we have seen, a remarkably vital music scene. Regardless of their specific geographic location, music scenes bring "together musical and business talent (e.g., agents, managers, taste-makers, gate-keepers, critics, and sophisticated consumers) across social networks and physical space (neighborhoods, communities, clubs, venues, recording studios and venues)."[21]

By bringing together creators, producers, and consumers of music, music scenes shape developing genres and popular taste. National and international musical trends are almost always rooted in local music scenes. The transformation from local to global is the result of a complex system of production and distribution, but the motivation is quite simple: the quest for larger audiences, increased revenue, and expanded cultural influence.

When the music created in and nurtured by such a musical scene is distributed nationally via recordings and broadcast media, the scope of the scene expands both culturally and economically. Though the means for production, promotion, and distribution change from one era to another, the process inevitably depends upon

> a shift in the geography of music—from locally-constituted and genre specific music scenes to music clusters located in larger regions which offer scale economies in the form of larger, multi- and cross-genre markets for performance and experience and scope economies that stem from the concentration and spillover effects of related artistic and creative producers and industries.[22]

In other words, the larger the scene and the city or region that hosts it, the greater the resources for production and distribution. This is why major music cities—New York, London, and more recently, Los Angeles and Nashville, not only attract a great deal of musical talent but also have a disproportionate impact on the musical economy and culture as a whole.

The rise of such preeminent music scenes is an inevitable consequence of two aspects of musical productivity. First, the social experience of music must be situated in a particular, localized place so that artists and audiences can come together and interact. Second, in order to support mass enterprise, music production and reception must be on a scale that is regional if not larger. The tension between these two imperatives explains both major and independent labels and the rise of mainstream, commercialized versions of initially disruptive underground musical styles.

The process of taking local music to a national or international level is not only a matter of scaling production and distribution accordingly. It also involves understanding audiences that are increasingly distant from the artist and the frame of reference of the artist's home music scene. It is one thing to build and maintain a connection when artist and audience live in the same city and share live musical experiences in a physical place. But scaling the artist-audience relationship beyond a local context involves a variety of logistical, marketing, and distribution issues. Many of these factors will be examined in later chapters. Perhaps the most fundamental issue, however, is to understand, even as numbers and distances expand, who the audience is, where they are, and what matters most to them.

METRICS AND CROSSOVER: DEFINING (AND REDEFINING) IDENTITY AND SUCCESS

By the beginning of the Second World War in 1939, the commercial styles of country, blues, and gospel were well established, selling millions of records and reaching millions of listeners on the radio. As the music business increased in geographic scale, audience size, and diversity, monitoring sales and measuring success grew more challenging.

The methods by which these genres were marketed and the sale of records tracked were based on a belief that musical styles were most usefully defined—from a business perspective—not by their musical characteristics, but rather by the ethnicity, economic status, and geographic location of their audiences. This way of looking at music and music audiences was created by the magazine that ultimately became the music industry publication of record.

Billboard

Billboard was founded in 1894 as a trade magazine for the billboard sign industry and soon added coverage of circuses, carnivals, minstrel shows, and vaudeville. In 1905 *Billboard* began to track the sale of sheet music and, later, records. *Billboard*'s sales charts tracked jukebox play and record sales beginning in 1940. Those charts became (and, to a large extent, remain) the most critical measurement of success in popular music.

By 1944, *Billboard* was sorting records and sales into the categories of race, hillbilly, and pop. The *Billboard* sales charts were so important to the record industry that their underlying assumptions—that race music was created by and sold to African Americans in both city and country locations; hillbilly was music by and for rural whites; and pop music was intended for relatively wealthy, educated whites—began to define how decisions were made at record labels and radio stations.

Even though those chart categories were never a truly accurate map of how music was created, by whom, or of who was listening to it, most music companies/labels, radio stations, and live music venues kept their operations in line with the ethnic and socioeconomic characteristics of those audience demographics. White radio stations didn't play race records. Black nightclubs couldn't feature white performers or cater to integrated audiences. Hillbilly music wouldn't sell in the city.

Certainly, this demographic framework paralleled the deep-seated belief held by many Americans in the mid-twentieth century that segregation based on race and social class was important to social stability. But *Billboard*'s growing influence in the entertainment industry definitely encouraged business practices to fall in line with the categories, keeping the races, regions, and economic classes musically distinct—at least on paper.[23]

As noted earlier in this chapter, many of the new entertainment consumption technologies had the potential to break down these arbitrary divisions. Jukeboxes, for example, crossed barriers because—at least in theory—any record could be put into any jukebox, regardless of location. Radio waves traveled everywhere, and you could listen to a record without looking at the artist's photo on the cover.

Despite these practical realities, the American music industry midway through the twentieth century was still fundamentally segregated in its production and distribution. The industry largely operated on the assumption that consumption followed the same patterns. Outside the corporate offices, in the bars, clubs, and parties where working musicians played, another kind of musical participation was evident—one suggesting that separating styles and audiences by demographics did not reflect the social reality of music.

For example, rhythm and blues (originally *Billboard*'s "race" category) was assumed to be made by and for African American audiences. Nevertheless, young white audiences would fill the dance floor when a band played an R&B song, a fact noted by many performers in the 1940s and early 1950s. With a booming national economy following World War II, teenagers had their own money to spend, and it became apparent that they were also buying records and listening to radio stations across racial lines.

This is a critical issue for several reasons. First, the fact that audiences would "cross over" from one demographic category to another to buy records meant that at any given point, the potential audience was larger than the record categories suggested. Further, such sharing of musical experience outside of ethnic categories and across socioeconomic status lines suggested that long-held attitudes about social segregation would not stand forever. As a result, the pop music charts seemed to point the way toward not only a different business model for the music industry but also a more diverse and inclusive culture and society.

From the perspective of understanding how music enterprise works, the crossover phenomenon suggests something in addition. The "barriers" between the genres as expressed by the *Billboard* charts were an artificial construct, but they seemed to make sense and be in alignment with lived experience. Music that "broke down" those barriers—real or not—proved to be economically valuable and culturally transformative.

There are two principles in play here. First, there is a power in music that crosses boundaries and connects previously disconnected styles of music and/or audience experiences. Second, by identifying—in any given cultural context—things that apparently "don't go together," there is an implicit opportunity for success by connecting them. Understanding this principle could—and does—shape programming decisions on live shows, partnerships on recordings, and business agreements involving licensing music and brand relationships.

> Widespread belief that musical styles, performers, audiences, or events "don't go together" indicates an opportunity for a valuable economic and/or cultural convergence.

There are many examples of this throughout the remainder of the twentieth century and thus far in the twenty-first. Music awards shows are a particularly good source of such pairings, where "old" and "young" artists perform together onstage (Taylor Swift and Stevie Nicks), or artists from a disparate genre are included in a show devoted to another style (Snoop Dog on the Country Music Association [CMA] Awards). Those events are not just examples of attempts to expand the audience for both categories of music and performers. They are also attempts to exploit convergence; to cross a barrier reveal a previously hidden connection, and capture the power that convergence can produce.

CONVERGENCE, COMMERCIALIZATION, AND CROSSOVER

Production, distribution, and reception/consumption in music changed significantly in the first half of the twentieth century. Music styles, business models, and distribution patterns (and mechanisms) at the beginning of the 1950s were profoundly different than they were in 1900. This transformation was the result of the synergy of technological innovation, expanding economic opportunity, and the evolution of social and cultural expectations about music and musical experience.

Musicians, record labels, and radio stations that combined regional styles and cultural sensibilities began to create, produce, and distribute new forms of music that not only blurred stylistic lines but also grew "from the ground up" for commercial mass distribution. Rock and roll, rhythm and blues, Nashville country, rockabilly, and more were genres created and marketed with a deep understanding of how music could cross over from one demographic to another, expand the market and further cross-pollinate musical styles.

As markets expanded and revenues increased, interest in understanding those markets and the consumers in them created new systems of measurement for audience demographics and sales. *Billboard* was the leader in this initiative and, in the process, created not only the record charts but also the categories—initially pop, hillbilly, and race—that defined audiences and the music intended for their consumption. It was the disruption of this thinking—by proving that listeners and therefore records could cross from one category to another—that drove the success of new musical genres, disrupted established business models, and paved the way for the globally dominant American popular music industry to come.

CORE PRINCIPLES

Widespread belief that musical styles, performers, audiences, or events "don't go together" indicates an opportunity for a valuable economic and/or cultural convergence

KEY CONCEPTS

Cultural convergence: social migration, record distribution, broadcasting

Hybridity and commercialization of musical styles

Bristol sessions

H. C. Speir

Border blasters

Billboard

Record charts

Crossover

FURTHER CONSIDERATION
Show Us What You Got, Stevie

Consider the performance of "Burnin' Up" by the Jonas Brothers with Stevie Wonder at the 2009 Grammy Awards, or of "Rhiannon" by Stevie Nicks with Taylor Swift at the 2010 Grammys, or the appearance of

Snoop Dog as a presenter at the 2008 Country Music Television Awards in terms of the power of crossover. Are these examples of bridging previously distinct categories of performer, music, or genre a way to create some new synergy of creation and audience? What boundaries (and whose) are being crossed?

If you think about things in music today—styles, people, events, formats, and so forth—what pairs seem like they particularly don't go together? Taylor Swift and Def Leppard? It's been done. Hip-hop and metal? Done. A punk band and Broadway musicals? Ditto. What are some untried barriers or divisions in society and/or in music?

Can you find examples of a barrier-transcending attempt that failed? Why did it fail? What's the difference between a successful "border buster" and one that is not?

Links

http://www.grammy.com/photos/jonas-brothers-and-stevie-wonder.

http://www.esquire.com/entertainment/music/a31961/grammy-surprises/.

EXPLORATION

"The Ballad of Geeshie and Elvie"

John Jeremiah Sullivan, "The Ballad of Geeshie and Elvie: On the Trail of the Phantom Women Who Changed American Music and Then Vanished without a Trace," *New York Times Magazine* (4–13–2014), http://www.nytimes.com/interactive/2014/04/13/magazine/blues .html?src = longreads&_r = 0.

Billboard's *Rhythm and Blues Charts: Who Counts?*

Chris Molanphy, "I Know You Got Soul: The Trouble with *Billboard*'s R&B/Hip-Hop Chart," *Pitchfork* (4–14–2014), http://m .pitchfork.com/features/articles/9378-i-know-you-got-soul-the-trouble -with-billboards-rbhip-hop-chart/.

Sasha Frere-Jones, "Fixing the Charts," *New Yorker* (5–9–2014), http://newyorker.com/online/blogs/sashafrerejones/2014/05/fixing-the-billboard-music-charts.html.

CHAPTER 6

Massification

Music is a big machine that would go on with or without me.
—Rob Thomas

The history of music enterprise is a progression from patronage—performance for small, elite audiences and single-source payment—to mediated mass production for mass audiences. Certainly tastes and styles evolved and technological means were revolutionized, but it has been the increasing scale of it all—audience size, geographic scope, and potential economic reward—that has undergone the most astonishing change. By the mid-twentieth century, the massification of production, distribution, and consumption of music had begun to seem both inevitable and limitless.

Even as early as the 1920s, a single performance or recording could—via radio—be heard by millions across North America all at the same time. As this increasingly became the norm, more and more musicians aspired to make records, be on the radio, and become celebrities. Others wanted to own a radio station or start a record label and begin aggregating and distributing talent themselves.

All of this demand, this boundless ambition, created a need for methods to channel and control it.

In radio, the number of available broadcast frequencies limits the number of possible radio stations. The Federal Communications Commission (FCC) was established in 1934 to manage the airwaves, ensuring public access and deciding which applications for broadcast licenses were approved. Once licensed, radio station owners, managers, and program directors had the power—within certain legal constraints—to decide who and what went out over the air.

Sales of single records approached 200 million copies in 1950, and were three times that a decade later. The more commercial success increased, the more aspiring recording artists appeared. In the recording industry, the artist and repertoire (A&R) representative was an artist's first point of contact with a label. Like program directors in radio, A&R people were the gatekeepers to access: recording contracts, studio time, a producer, and all of the other resources of the popular music business. Getting a record deal became the prize for aspiring artists, a symbol of success and validation, and the gateway to fame and fortune.

Music publishing was already big business before records and radio. By midcentury, however, the sale of printed music was declining and, although publishers received publishing royalties from the sale of records, those profit margins were far less than for "copy sales."[1] Though publishers were also positioned to license the value of the musical creativity across live and mediated performances generally, the value of such licenses was not yet well established.

On the surface, the mass music era appears to be mostly about the synergy between the recording and radio industries, but publishers were also important managers of musical content—though much more behind the scenes. Radio DJs and even some record producers (Phil Spector, for example) achieved fame. Publishers rarely became famous, yet a publishing deal could open the same doors to an aspiring songwriter as a recording contract. In fact, a recording contract without a publishing deal was a recipe for exploitation. And, due to the radio exemption (see chapter 5), publishers controlled the only means to receive royalties from records played on the radio.

The necessity for control mechanisms and "decider" roles in the radio, recording, and publishing industries put them all in a position to be both nurturers and gatekeepers of musical culture in the twentieth century. Though these roles had existed previously, as the reach and impact of recording and broadcast media were realized in the twentieth century, the roles of gatekeeper and nurturer became more powerful than ever before. This chapter looks the emerging mechanics of star and hit making in the mass popular music industry, and the people who built and fine-tuned that machinery.

CONVERGENCE AND CROSSOVER INTENSIFY: ROCK AND ROLL

The years between the two world wars was a time of migration for Americans seeking better opportunities, and the end of World War II only intensified that impulse and mobility. Between the return of American soldiers to civilian life, general economic growth in the 1950s, and national initiatives like the interstate highway system, it was an era of great energy. It was also a time when teenagers had an unprecedented amount of money of their own and products—movies, drive-in movie theatres, clothing, and music—were produced and marketed with teens in mind.

This teen market was immensely profitable and also controversial. Teen-oriented culture struck many adults as dangerous to young people and to society as a whole. Fears about drug use, "juvenile delinquency," and "sexual hysteria" were seriously discussed, and popular music for teens was at the core of many of those discussions. Before the 1960s were over, fortunes had been made, businesses disrupted, and popular culture irrevocably altered by records made for teenagers.

In many ways, rock and roll was the epicenter of the postwar teen culture and commerce explosion. The music, the lyrics, the performers, the dances, and the audience demographics all represented both opportunity and disruption, commercially and socially. Rock and roll's capacity to transcend musical boundaries, as well as age, racial, and geographic identities, not to mention sexual conventions, made it a powerful driver of convergence. As noted in chapter 5, a widespread belief that musical styles, performers, audiences, or events "don't go together" indicates that there is an opportunity for an economic and/or culturally valuable convergence.

Rock and roll did all that on a previously unimagined scale. Some few entrepreneurs were looking for a way to make that convergence happen, while others simply observed what was already happening.

A number of pre–rock and roll performers—working in various sub-genres of rhythm and blues and country—began to experiment with performing songs and then making records that deliberately crossed identity lines and mixed musical streams. This worked very well, and soon crossover became a standard approach in the record business.

In addition, rock and roll democratized songwriting and performance in a way that blurred the distinctions between amateurs and professionals. This led mainstream music businesses to underestimate the potential of rock and roll, which in turn created opportunities for independent labels and radio stations to promote and exploit it. This democratization also inspired a generation of young people to make the leap from the seats to the stage, to start bands, and to dream big.

Garage Bands

By the end of the 1950s, the number of amateur rock and pop bands had skyrocketed. No accurate count is possible, but it is undoubtedly in the tens of thousands, if not more.[2] Often called "garage bands" because they frequently rehearsed in the garage of one of the band members' parents, they learned how to perform by copying the records of established artists. The members of these bands were often motivated by recreation and social connection. But the bands could also be a kind of apprenticeship for aspiring performers. Virtually every band and artist that rose to prominence in the 1960s began in a garage band covering the hits of American rock and roll and rhythm and blues.

Of course, very few bands rose to international fame. Most never got out of the garage, or in any case, not much further than a local teen dance. But some garage bands fit neither category. Some were able achieve a musical originality that sparked the emergence of a new musical style, local music scene, or even a hit record, becoming "one-hit wonders" before they disappeared.

Both the pure amateurs and the one-hit-wonder professionals were also important consumers of music and music-making products. They helped build a huge market for musical instruments—especially electric guitars and amps—and accessories.[3] And they also represent a particular type of consumer: one that also produces—a type described by Alvin Toffler as a "prosumer."[4]

In the second half of the twentieth century, musical amateurs continued to start and play in bands, sometimes for social and sometimes for professional reasons. In addition, although there were still "stars" and "fans," the idea of the amateur talent show gained traction. Increasingly, as the twentieth century ended and the twenty-first began, aspiring musicians didn't dream as often of starting bands; they wanted to be discovered on nationally televised talent searches (for a more detailed discussion, see chapter 9, "Artists, Audiences, and Brands").

In the 1950s and early '60s, most musical amateurs and semiprofessionals—in garage bands, local scenes, and even at smaller independent labels—were invisible to the major labels and publishing companies. In part, this was a consequence of the major label, publisher, and broadcast network attitude that rock and roll was crude, amateurish, and destined to be a short-lived fad. But it was also was due to a sense that established publishing, recording, and broadcasting already controlled the most valuable music products and—secure in their gatekeeper roles—didn't need to concern themselves with upstart competition.

Eventually, though, as the popularity of youth-oriented pop music showed no sign of diminishing and its market share continued to increase, mainstream music businesses began to respond. They used various creative, social, and legal methods to slow down the independent competition. In the process, they reshaped music production and consumption for the second half of the twentieth century and defined the "battlefields" among the stakeholders—producers and consumers—in recording, broadcasting, publishing, and live performance.

MIDCENTURY RECORD LABELS

The difference between "major" and "independent" labels is primarily one of size. Major labels are bigger. They represent more artists, have more resources for promotion and distribution, and have the relationships and the means to handle international distribution. Majors may produce records in more than one musical genre, using sublabels or imprints to distinguish product areas. These imprints, organized as subsidiaries of the main label, may be the result of the acquisition of smaller labels or have been created by the major itself in order to take advantage of an emerging or specialized musical trend or audience. Major labels and their sublabels function as massive aggregators and distributors of content and, as such, became major gatekeepers of public access and shapers of musical culture.

Independent labels are smaller and represent fewer artists in a narrower spectrum of styles or a single style. Typically, independents have fewer resources for promotion and historically have entered into agreements with larger labels to handle their distribution, both nationally and abroad. Conventional wisdom holds that independent labels are best for developing new and especially outside-the-mainstream musical styles. Bands and solo artists have often gotten their first big break and exposure to regional radio play and record sales via an independent label. Then, after some commercial success, they sign with a major to take their career to the next level of exposure, success, and both national and international audiences. Independent labels have often been perceived more as nurturers than gatekeepers, discovering artists near the beginning of their careers, helping them to find their voice, providing public exposure, and developing the beginnings of an artistic brand.

Evolution of Major Labels

Many major labels, of course, contributed to the development of the recording industry. For reasons of space and focus, two are discussed here, Decca Records and RCA Records; they exemplify the major label category in the era when majors first emerged.

Decca Records

Decca Records was a British label established in 1929. The US label, American Decca, was added in 1934. American Decca was particularly effective, even during the years following the stock market crash, because of its felicity in signing several of the major popular artists and the marketing expertise of its general manager, Jack Kapp.[5]

The US label emphasized mainstream pop music like Bing Crosby ("White Christmas," 1942), easy listening, Broadway musicals, country music, and compilations. Decades later, British Decca, after passing on recording the Beatles, bounced back and signed the Rolling Stones and several other rock acts in the 1960s. Today, Decca in both the US and the UK is part of EMG.

RCA Records

One of the oldest brands in recorded music began as a result of the purchase, by the Radio Corporation of America, of the Victor Talking Machine Company in 1929. As a company, RCA was always interested in playback media, unsuccessfully attempting to introduce the 33 1/3-rpm record in 1931 and then successfully introducing the 45-rpm record in 1949—which became the industry standard for singles.

During the 1950s, RCA expanded its operations to Nashville in order to take advantage of the growing country music market. During this time RCA built the now legendary Studio B recording studio and signed Elvis Presley to his first national record deal.[6]

In 1983, RCA merged with major Bertelsmann to form Bertelsmann Music Group (BMG).[7] In 2003 Sony and BMG agreed to merge their interests to form Sony BMG, and in 2008 Sony bought out BMG to form Sony Music Entertainment. RCA was part of the newly formed RCA/Jive Label group until 2011, when RCA shut down both Arista and Jive to focus on "artist development and making better records."[8]

The "Bigs"

The complex business transactions that shaped the last thirty years of RCA Records history are typical of the era of the conglomerate major labels, now usually called "music groups." Over the past several decades, large-scale mergers and ever-larger music groups have increasingly defined the upper end of the music industry. The largest of these groups have come to be defined as the "Big Six," the "Big Five," and so on. The fact that the number of "Bigs" declines points out another trend. The number of Bigs is getting progressively smaller, indicating that the production and distribution of more and more musical product are being concentrated into fewer and fewer hands.

During the 1990s—the boom years for record sales after the CD was introduced—industry analysts and journalists talked about Warner Music Group, EMI, Sony Music, Polygram, Universal Music Group, and BMG as the "Big Six" labels. In 1998, the merger of Polygram and the Universal Music Group brought the "big" number down to five. The new, combined Universal controlled over 25 percent of the world's recorded music market, and the Big Five together controlled somewhere between 75 and 90 percent. As noted, in 2003, Sony and BMG agreed on a merger, yielding a "Big Four" consisting of Universal Music Group, Sony Music Entertainment, Warner Music Group, and EMI.

The latest consolidation to date was the most complicated. The *New York Times* described it this way in 2011: "In a complex sale brokered by Citigroup, the Universal Music Group, a division of the French conglomerate Vivendi, will absorb EMI's recorded music operations for $1.9 billion, while EMI's music publishing division will be sold for $2.2 billion to a consortium of investors led by Sony, the companies announced on Friday."[9]

Ben Sisario, the author of that article, goes on to discuss the dominant position, in terms of market share and song catalogs, that Sony and Universal Music Group would hold as a result of the deal. The article reports that in 2010, revenues for Universal were near $6 billion, for Sony $5.7 billion, and for Warner $3 billion. Factoring in the value of EMI's catalog ($1.8 billion) and publishing (nearly $750 million), the financial advantage of the two largest of the Big Three labels increases significantly. As Sisario notes, "With Universal and Sony now far outweighing the third major, the Warner Music Group, the competitive landscape of the industry is expected to shift."[10]

A critical issue raised by the progressive consolidation of the majors from six to three is market share—the competitive advantage that it confers and what it implies about the relationship of gatekeeper and nurturer roles in record production.

As we will explore in later chapters, the emergence of online services for downloading and streaming music has further aggregated music, musicians, and even major labels, intensifying concerns about nurturing new music. Other issues, such as what the consolidation of majors does to create opportunities and constraints for independent labels, are discussed in the next section.

Evolution of Independent Labels

Other than size, perhaps the most important difference between major labels and independents is connection to local musical culture. The history of independent labels in the US shows over and over that labels start out small and as part of a local music scene (see chapter 5). From that position, independent label owners and management can be more accessible to performers and, potentially, more personally invested in the local community, better connected to audiences, and more knowledgeable and passionate about local/regional styles. Taken together with the tendency of majors to be less accessible, particularly to young, unsophisticated artists, independent labels have a history of being leaders in "breaking" not only undiscovered talent but also new musical styles.

Further, there is the consideration of authenticity. While no one goes into business to lose money, independent labels have in general been more invested in capturing a particular sound and flavor of music and musical experience and relatively less concerned with marketplace considerations. Majors, on the other hand, with larger investments in infrastructure, are inevitably more concerned with the broadest commercial potential of a given act, sometimes reshaping an original, locally inspired and developed sound in order to achieve that goal. The following discussion examines a few specific examples of how these tendencies played out for independent labels at midcentury.

Sun Records

Sun Records opened in Memphis, Tennessee, in 1952.[11] Founded by Sam Phillips, Sun Records (originally as the Memphis Recording Service) became known for giving unknown performers such as Elvis Presley, Carl Perkins, Roy Orbison, and Johnny Cash their first recording contracts. Ultimately, these and other Sun artists went on to sign with major labels and establish international careers. But it was Phillips's vision, as well as his musical and business acumen, that not only launched specific careers but also established "rockabilly" as a musical style; Phillips had a significant role in launching the transformative force of rock and roll into the world.

Perhaps the best recognized Sun artist today is Elvis Presley. Presley was a local Memphis teen who wanted to make gospel records. He began hanging around Sun studios, hoping to be discovered—an obvious example of how a local independent can be more accessible than a major. After some time and a period of uncertainty at Sun about his potential, Presley recorded a cover version of "That's All Right."

That recording, originally an R&B classic by Arthur "Big Boy" Crudup, cast the song in a country style. That single was "backed" with the song "Blue Moon of Kentucky," a bluegrass hit by the then huge star Bill Monroe. The Monroe cover was also retooled into an up-tempo rockabilly style. Both sides of this 45-rpm release were successful, appearing on the R&B, country, and pop charts. As a result, not only did Phillips launch Elvis Presley's career, but he also demonstrated the crossover potential of rockabilly, as well as the tactic of treating both sides of a 45 as potential hits targeting different market demographics.

A successful strategy? Absolutely—but, typical of small independent labels, one limited in scale.

Phillips sold Presley's recording contract to RCA Records for $35,000 (with a $5,000 bonus for Elvis) in 1955, recognizing that he did not have the promotion or distribution resources that Presley's career was soon going to need. In addition, Phillips planned to use those funds to develop new artists, which was always his primary motivation. In many ways Phillips's decisions define the strengths and limitations of independent labels.[12]

Sun Records Strength/Limitation Summary

Strengths: accessibility, artistic development, personal touch, commitment to particular style
Limitations: resources for promotion and distribution

Phillips developed a number of other successful artists after Presley. He also turned down offers to produce records for larger labels, including a generous one from RCA Nashville to help with Presley's early records. Independent to the end, Phillips sold Sun Records in 1969.[13]

Chess Records

Brothers Leonard and Phil Chess came to Chicago from Poland in the 1920s. After some years in nonmusic ventures, they entered into a partnership in 1947 with the owners of Aristocrat Records to make blues and R&B recordings. An early Aristocrat artist was McKinley Morganfield, known professionally as Muddy Waters. At Chess, Waters became one of the foremost exponents of the Chicago blues.

In 1949, the Chess brothers bought out their partners' interest in Aristocrat and changed its name to Chess Records. Chess became one of the major players in R&B, along with other independents like Atlantic. Sam Phillips, before he established Sun, leased the master recordings of one of his discoveries, Chester Burnette, to Chess Records. Burnette, known onstage as Howlin' Wolf, became—perhaps only second to Waters—one of the most influential American blues and R&B artists of the 1950s and beyond.

During the 1950s, the Chess label also experimented with making records by African American artists intended for white audiences. As a result, Chess was an early proponent of the so-called doo-wop style of pop, producing the Flamingos and the Moonglows. Though it was so-called white covers of those songs (on other labels) that made the most money, ultimately Chess's reputation as a hit-making label was further solidified.[14]

In 1955, based on the recommendation of Muddy Waters, Chess recorded Chuck Berry's "Ida Red," which was reworked to be the single "Maybelline." It was the first of many Top 40 hits by Berry on Chess, though it turned out to be a mixed blessing. The name of popular radio DJ Alan Freed, ended up on the label of "Maybelline" as coauthor with Berry. It was a common exploitative practice in the 1940s and 1950s for a person not involved in the creation or production of a record to have his name put on the record label to get a percentage of publishing royalties as payment for some service rendered. In the case of "Maybelline," it was in exchange for Freed playing the record on his popular New York–based rock and roll radio show.[15]

Despite engaging in such practices, the Chess brothers and their label maintained a generally positive relationship with most of their artists for a long time. According to journalist Joel Francis's history of the label, "With the exception of Berry, who briefly recorded for Mercury in the mid-'60s before returning to Chess, and Dixon, who took a short-lived job at Vee-Jay, all of Chess' major artists stayed with the label until its sale."[16]

Motivated by the desire to move in new directions, the Chess brothers sold the label to General Recorded Tape in 1969 for $6.5 million. Under the new management, Chess quickly lost relevance in the marketplace and was dissolved in 1975.[17]

Vee-Jay

Another Chicago-based label associated with the blues provides a contrast to Chess Records. Vee-Jay Records was founded by wife-and-husband team Vivian Carter Bracken and James Bracken. They began with a $500 loan to record a group in Gary, Indiana, where they owned a music store at the time.[18] That record, "Baby It's You," by the Spaniels, was so successful that it had to be leased to another label for distribution.

Vee-Jay soon relocated to Chicago and produced additional singles with the Spaniels as well as other blues artists attracted by the label's success. Unlike the Chess brothers, during the 1950s the Brackens were much more aware of changing tastes and emerging styles. From early doo-wop greats (and soul music forerunners) the Dells to Gene Chandler's "Duke of Earl" in 1961, Vee-Jay made itself into "one of America's top labels."[19]

Ironically, Vee-Jay's problems and eventual downfall began with its most successful record, "Sherry," by the Four Seasons. Vee-Jay did not have the resources to press enough copies of the record to keep up with demand. In part, this was due to the label's record promotion practices. Vee-Jay's business manager, Ewart Abner, was known for his extravagant gifts to DJs, as well as for, reportedly, gambling with the label's payroll in Las Vegas.[20]

While Vee-Jay could not meet its current obligations to press records for successful acts like the Four Seasons, they continued, impractically, to ride the front edge of popular music styles and sign new acts, and—as part of a package deal in 1963—took on the Beatles from British major EMI. The label sold 2.5 million records the first month, but could not pay for more pressings or even the artists' royalties. A series of lawsuits from artists and even other labels soon followed. Vee-Jay closed in 1964, nominally at the height of its success, but unable to meet its financial obligations.

Sun, Chess, and Vee-Jay illustrate—in different ways—a fundamental challenge for independent record labels in the massification era of music. They each excelled at capturing a local music "vibe" and cultivating the artists within it, achieving creative success with relatively minimal capital resources. But meeting the expectations of a market based on mass production and distribution required significant resources and particular kinds of expertise. Phillips was willing to sell artist contracts outright. Chess worked successfully through licensed distribution arrangements with larger labels. Vee-Jay, however, was unable to adopt either strategy and did not thrive, despite, and to some extent even because of, their success.

RECORD LABEL AS PROCESS

In examining a number of specific labels—large and small—it is easy to see the broad similarities and differences between them. But if we strip away the contextual details and look deeper, we can uncover structural elements that define how record labels work, regardless of specific situations. To do so, we will define and examine the elements common to all record label enterprises: the resources, roles, and activities used to produce the output—bringing a commercial musical product to a mass audience.

To begin, let's return to the diagram representing the transactional musical experience in its most basic form (see figure 6). As discussed in the first chapter, the upper arrow indicates the delivery mechanisms for connecting the musical artist to the audience. The kinds of response that flow back to an artist include those in the social realm—recognition and status—as well as the economic.

A variety of systems have been created to manage and exploit this dynamic relationship. Record labels function as an optimization system for the entire transaction of creating and experiencing music. As such, in the context of the diagram shown in figure 6, any record label sits in the middle, comprising both arrows and overlapping with producers and consumers. This can be graphically represented as in the diagram shown in figure 7.

Let's look more deeply at the center circle.

Fundamentally, any record label—regardless of size—is in the business of creating recorded product to sell to the public. Achieving this on any scale depends on a multistage process: discovery, development, production, promotion, distribution, sales, monitoring, accounting, and royalty payments. The first six stages—discovery through sales—correlate with

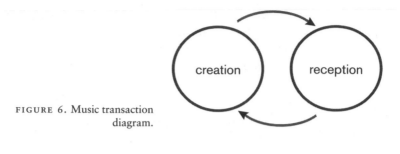

FIGURE 6. Music transaction diagram.

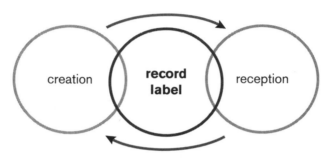

FIGURE 7. Music transaction diagram: record labels.

the arrow on top of the circle. The last three—monitoring, accounting, and royalty payments—correlate with the bottom arrow. The record label process is expressed graphically in figure 8.

Discovery: Artists and Repertoire

The record label process begins with finding artists with creative and commercial potential, which includes the artist personally as well as her music. This has traditionally been the province of A&R, or artists and repertoire. Finding talent can be both simple and difficult. Simple, because all you have to do is go out and listen to music. In addition, after a certain amount of success, musicians find the label. Sun, Chess, and Vee-Jay all achieved sufficient success to attract aspiring performers. The difficulty in discovery arises in moving from the personal and local to larger markets. A&R representatives used their personal taste to identify potential talent, but without a capacity to connect to a larger audience, the discovery had little potential to generate value. Likewise, an artist perfectly suited to the audience in a specific location who did

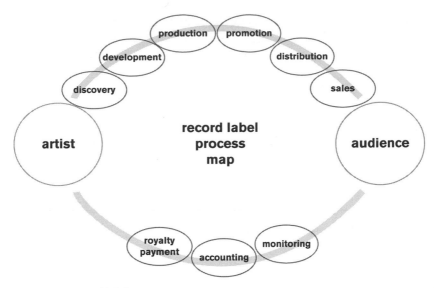

FIGURE 8. Record label process map.

not "travel well" would also be of limited commercial value. To some extent, however, such issues could be mitigated by the development of the artist and his music.

Development: Images and Singles

Since marketability in music has consistently depended on the right song combined with the right performer, artist image and hit singles have gone hand in hand since the earliest days of recording. Even in the prerecording days, when sheet music rather than records drove music commerce, having the photo of certain artists on the cover of the music meant bigger sales. To that end, the A&R person will often continue to work with artists during this phase, though it might also become the responsibility of a producer to guide the development process.

Production: Commercially Viable Master Recording

The production process takes over from A&R to bring the performer and her material into a studio, where a recording engineer captures performances on disc, tape, or (later) digital media. The performance-to-recording process is guided by a producer, who must balance creativity, technical limits (with the engineer), marketability, and budget. The end point of the production process is a commercially viable master recording.[21]

Promotion: Advertising, Appearances, and Media Play

The delivery of a finished master marks the point at which an artist's song—now transformed into a commercial product—can be marketed to an audience. Historically, this has been the domain of the record promoter, whose job was to encourage radio stations to air selected singles.

Radio play was typically coordinated with live appearances in order to generate media coverage and consumer excitement, as well as to increase audience access to both the song (via radio and retail) and the artist herself (via television, print, and radio interviews and performances). Promotion is critical to enhancing familiarity with a song, boosting record sales, and circulating the artist's brand (see chapter 9, "Artists, Audiences, and Brands").

Of all of the record label process elements, few have been more cash intensive than promotion. Historically, this has been one of the key factors differentiating major and smaller labels, as well as often (but not always) making the difference between success and failure.

Distribution: Providing Access

Just as product has little value if people don't know about it and want to buy it, so promotion has little value without available product. In the twentieth century, distribution primarily meant shipping physical recordings: albums or singles. Even as formats changed to tape and then the CD, there was a physical product typically shipped to a brick-and-mortar retail store. Much like promotion, the distribution (and manufacturing) of recorded product is relatively expensive and requires the expertise and resources of a large-scale logistics network.

Sales: Profit and Loss, Gatekeepers and Nurturers

Monetizing the musical experience depends upon turning listeners into customers. In the retail store environment, customers traditionally purchased a recording in order to have access, on demand, to the music in question. It was only at this step—the sixth in the process—where the record label stopped spending and began making money—at least potentially.

The majority of records released in the second half of the twentieth century never made a profit. While the relatively few hit records could and did create massive profits, the business model required large, relatively risky investments to move musicians' creativity to the point of sales.

But the importance of hits was more than keeping the profit-and-loss statement "in the black" for the year. Without sufficient revenue, the high-risk investment in discovery, development, production, promotion, and distribution would become impossible. The gatekeeper role would get stronger to protect a label from risk, and the nurturer role would get proportionately weaker.

In the latter twentieth century, record labels nurtured a great deal of rising talent. As we will see in chapter 10, "Digitization," things would change greatly in the twenty-first.

Monitoring, Accounting, and Royalty Payments

Since record sales have been so closely related to radio play (and vice versa), one of the most significant success metrics has been *Billboard* chart placement, as well as the RIAA certification as a "gold" or "platinum" record.[22] Additionally, there are forms of direct sales accounting among labels, distributors, retailers, publishers, and performers. Likewise, publishing royalties (typically shared by songwriter and publisher) must be tracked. Licenses for the secondary use of master recordings are also part of the monitoring phase. Keeping track of who is buying and using an artist's and label's music is critical to capturing the value produced.

The disbursement of artist royalties is a particularly complex and potentially contentious phase. Since record labels incur significant expenses in all steps of the process up to and including paying royalties, there are significant costs to be covered, or "recouped," before any profit is realized.

Most standard recording contracts do not provide for artists to receive royalty payments until all costs are recovered by the label. Another standard contractual provision is that labels get to use their own accounting to determine when that point is reached. Thus, accounting and royalty payments are interconnected and often a source of disagreement between artists and labels. Accounting and royalty payment disputes exemplify the challenges inherent in every interface between creativity and commerce and the "artist versus label mentality" prevalent in the music industry.

Understanding this adversarial relationship is important to being able to understand how music enterprise works in the recording business and beyond. Without access to an audience, music doesn't get heard and money doesn't get made. In effect, creativity must be exploited to make it available enough to create value. There are costs associated with this, and the larger the scale of the exploitation, the higher the cost. One reason that established artists can make more favorable revenue-sharing arrangements with labels is that with a history of commercial success, they represent a lower risk.

RECORD LABELS AND PUBLISHING COMPANIES

Although by midcentury total record sales surpassed even the best years of sheet music sales, publishing continued to have a significant value. Not so much because people were eager to buy the sheet music to "Blue Suede Shoes" and play it on the piano in their parlor—although that did still happen—but rather because owning the publishing rights (the underlying words and music) of a hit record had an economic potential that was just beginning to be realized.

Carl Perkins's recording of "Blue Suede Shoes" was Sun Records's first million-selling hit, and the sheet music for it was released in 1956 by Hill and Range publishers. The "Blue Suede Shoes" record made money for Carl Perkins, Sam Phillips, and Elvis Presley (when he covered it), as well as for Hill and Range. Perkins, along with Hill and Range, received royalties from all recorded versions (including Presley's) as well as from the sheet music sales in 1956 and for many years to come. Various arrangements of "Blue Suede Shoes" are still for sale today in print and via digital download. Thus, in practical terms, the revenue-generating potential of publishing went far beyond the sale of printed copies.

If we map the music publishing process as we did for record labels, we find a model that creates more revenue pathways than recordings do. In addition, because publishers manage the revenue created via mechanical licenses—necessary for records to be made—the publishing process supports and to some extent incorporates the record label process (see figure 9).

The relationship between publishing and performance was also critical to production and consumption on a mass scale. Perkins, for example, wrote his own hit song. But Presley, like many famous performers, did not write music. The majority of the music Presley and other non-

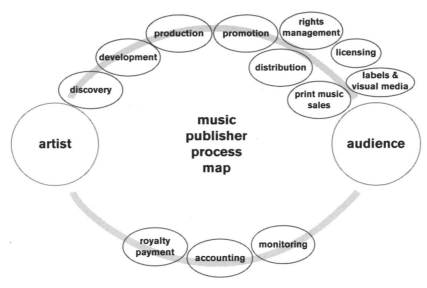

FIGURE 9. Publishing process map.

writing performers recorded was provided by professional songwriters like those who worked in Tin Pan Alley and, later, in Nashville. Getting a song "placed" with a performer who was proven hit maker was a critical objective for songwriters and their publishing companies.

Song placement was not a matter of luck. Publishers worked with artists, managers, and record companies to get their names on the record label. Several of the more influential and effective publishers—and therefore the best connected with artists and their labels—are discussed below.

Acuff-Rose

One of the most powerful music publishers of the recording era was founded in 1942 by popular country music performer Roy Acuff and songwriter Fred Rose. Acuff was already selling songbooks of his music at his live performances and was looking to increase revenue. Rose had written hit songs for recording and movie performers. As a writer, Rose had played a major role in the conversion of Nashville songs from their traditional origins to a successful commercial style.[23]

One of the ways that publishing companies maintained relevance and increased revenue production in the recording era was by discovering and signing talent to their companies. Acuff-Rose signed Hank Williams to a publishing deal in 1946 and got him his first recording contract shortly thereafter. Williams's songs became a cornerstone of the Acuff-Rose catalog, but Acuff-Rose also went on to sign and publish the music of dozens of country music celebrity performers as well as influential composers.

Their catalog and contracts gave Acuff-Rose significant leverage on Music Row in Nashville. Record producers wanted access to their artists and songs. Artists wanted access to their songwriters. As a result, being represented by or having a productive working relationship with Acuff-Rose was a ticket to success. Conversely, not doing what they wanted could become problematic very quickly. The story of the Everly Brothers is a perfect example.

Don and Phil Everly began performing in a family group along with their father. Famed guitarist and RCA music executive Chet Atkins, a longtime family friend, helped the brothers get their first record deal in 1956. When an early single failed to perform, their label dropped them. Atkins then introduced them to Wesley Rose, who had taken over for his father after Fred passed away in 1954. After the introduction from Atkins and an audition, Wesley agreed to manage the Everly Brothers, promising them a new record deal if they would sign a contract making Acuff-Rose the exclusive publisher of their songs.

Three successful years at a small label were followed by a ten-year, multi-million-dollar contract with Warner Brothers. Everly Brothers records sold millions, and they became a household name. But the source of their success—the publishing deal with Acuff-Rose—soon became their undoing.

Around 1961, the brothers began expressing interest in performing songs by writers other than those represented by Acuff-Rose. This was contrary to the wishes of Wesley Rose, who had them use only his writers when they weren't performing their own songs.

The economic motivation for this should be obvious. If Acuff-Rose owned the publishing on every song performed by the Everly Brothers, then Acuff-Rose got a piece of the royalties on every record, album, piece of sheet music, radio play, cover version, and live performance by or in any way related to the Everly Brothers. In effect, Acuff-Rose profited more than the brothers' label or, conceivably, the brothers themselves.

Wesley Rose was displeased, and the Everly Brothers lost access to the "A list" songwriters represented by Acuff-Rose, several of whom had previously written hits for the brothers. In addition, since Don and Phil were represented by Acuff-Rose as songwriters themselves, they also lost access to their own, more recent, songs for recording purposes. As performers they could do as they wished, but in terms of publishing and recording, they were confined to covering songs by writers that were published by publishing houses other than Acuff-Rose.[24]

Being blacklisted by Acuff-Rose (from 1961 to 1964) seriously damaged the Everly Brothers's career. Though they tried to work around their problems with the publisher, they were limited primarily to covering the music of other writers and artists and their popularity suffered. The harm to their reputation was amplified by the rise of the Beatles and other British invasion bands during the period. They were never able to recover their pre-blacklist audience. Acuff-Rose was sold to Gaylord Entertainment Company in 1984 and is today owned by Sony/ATV Music Publishing, a subsidiary of Big Three music group Sony Music Entertainment.

Elvis and Julian

Hill and Range, the publishing company that published the sheet music for Carl Perkins's "Blue Suede Shoes," was established in Los Angeles in 1945 by Julian Aberbach. Originally from Austria, Aberbach came to the US shortly before World War II, served in the military and secured a $3,000 loan from his father. Aberbach later recalled, "I rented three chairs, a desk, and a carpet and I was in business."[25] Aberbach had been stationed in Georgia, and it was while training there that he became familiar with American country music, which became the focus of his new business.

Business was good. Aberbach's brother Jean established offices in New York in the Brill Building (in Tin Pan Alley), and the company soon expanded into the Nashville market. Aberbach describes it this way: "Next, I went to Nashville, Tennessee. This was very strategic as I became friendly with the people at the Grand Ole Opry. I organized agreements or exclusive songwriting contracts, or, jointly owned publishing companies with the following artists, among others: Red Foley, Ernest Tubb, Hank Snow, Lefty Frizzell, Bill Monroe, Eddie Arnold, and Johnny Cash."[26] Like Acuff-Rose, Hill and Range was extremely aggressive about publisher, performer, and record label relationships. It has been estimated that at one time Hill and Range represented 75 percent of the music produced in Nashville, in no small part because they were able to aggregate—purchase outright—entire catalogs from other publishers.[27]

The relationship between Hill and Range and Elvis Presley is in a category by itself. One of the artists Aberbach represented was the country star Hank Snow. At one meeting, Snow mentioned that he had seen a young performer on the road who "was so popular that the girls chased him off the stage."[28]

Shortly thereafter, Aberbach heard that Eddy Arnold was breaking with his longtime manager Colonel Tom Parker. "So I told Parker about Elvis Presley and that I would go to Louisiana the next week to check him out."[29]

Aberbach saw Presley performing on the popular television show *Louisiana Hayride* and was so impressed by his potential that he helped Parker become Presley's manager and ultimately brokered the deal for Presley to go to RCA Records. "So Elvis became an RCA Victor recording artist with the contract done by our attorney," Aberbach recalled.[30]

Aberbach made his cousin, Freddy Bienstock, the supervisor for all of the music recorded by Presley both on records and in films. As Acuff-Rose did with the Everly Brothers, Hill and Range controlled the music to which Presley had access and strongly resisted the inclusion of songs from other publishers on Presley records. Perhaps the most striking detail of the arrangement was that Hill and Range received 50 percent of all royalties for the songs, with the other 50 percent split (also 50/50) between Presley and Parker. In 1975, Hill and Range sold the majority of its catalog to Chappell Music, but retained 50 percent of the royalties for Elvis Presley songs. The net value of Hill and Range's Presley catalog is unknown, but it was almost certainly worth many millions at the time of Presley's death and it is certain to have increased since then.

Mechanical Licenses Revised

Publisher and record label collaborations became an economic cornerstone of the music industry. One of the key factors of this relationship was the mechanical license.

As noted in chapter 3, the 1909 revision to US copyright law was both practical and prescient enough to remain an effective framework for the music business for decades. While mechanical licenses were a well-established part of the business—foundational, for example, to the proliferation of "cover versions"—by the 1970s, there were problems with the law as originally configured. The Register of Copyrights wanted mechanical licensing simplified or even eliminated, while publishers wanted to see rates adjusted upward from the two-cent-per-copy rate that had been in effect for over sixty years.[31]

With the Copyright Act of 1976, Congress implemented effective remedies for these concerns. Section 115 simplified the required notifications, put limitations on how much a "cover" version could rearrange an original sound recording, and established the Copyright Royalty Tribunal to oversee and adjust the statutory rate of payment.[32] This revision to Section 115 proved very workable and remained in effect until the emergence of digital formats in the 1990s (discussed in some detail in chapter 10, "Digitization").[33]

The midcentury music publishing industry is a particularly significant and complicated example of the power of aggregating creativity. Publishers could sign songwriters to their companies and control performers' use of their music. Both songs and performers were vital ingredients of the record production process. So music publishers not only could aggregate the creativity of many songwriters but also could aggregate and control access to this valuable resource. In the three-part structure that included publishing, performance, and record production, it was the songwriters and performers who had the least opportunity to aggregate creativity and the least leverage to negotiate the value of their creative productivity.

In another transactional structure—recording and broadcasting, discussed below, songwriters had even less leverage, and performers none at all.

RECORD LABELS AND RADIO: PROMOTION AND PAYOLA

By the late 1940s and 1950s, the radio business bore little resemblance to the early days of insurance and flour company–owned stations and "border blasters" (see chapter 4). It was a time when network radio programming dominated much of the airwaves and—in the early part of the period—the use of recorded music was constrained by the American Federation of Musicians (AFM).

For local, non-network stations, this period was a time of programming autonomy. To a large extent, a song made it on the air locally because an individual program director or DJ liked it, or perhaps as a result of a significant phone-in request campaign by listeners. In addition, direct record promotion from label to radio station was a quid pro quo business, with various kinds of compensation offered to radio people by label representatives in exchange for airtime. This "pay for play" concept was very much an established part of the record and radio business by the 1950s.

Payola is a combination of the words *pay* and *Victrola*—as in record player. It was the term used to describe the common practice of paying DJs or radio executives some form of compensation for putting records on the air. In the 1950s, this practice was common; it was also legal almost everywhere.

The increasing scale of payola in the 1950s paralleled the rising status of DJs. According to a 2013 review of the payola era by Lydia Hutchinson: "These on-air personalities had so much clout with younger listeners, *Time* magazine called them the 'Pooh-Bahs of musical fashion and pillars of U.S. low- and middle-brow culture.'"[34]

Hutchinson continues:

> Aware of their rising status, jocks established flat rate deals with labels and record distributors. A typical deal for a mid-level DJ was $50 a week, per record, to ensure a minimum amount of spins. More influential jocks commanded percentages of grosses for local concerts, lavish trips, free records by the boxful (some even opened their own record stores), plus all the time-honored swag. As Cleveland DJ Joe Finan later described the decade, "It was a blur of booze, broads and bribes."[35]

The issue was seen as a problem in certain sectors of the business. *Billboard,* ASCAP, and BMI came out against it mainly because of apparent competitive advantages the practice of payola conferred on independent labels and the nonmainstream music they produced. But public statements were not sufficient to change established payola practices.

In 1959, the US House Oversight Committee investigation into alleged cheating on the popular television quiz show *Twenty-One* was expanded to include the practice of record label and radio station payola. Over three hundred disc jockeys from around the country testified to having received over $260,000 in fees for playing specific recordings. Most industry insiders considered that a fractional part of the real total.

Congress amended the Federal Communications Act to make payola a misdemeanor. There was a short-term impact on the music business. Some DJs were fined or even lost their jobs, and for a while access to radio was reduced for some independent labels. But in the long run, little changed. Payola continues to be a routine practice in the recording and broadcast industries through the present day. Periodically, labels and radio stations are investigated and sometimes prosecuted for the practice.[36] Ultimately, though, it was the rise of nonbroadcast discovery platforms on the Internet that marginalized radio and reduced incentives and resources to promote records there.

ARTISTS AND THE MACHINE

Though essential to the business of records, radio, and publishing, songwriters and performers had little influence or leverage in the pre-Internet era (and perhaps even less since). The explanation for this imbalance of power is simple: artists are rarely if ever in a position to aggregate anything other than their own talents. Aggregation is power—and all sectors of the midcentury music industry were specifically designed to aggregate the musical creativity of others. Artists and songs progressively became the raw material fed into the music industry machinery to create stars and produce hits.

Both musicians' unions and artist representatives (or agents) first appeared in the 1800s, but as the power of mass production increased, the need for someone to speak for the artist became more urgent, and eventually two forms of artist representation developed: collective and individual.

One of the most hotly contested areas of music enterprise was the relationship between live performance (and performers) and recorded music. As it became ever more clear that recorded sound on records, on the radio, and in the movies was reducing live performance opportunities, professional performers became increasingly desperate. The ongoing struggle between music as a good and music as a service became a war.

One person to take a stand against the technological tide and the rise of recorded music was the charismatic and pugnacious president of the American Federation of Musicians (AFM), James Petrillo.

Petrillo: The Musician's Union War against Records

James Petrillo was born in 1892 in Chicago. He grew up in a workingclass family and began playing the trumpet when he was eight years old. According to his obituary in the New York Times, "He left school for work at the age of 14, driving a horse and wagon for an express company and working as a railroad sandwich vendor. He also continued his music, for a four-piece band known as Petrillo's."[37]

Petrillo joined Local 10 of the AFM in 1918 and became its president in 1922. He was elected president of the AFM national in 1940. As a musician and a leader, Petrillo had experienced some of the most disruptive innovations of the twentieth century, including Prohibition, sound in motion pictures—which threw thousands of theatre musicians out of work—and the emergence and explosive diffusion of recordings and radio. Given these experiences and his notorious temper and flair for the dramatic, it is perhaps no surprise that he decided to draw a line in the sand.

Petrillo called a general strike of the AFM in 1942 and kept it going until 1944. Inspired by rising concerns about the impact of records on opportunities for live music, AFM members stopped making records entirely. In his obituary, the *New York Times* wrote of the strike:

> After 27 months, the big record companies gave in and agreed to pay royalties of 1 cent to 2 1/2 cents per record to the union; a 10-inch 78 revolutions-per-minute popular record then cost about 50 cents retail. The royalty fund, with royalties varying over the years, is called the Music Performance Trust Fund and is "his legacy to the nation's music world," Mr. Fuentealba [AFM president in 1984] said.[38]

Obviously the number of new recordings made during the strike was significantly reduced, but that reduction was not distributed equally across all musical genres. Musical styles such as country and R&B, plus other music that had emerged from regional traditions, rarely employed union musicians in the first place. Public demand for records did not decrease during the war, so there was a significant opportunity for non-union "outsiders" to get past the "gate" and make records for the general public. For many players, performers, recording engineers, and entrepreneurs, the musicians' union strike, social and economic conditions, and the overall "vibe" of change and growth meant opportunity. For the working-class union musician it was just one in a series of disruptions to established employment models.

In addition to the representation and advocacy offered by collective bargaining units like the AFM, individual artist representatives became an important part of the industry in the twentieth century.

Artist Managers

As noted in chapter 3, the emergence of a public, paid music marketplace created a need for management services to support the work of musical artists. Organizations like Columbia Artists Management International (CAMI) were established to facilitate the presentation of public concerts by celebrated classical artists. As the opportunities and demands created by recording and broadcasting grew, CAMI's services and operations evolved, and it remains an important voice for classical and other artists today.[39]

In the 1950s artist management services for popular musicians evolved with changing musical styles and new ways of connecting artists and audiences. In the early years of the rock and roll era, when independent labels dominated the talent discovery and development process, many label owners were also talent agents or managers. Though not referred to as such, Sam Phillips certainly fulfilled the managerial role for many of his artists. Others, such as Robert Marcucci, who promoted the careers of teen idols Frankie Avalon and Fabian in the late 1950s, also operated in the multiple roles of record producer, label owner, and artist manager.[40]

Later in the rock era, talent managers became more independent of labels, but because complex relationship between performance, recordings, radio, and live performing was essential for success, rock managers were still more likely to operate from a corporate than a creative perspective.

An artist representative needs to be connected with the deciders in multiple music business sectors but also sympathetic to the concerns of creative artists. An artist manager who gets a percentage of all of an artist's productivity—regardless of the venue or medium of production—likely has a greater incentive to invest in the client/artist's success.

In many cases this arrangement worked. Whether for the standard 15 percent commission on artist fees or something more substantial (Colonel Parker made a flat 50 percent of everything Elvis Presley earned), the value of professional representation by a skilled and knowledgeable negotiator proved to be quite high in most cases. At the same time, there are many examples of exploitive relationships—whether actually fraudulent or just uncaring—between artist managers and those they represent.

The second wave of the rock era, beginning in the 1960s, brought a new generation of artist managers who contributed to both the business and the artistic arenas. This era produced a number of colorful, controversial, managers—some of whom became celebrities themselves. Some will be discussed in chapter 7, "Scaling and Selling Live Performance," and in chapter 11, "State of the Art."

SUMMARY: MIDCENTURY MODERN

If the 1950s opened the door to the rock and roll revolution in music and business, the 1960s blew the doors off entirely. By the beginning of the 1970s, popular music was almost unimaginably profitable and incredibly diverse in terms of musical styles, artists, and audiences.

The 1970s brought the first major revisions to US copyright law since 1909. The Copyright Act of 1972 established the first copyright protection for sound recordings, extended the duration of copyright terms, and created the doctrine of fair use (Section 107) as a limitation and balance to extended protections.[41] It also introduced substantial revisions to mechanical licensing and—critically—affirmed the principle that broadcast radio was exempt from paying performance royalties to copyright holders.

Over this same period we see the progressive consolidation of the major labels, along with occasional outbursts of radical creativity from independents that were often quickly absorbed into the commercial mainstream. Radio remained an important component of the record industry, providing "free" promotion while not paying for the use of recordings. Publishers increasingly controlled and profited from the varied uses of musical ideas rather than printed copies.

This is the era when the term *music industry* was first consistently used, and when the practices that defined mass production, mass distribution, and mass consumption in music were defined, refined, and nailed down. Increasingly, *massification* defined all aspects of musical commerce and culture.

The era of "Big" had begun.

OPERATIVE DYNAMICS

Record label as process

Publisher as process

KEY CONCEPTS

Major labels

The "Bigs"

Independent labels: Sun, Chess, Vee-Jay

Acuff-Rose

Hill and Range

Aggregation and aggregation of access

Payola

EXPLORATION

Other Midcentury Independent Labels

Ric-Tic—"Ric-Tic Records," Soulbot (2016), http://soulbot.com /ric-tic-records-2.htm.

Philadelphia International Records—Mark Anthony Neal, "Who Owns the (Philadelphia) Soul of Black Music?" *The Root* (2–19–2014), http://www.theroot.com/articles/culture/2014/02/black _owned_philadelphia_international_records_remaining_songs_sold .html.

Twenty-First-Century Convergence of Publisher and Label

Evan Kramer, "The Publisher as Record Label," *Music Business Journal* (October 2010), http://www.thembj.org/2010/10/the-publisher-as-a-record-label/.

CHAPTER 7

Scaling and Selling Live Performance

If you told me I could only do one thing, I would choose live concerts.

—Mandy Patinkin

A live concert to me is exciting because of all the electricity that is generated in the crowd and on stage. It's my favorite part of the business, live concerts.

—Elvis Presley

For aesthetic, practical, and economic reasons it is always necessary for a musical performance to be on a scale appropriate to the circumstances. During the patronage era, for example, scale was primarily determined by the patron's status, as well as the layout of the patron's home (or church), the purpose of the event (social/liturgical), available financial resources, and the patron's personal preferences. The "sale" of performances (and other creative services) was most often part of a long-term relationship between artist and patron.

With the shift toward market-based performance, scaling public concerts became a function of venue capacity and potential audience size. Economic relationships were short term and services were sold concert by concert. Audience characteristics such as social status, taste, and affluence remained relevant, but primarily because of their effect on audience size and ticket sales. Programming, venue selection, and every other performance element were designed to maximize tickets sold. In practice, in a market-based performance model, scaling a public concert is inseparable from selling it.

> In a market-based context, scaling a concert is inseparable from selling it.

During the mid-twentieth-century massification of music and culture, one of the things that got bigger was the live show—especially in popular music. In genres where there were limitations on how much audience/venue size could be expanded—classical music, for example—concerts became more frequent, more fully subsidized, or both. Artists and institutions in those sectors came to be defined as "nonprofit" and to depend upon public and private grants and gifts. In effect, music organizations in the nonprofit sector moved back toward patronage—though with (mostly) new kinds of patrons—and away from the marketplace. But even this development is based on how to scale and sell the live "show."

In the previous chapters, we looked at emerging technologies, patterns of social migration, the convergence and commercialization of regional styles of music, and the emergence of "big" music—the music industry. Across all of these changes, regardless of how the landscape was altered, there was always an assumption that live performance would continue to be a central component of the music enterprise.

This chapter focuses on how concert promotion/presentation evolved and adapted to remain relevant and continue to create value in the second half of the twentieth century. For popular music the period was one of big audiences, big venues, and big tours. For classical music it was one of fund-raising and audience development in the face of declining attendance and reduced opportunity.

CLASSICAL MUSIC MANAGEMENT AND FUNDING

As discussed in chapter 3, the shift to market-based productivity changed the European musical world dramatically in the 1800s. Many of the leading figures that paved the way for this shift were trained in the European classical music tradition, and many began their careers under the patronage model. Yet it was their work in the public sphere that established the economic and cultural value of "fine art" music in the marketplace.

In the earliest years of the twentieth century, young "classical" composers continued to pursue market-driven opportunities. Igor Stravinsky wrote music for ballets (on commission) as well as symphonic music. He was an aggressive exploiter of his own creativity, marketing his music "within and beyond the concert hall."[1] Stravinsky, like Beethoven, was particularly astute about the value of music publishing and—unlike Beethoven—had the advantage of nearly one hundred years of copyright law development. According to Saint-Amour, in *Modernism and Copyright,* Stravinsky also "had no qualms about rearranging his own works with only slight modifications in order to claim new copyrights and cash in on new revenue streams."[2]

In the 1930s, another generation of young American composers, including Aaron Copland, explored writing music for movies as well as for the concert hall. Hybrid composers such as George Gershwin bridged popular dance music, musical theatre, and concert music. In the later twentieth century, classical composers continued to explore music for film, and this was one place where formally trained and popular music composers interacted in the same creative and market space. The integration of popular musicians with symphonic performances either as composers or performers is another.

Despite individual innovations, there was a steady decline in financial support for institutional classical music performance over the course of the twentieth century. This is particularly true for the instrumental concert forms, primarily chamber music and symphony orchestras.

Chamber music refers to small-scale instrumental performances, for example, string quartets. This genre was originally designed for smaller performing spaces (rooms or "chambers") and more intimate audiences. Professional chamber music performances in the US have most often been presented as part of a series—a concert season lasting from six to nine months and consisting of various artists and groups. Based on nineteenth-century presenting methods (and the "touring" model discussed in chapter 3), chamber music ensembles travel from series to series, city to city, performing one concert before moving to the next one.

Symphony orchestras are much larger and more expensive to manage and maintain than chamber music groups. Symphonies are typically city based, operating primarily on the "tourism" model, with audiences cycling through to hear a series of concert offerings over the course of a season. A symphonic season typically consists of a varied menu of concerts, each repeated several times to maximize audience attendance.

As the twentieth century advanced, it became evident that the market for symphonic and chamber music was not going to keep pace with that of popular music—particularly in the US. In fact, after the explosive market growth for rock and roll and other popular music styles in the 1950s, some feared that the end of classical music in America was near.

This was the period when philanthropic organizations increasingly provided financial support for classical music in order to insulate it from the constraints of the marketplace. Gifts and grants made it possible for organizations to continue performing and presenting even when they were not able to sell enough tickets to support the cost of operation. In many cities, elite citizens formed local nonprofit organizations to encourage fine art music. Competitions and prizes were established for classical performers. Federal and state arts councils also began to provide funding for classical concert programming and educational projects.[3]

Nothing, however, had a greater impact on classical music and classical music business models than the Ford Foundation.

Matching Fund Grants

Beginning in 1956, the Ford Foundation began providing funds to support classical music and other fine arts organizations by offering "matching funds" grants intended to be seed money for local arts organizations.[4] In this model, the foundation would offer an amount that had to be matched locally (or perhaps doubled or increased by some other multiplier). The grants were intended to encourage the production of high-quality art in communities. The idea was that after the value of such art was demonstrated to the community, local funding for fine arts and music initiatives would take the place of foundation contributions.[5]

In practice what happened was that local arts groups, including symphony orchestras, tended to use the external funding to expand the number of concerts they offered to the public and the number of musicians they employed, without regard to ticket sales or cost-revenue balance. New musical organizations also proliferated. Between 1966 and 1974, the number of US orchestra concerts increased by 80 percent. There were 58 professional symphonies in the US in 1965 and 225 in 1988. Seasons crept up from twenty-five to forty-two to fifty-two weeks and included paid vacations.

This was the *massification* of the symphony orchestra. Longer seasons, larger personnel rosters, and full-time benefits for employees drove costs sky high. Previously adequate endowments were consumed and, to make matters worse, attendance dropped steadily as audiences aged.

Everything was big except the revenue generated.

Anxious and increasingly desperate to defray rising costs with ticket sales in a shrinking market environment, symphony managers began to replicate the strategies of nineteenth-century London. Symphonies engaged highly paid soloists with international reputations, as well as more popular music stars to present crossover "pops" programs. By the 1980s, most professional orchestras had full-scale marketing departments. Deficits continued to increase.

The crisis peaked during the 1980s as economic stressors caused many corporate sponsors to cut back on charitable donations, particularly to fine arts initiatives. Tax cuts during the Reagan presidency also reduced the availability of public funds. In addition, many nonprofit experts, including those at the Ford Foundation who had conceived the matching funds model, declared the situation to be a disaster and an unsustainable use of donated funds.

In 1987, writing in the *New York Times,* Donal Henahan described the situation this way:

> The irony is that arts administrators, orchestra trustees, critics and others in influential positions have worked hard for generations to help bring about the current state of doubt and confusion. Driven by economic winds and, in some cases, fearsome ambition, they have sold the American public on the need for quantity in music rather than quality, on the necessity for glamour at the podium and on the crippling belief that music is a product that must be promoted, advertised and devoured like so much fast food.[6]

In the 1990s (and beyond), these issues led to bankruptcies and severe reorganizations for many professional orchestras; they were also recognized as signs of a fundamental cultural shift. Ideas about what makes a city and what constitutes a culturally rich life were changing. It's not that people didn't still love music. Rather, what constituted musical participation and consumption were shifting away from long-established forms and patterns.

The 2008 National Endowment for the Arts Survey of Public Participation in the Arts showed that attendance at concert events was declining, especially among younger adults, and that fewer than 10 percent reported attending a "classical or jazz" event in the previous twelve months. That still represents somewhere between 16 and 17 million attendees, not a negligible number. But those 16-some million also represent a 29 percent decline since 1982. In addition, the survey identified a continuous rise in the median age of classical concert attendees. Perhaps most critically for concert presenters, there were also significant increases in the number listening to classical music via physical or Internet-based media.[7]

Taken all together, the NEA research seems to indicate that while classical music continues to be valued by the American public, people are increasingly choosing to experience it via electronic and digital media rather than by attending concerts.[8]

Still, the sound of the classical (or more accurately, the romantic) orchestra is embedded in our cultural experiences. Consider, for example, film scores. It's a rare "blockbuster" film that does not include a musical soundtrack scored for full orchestra. Because that sound is part of our culture, it is very likely that the symphony orchestra in some form will persist. That does not mean, however, that the scale of the symphonic enterprise achieved during the peak of the late twentieth-century matching funds era will ever return.

Many advocates for classical music believe that being subjected to the constraints of the marketplace will threaten the aesthetic value of the music. At the same time, there is a valuable lesson in the rise and fall of the symphony orchestra in the second half of the twentieth century. There is inherent danger in disconnecting any musical enterprise from market demand. Doing so leads to disengaging with the public and becoming increasingly disconnected from its audience, its musical interests, and the value its members place on musical experience.

> There is inherent danger in disconnecting from the marketplace because that is where the public both gains access to and demonstrates the value it places on musical experience.

Opera presenters initially fared a bit better than symphonic ones in terms of attracting audiences with a younger median age, though they ultimately faced a similar—if slower and later—decline (see chapter 11). Both touring and city-based opera companies persisted throughout the twentieth and early twenty-first centuries, with similar funding challenges and increasing dependence on gifts and grants. Additional burdens for opera include the language barrier for lyrics (subtitles became a standard part of the modern opera experience), higher per-opera production costs, and competition from pop-music-infused Broadway-style musical theatre.[9]

For all forms of music in the classical tradition, beginning in the 1950s and continuing long afterward, the "800-pound gorilla" of the music entertainment market was the rock concert. Audiences of fifty thousand–plus and tours grossing in the hundreds of millions of dollars (not to mention record sales) created entirely new metrics for success. Traditional fine art forms of music simply could not compete on this scale.

The reason that concerts in the rock era produced such remarkable numbers is actually the same reason that the matching funds model ultimately didn't work. Both were based on market demand. Matching funds models were intended to insulate classical music from the market long enough for audiences to become aware of the value of the music, which, it was believed, would stimulate new market support.

In contrast, rock was always about lots of screaming kids and lots of dollars. One approach worked; the other didn't.

CONCERTS IN THE ROCK ERA

The first rock and roll concert was a dance party thrown by a Cleveland radio DJ. The "Moondog Coronation Ball," hosted by Alan J. Freed of WJW radio on March 21, 1952, marked the beginning of the rock concert era.

According to Freed's son, Lance:

> Together with Mintz [the radio show's sponsor] and concert promoter Lew Platt, my father hatched the inaugural Moondog Coronation Ball, billed on posters as "The most terrible ball of them all" and scheduled for March 21, 1952 from 10 pm—2 am. The bill for the evening included Paul Williams and his Hucklebuckers, Tiny Grimes and his Rocking Highlanders, the Dominoes, Danny Cob and Varetta Dillard. Pre-sale tickets were $1.50 and $1.75 at the door. My father and his partners never envisioned a sell-out—much less the near-riot the concert sparked—given that the advertising for it was largely relegated to the *Moondog* radio show and at Record Rendezvous [Mintz's store].
>
> On the evening of March 21, an unprecedented swell of humanity descended on Cleveland Public Hall. A crowd of thousands lined the streets and soon the festive atmosphere turned discordant, as the venue quickly reached capacity and thousands of fans broke through the arena's doors. The resulting hysteria cut the show short after only one song by the opening act, Paul Williams and his Hucklebuckers. It was the first rock and roll concert and my father was heartbroken.[10]

The problem was too many people who were too enthusiastic. It was both the literal opposite of concert presentation in the classical music world and a realization of polite society's darkest fears about the effects of popular music on the nation. It was also an accurate predictor of the main challenges of producing rock shows: managing large, excitable audiences for their safety while preserving the entertainment value and musical integrity of the event. That first rock concert also demonstrated a fundamental principle: the importance of radio to concert promotion.

The scale of the event was also a complete surprise. Afterward, on his radio show, Freed discussed the Moondog Coronation Ball this way:

> When we attempted to bring you, with every sincere good intention, the finest event you'd ever attended in Cleveland or elsewhere, we had no idea that the turnout would anywhere come close to the tremendous number of folks who turned out last night at the Cleveland Arena. If anyone—even in their wildest imagination—had told us that some 20- or 25,000 people would try to get into a dance, well I suppose you would've been just like me: you probably would've laughed and said they were crazy.[11]

That disbelief lingered for quite a while for many music professionals. For some, it was a matter of distaste, finding the music and its effect on teenagers disturbing; a 1956 article in the *New York Daily News* was openly critical of Alan Freed and declared rock and roll music to be an "inciter of juvenile delinquency."[12]

To others, Freed's concert seemed to be an anomaly, a fad that was destined to pass quickly. Freed, however, kept producing shows and was soon imitated by others, often those in the radio business who saw it as an obvious way to build their listener base.

Murray Kaufman was another influential rock and roll DJ and concert promoter. Better known as Murray "The K," he was on the radio in New York from 1958 to 1967 and produced shows during school holiday breaks at the Brooklyn Fox and Brooklyn Paramount theatres. These shows (as the Moondog Coronation Ball was supposed to have been) were a series of performances by a variety of acts, both famous and less well known.[13]

Package Tours

The concept of the variety show or concert, featuring many acts performing in styles from across the 1950s pop music spectrum, became a template for touring shows of the era. When a group of artists were put on a bus or in cars to take this kind of show on the road, it was called a "package tour."

According to Chris Nickson: "The idea was quite simple—assemble a couple of big names, some lesser ones, and send them out to play in theatres all over the country. The relative unknowns would receive exposure, the stars would play a few of their hits, and everyone would go home happy."[14] Tours could reach smaller, less cosmopolitan cities with less competition for entertainment dollars. Overhead was kept low by traveling cheaply (and often uncomfortably) and using only the staging available at each stop on the tour. Frequently, accompanying bands were shared among multiple singers, further reducing production costs.

Part of the logic of the package tour was a belief that only a very few solo artists could fill a theatre on their own. Since many considered rock and roll to be a temporary fad, it was considered important to put artists in front of audiences early, while they were "hot," regardless of how much success might be in their future. Virtually all recording artists of the era participated in package tours. Even the Beatles, as they first rose to fame, "played the packages—there was no other game in town."[15]

But by the end of the 1960s, although there were still package tours, the market was changing. Audiences demanded longer shows from the main act, and artists wanted to play longer sets. The residual impact of the package era can be seen in the use of an opening act or acts by major artists on tour.

Touring "Festivals"

The concept of the package tour was later revived and implemented by a number of artists, promoters, and businesses. The motivations for doing so varied, ranging from the social and political to the artistic and economic. Group tours, or, as they are sometimes called, touring festivals, are quite common and operate on a variety of scales in terms of celebrity and cost.

One of the first and most successful of the newer generation of "package tours" was Lollapalooza. It was established in 1991 by Jane's Addiction singer Perry Ferrell and continued annually until 1997. It was revived in 2003 and converted to a "destination" festival in Chicago in 2005. Lollapalooza has commitments there through 2018.

Lollapalooza was a massive success in both its original and more recent iterations, presenting more than a thousand acts to hundreds of thousands of fans over more than a decade. After 1991 the tour included a second stage and then later (in 1996) a third to provide additional performance opportunities for rising and emerging artists.[16]

In 1997 the first Lilith Fair tour was established as a touring festival celebrating women and women in music. Founded by singer and song-writer Sarah McLachlan, Lilith Fair was intended to provide a "platform to talk about a lot of issues that are important to me and a lot of us as women and human beings."[17]

It was a solid success: "What started out as a 35-city fledgling tour in 1997, racked up $16 million in ticket sales last year. Overall, Lilith Fair was the top-grossing festival tour of 1997 and ranked 16th among the year's Top 100 Tours. This year's tour is expected to generate $25 million in ticket sales."[18]

Another type of package developed in the 1990s was the corporate-sponsored tour. To cite a very successful and long-lasting example, the Warped tour was conceived in 1994 by Kevin Lyman, who was then working on skateboarding events that incorporated music into the contests. Since 1995 the Warped tour has been sponsored by the Vans Shoe Company, a major supplier of skateboarding footwear and sponsor of skateboarding teams.

Though the term *package tour* has fallen out of general use, the format remains an attractive option for artists wishing to share costs and build audiences, for promoters hoping to generate a buzz from a touring festival, and for corporations seeking to extend their brand value with the concert-going public.

Package tours and opening acts on tour provide opportunities for emerging artists to perform in front of larger audiences and in better venues than they would be able to do on their own. Some musicians, however, see touring festivals as an impediment to new acts.

According to punk musician Brendan Kelly:

Summer touring season used to involve a bunch of bands, like Alkaline Trio for example, jumping on buses and taking smaller bands, like us and The Black Maria for example, on tour. There would be all these bands that would do that, so all these support bands would have great tours to go on. Kids in every town would have a bunch of different shows to go see, like over the summer. Small clubs would have big, good shows at least once a week if not twice a week, three times a week; and kids would have stuff to do. Now, all those big bands go on the Warped Tour. When they come to town, it's for one day. It's in a band shell, small clubs all across the US are closing down, they can't afford to be open.[19]

The pros and cons of touring festivals reflect the tensions between the gatekeeper and nurturer roles found elsewhere in the music industry. Certainly package tours with many slots for upcoming musicians have nurtured emerging artists while connecting established ones to younger fans and colleagues. At the same time, the large-scale, big-ticket touring festival is designed to make money and extend the value of already established artists and of the tour/festival itself. As such, festival management is not so much involved with nurturing new value as with promoting and protecting existing value. During difficult economic times, the gatekeeper perspective typically dominates and, as a result, emerging acts struggle.

ROCK CONCERT PROMOTION

In earlier eras, publicity, talent, and name recognition were key factors in the concert promoter's playbook. That's exactly how Barnum promoted Jenny Lind. But Barnum began with someone whose talent was established and who was already celebrated. He only needed to optimize and exploit those elements, not create them.

Colonel Tom Parker's approach to management teaches us, by comparison, what can happen when you have a talented and charismatic, yet relatively unknown, performer. Parker demonstrated how to manipulate press coverage and manage public perception to create celebrity status for Elvis Presley from the ground up.

In doing so, Parker's management also demonstrated that everything about the performer—not just what happens on stage or at public events—can be used to increase celebrity value. In this, perhaps more than anything else, we need to acknowledge Andreas van Kuijk and his invented persona, the Colonel, as an archetype for twentieth- and twenty-first-century impresarios.[20] At the same time, the Parker-Presley relationship was not typical of the midcentury manager-artist dyad, functioning more as a cautionary tale than as an exemplar.

Three promoters who shaped the mainstream of rock concert promotion—creatively and commercially—in the 1960s and beyond are discussed below.

Chet Helms and the Summer of Love

One of the first promoters of the psychedelic music era, Chet Helms, failed to follow the Barnum/Parker guidelines for success in virtually every way. Part of the hippie scene himself, Helms espoused communal values that ran contrary to financial success. He was devoted to the musicians and their art. He trusted fans to be able to discern what was good in music. He believed that music and community were more important than money.

When Helms arrived in San Francisco in 1962, he saw a wide array of creativity and talent and realized that there were not enough affordable performing spaces available to present it. He found a boardinghouse basement and began to put on live music shows there.[21] The basement shows became so popular that Helms looked for larger venues.

On the advice of friends who admired the blue-collar work ethic and common man ethos it represented, Helms began producing shows at the International Longshoremen's Union Hall. Those friends were associated with a group that mostly sold marijuana but also sometimes put on light shows for concerts. Having decided that the marijuana trade was becoming too dangerous, that group—called the Family Dog—decided to put on rock shows instead, and they formed a partnership with Helms.

Their first show at the International Longshoremen's Union Hall was on October 16, 1965. Admission was $2.50 ($2.00 for students). Over four hundred people attended, even though the show was not widely publicized. This success indicated the need for an even bigger space where they could stage larger shows with more amplification and light displays. Helms and Family Dog identified the Fillmore Auditorium, which, because it was in some disrepair and located in a rundown neighborhood, could be rented for $60 per night. With a capacity of over a thousand seats, the profit margin was potentially enormous.

In a casual conversation, members of the Family Dog mentioned their plans for the Fillmore to another SF promoter, Bill Graham. Graham quickly negotiated a three-year lease on the hall. Although Helms did go on to present his own shows at the Fillmore and was occasionally hired by Graham to promote others, he and the group felt that Graham "blew us right out of the water."[22]

Chet Helms was a visionary who put on some great concerts and pioneered the use of the "psychedelic" poster to promote his shows. He was not, however, as successful from a business perspective. In many ways, Helms and Graham represent opposite sides of the concert promotion business of the era: "Bill Graham had a reputation as an aggressive, no-nonsense business man, whereas Chet was seen as a more down-to-earth guy who was less interested in money and more focused on throwing a great party. His lack of business skills is one of the reasons Chet never made a huge fortune in the music business, but he was never short on ideas."[23]

Bill Graham—The Business of the Future

Originally from New York, Bill Graham started out trying to make a career for himself in the theatre, waiting tables and working other odd jobs to support himself. He moved to San Francisco in the 1950s to continue his pursuit of acting.[24] While working at an office job during the day, Graham frequently attended plays at night. It was at one of these that he met Ronny Davis of the Mime Troupe.

The Mime Troupe was formed in the late 1950s as an experimental theatre group. It soon became involved not only with alternative dramatic techniques but also with social and political protest themes.[25] Graham began managing the Mime Troupe and produced a series of "benefit" shows with them and others, including the band Jefferson Airplane.

The first benefit (November 6, 1965) was held at the Mime Troupe's loft, which had a capacity of six hundred. Nearly four thousand people tried to be admitted. The second benefit was at the Fillmore. According to Robert Scheer (then editor of *Ramparts,* a political magazine), when Graham arrived and saw a line of people going around the block he said, *"This* is the business of the future."[26]

After that, there was no looking back for Graham. He became one of the most influential and successful promoters of the twentieth century. He presented virtually every significant band of the era. He left the decaying Fillmore Auditorium for a better location and named it Fillmore West, and then opened another venue in New York, Fillmore East. According to his biography at the Rock and Roll Hall of Fame (he was admitted in 1992), "A high percentage of the most significant pop-music events in the Sixties, Seventies and Eighties were produced under the banner 'Bill Graham Presents.'"[27]

Barry Fey: The "Rockfather"

For most of his career, Barry Fey was based in Colorado, where his production company was located. Fey was one of the most prolific and successful concert promoters in the country. According to his obituary in the *Denver Post,* "Fey promoted tens of thousands of concerts and other events from the 1960s until he retired from his Feyline Corporation in the late-'90s."[28]

Originally from New Jersey, Fey became a concert promoter in 1965, booking college bands into American Legion halls and fraternity parties. He traveled to Denver to promote a show in the mid-1960s, liked the city, and stayed. He produced festivals and promoted tours for both established and rising stars. He was liked by most of the musicians he booked, and many remembered him fondly long after working with him. "When Fey's biography was published in 2011, Ozzy Osbourne was one of the musicians to write an appreciation. 'Barry was the first promoter to book Black Sabbath in 1971,' Osbourne wrote. 'He was the first one to believe in us.'"[29]

Fey was fondly remembered even by competitors. Chuck Morris, head of AEG's Rocky Mountain office, recalled: "When he was into it, there was nobody close to him as a promoter . . . When his head was around promoting a rock 'n' roll band, there was nobody better, and I knew 'em all—Bill Graham, you name it. But there was nobody better at selling tickets. Father's Day baseball games, for God's sakes? He was a magician."[30]

Helms, Graham, and Fey, like Barnum and Parker before them, were independent promoters. As the scale of concerts in the rock era increased, along with costs and potential revenues, more and more promotion was handled by groups and corporations. Below, we examine the three largest; together, they represent some 60 million tickets sold annually.

CONCERT PROMOTION GROUPS AND CORPORATIONS

C3 Presents

C3 Presents is a promotion company founded by Charles Attal, Charlie Jones, and Charlie Walker. Attal was the owner of a barbecue restaurant in Austin, and a longtime promoter of shows in Texas. Charlie Jones previously worked for Capital Sports and Entertainment, a major management company for sports celebrities. Charlie Walker was an executive with Live Nation, the largest concert promoter in the world. Before teaming up with Walker, Attal and Jones created the Austin City Limits Music Festival in 2002, now one of the largest festivals in the US. In 2003, they revived Lollapalooza, reinventing it as a destination-based festival in Chicago.[31]

In 2007, Attal, Jones, and Walker formed C3 Presents. While deliberately maintaining a laid-back attitude and an artist- and audience-friendly philosophy, C3 has became known for a high level of organization and professionalism. According to Ben Dickey, manager of the band Spoon, "They are always trying to make it better, and they spend more every year to do that. I don't think that's generally the first thing that comes to mind with a corporate rock festival, which, once they have 60,000 or 70,000 people a year, have a tendency to cut costs and start shortchanging the middle-of-the-bill artists."[32]

On the business side, C3 used its own ticketing system, managed some artists, and had an active relationship with corporate sponsors of the Lollapalooza festival. Some observers have criticized the degree of sponsorship, but C3 believes that sponsorship keeps ticket costs down, and according to the *New York Times,* "Lollapalooza's [2010] $215 price—with no surcharges—is significantly less than Coachella's ($269) or Bonnaroo's in Tennessee ($250)."[33]

The company maintains an intense awareness of branding, licensing the "Austin City Limits" name to brand that festival and obtaining the rights to "Lollapalooza" before reviving that event. "If we were launching the Grant Park Music Festival, you might pay attention to it, you might not," Mr. Jones said. "But with the name Lollapalooza, whether it's a good association or a bad association, when it rolls by you the first time you are going to pay attention."[34]

Local promoters in the Chicago area are less enthusiastic because the "radius" clauses in Lollapalooza contracts prevent their artists from playing in the area for six months before and three months after the festival. Though radius clauses are a common practice, their use by C3 has been investigated by the Illinois attorney general as anticompetitive.[35]

Live Nation acquired C3 in 2014.[36] Some consider the merger to be bad for independent festivals—an opinion aggravated by Live Nation's acquisition of the Bonaroo Music and Arts Festival in April 2015. Regardless of your opinion about corporations taking over indie festivals, this has been the trend, a pattern similar to the rise of the owner/producer companies in London during the 1800s (see chapter 3, "The Rise of Commercial Markets").

AEG Live

The second largest concert promotion organization in the world is AEG Live, which had $912 million in ticket sales in 2014.[37] AEG Live is a wholly owned subsidiary of AEG (Anschutz Entertainment Group), one of the largest music and sporting event companies in the world.

AEG Live covers touring, festival, broadcast, and merchandise. It has fifteen regional offices "and owns, operates, or exclusively books thirty-five state-of-the-art venues." AEG Live also produces the Coachella

Music and Arts Festival and the New Orleans Jazz and Heritage Festival, along with many others. Tour management is handled through various subsidiaries, including Concerts West in the US; AEG Live's regional offices produce some forty-five hundred musical events per year.

Through its many subsidiaries, AEG Live also manages merchandise, multiple media platform entertainment streams, and a wide variety of Las Vegas–based acts and reviews. Much of the concert promotion done by AEG Live falls under the umbrella of wholly owned subsidiaries, so the scale of the company's enterprise may not be evident at first glance. For example, the promoter of record for the Coachella festival is Goldenvoice, which also is the producer for the Stagecoach Festival, a country music festival in California.[38]

Live Nation

Live Nation is the giant of the concert industry, the biggest of the big, operating on a scale that dwarfs most other presenters. In the third quarter of 2013, Live Nation reported $43.8 million in net income (for that single quarter), drawing 21.2 million attendees to not quite fifty-one hundred events. According to the company's prospectus, from 2011 to 2013 Live Nation served between 50 and 60 million fans, with over twenty thousand events internationally. The company owns or operates some 140 venues. Its subsidiary, Ticketmaster, reported revenues in 2013 of $1.37 billion.[39] Live Nation's total revenue for 2013 was $6.5 billion (which was a net loss of $36 million); the company presented 22,852 live events to nearly 60 million people.[40] Its acquisition of C3, finalized in December 2014, brings "much needed muscle in the North American festivals arena."[41] Obviously Live Nation has aggregated concerts, festivals, other promoters, and audiences on an unprecedented scale, giving them an immense competitive advantage in the concert marketplace.

ECONOMICS OF LIVE SHOWS

There is a tendency to study only the top of the pyramid in any aspect of music enterprise: major labels and the largest independents, arena shows, massive festivals, and so forth. Certainly, we need to understand these things. But the concept of scale goes both ways. The music business as a whole does not consist only—or primarily—of the biggest stars, tours, venues, or labels.

In terms of scale, Live Nation is at the top of the pyramid for the concert business. But it is not necessarily the most important promoter, particularly if one considers all segments of the live music marketplace, the range of social purposes that music fulfills, the varying roles for musical artists in the marketplace and society, and the developmental arcs that define musical careers.

In other words, no one starts out playing arena concerts. Understanding the progression from bar to arena or indie to major and, more critically, how to manage that progress depends upon understanding not just scale, but scalability.

Scale and Scalability

Live musical performances can be organized into a hierarchy based on size, both of the venue and the audience. This section focuses on paid public performances in several genres of music in the second half of the twentieth century and early decades of the twenty-first.

Jazz and classical music differ from popular genres (as well as from each other) in terms of musical style, potential audience size, and the typical scale of the performance venue. In addition, the business models of jazz and classical artists/organizations are rarely supported through ticket sales alone and are most often dependent on some form of private, governmental, or corporate subsidy.

Conversely, pop concerts in the rock era are market driven and for the most part have been designed to make money from ticket sales. There was, however, a period of time in the later twentieth century when concerts were viewed (or at least viewable) as loss-leaders for selling records.

David Byrne (Talking Heads and other projects) describes that relationship as follows: "Live performances used to be seen as essentially a way to publicize a new release—a means to an end, not an end in itself. Bands would go into debt in order to tour, anticipating that they'd recover their losses later through increased record sales."[42]

As the 1990s progressed and sales began to decline, the record industry was forced to reassess what large, lavish tours cost to produce and keep on the road, how they were to be funded, and how their profitability could be improved. A major incentive for this cost-benefit analysis trend was that as the twentieth century ended and the twenty-first began, revenues from physical recordings declined significantly. As a result, live performance revenue streams became more important, perhaps on their way to becoming the primary revenue stream for the industry. Some even speculated that at some point in the not too distant future, recordings (in whatever format) would become primarily a tool to promote live shows, thus turning the twentieth-century "shows promote records, record sales pay for shows" strategy upside down.

In his analysis of the concept of "concert as loss leader," Byrne observes: "This, to be blunt, is all wrong. It's backward. Performing is a thing in itself, a distinct skill, different from making recordings. And for those who can do it, it's a way to make a living."[43]

That is the focus of this section: how a living is made by playing live music and how successfully doing so is most often a matter of moving from smaller to larger audiences and venues and from lower to higher levels of compensation. Managing this progression—as opposed to hoping and waiting for it to happen—is a matter of both understanding what the scale of opportunity is and your capacity to move along it. The latter—the scalability of your approach—is arguably the most critical factor to producing success or failure.

Venue Size

The state of a given musical enterprise—where a band is in its professional development—can be measured by the venues where it performs. Venues can be placed into a hierarchy that ranges from small to large in terms of audience capacity. The following represents a fairly standard framework for venue audience capacities:[44]

Small: <300
Lower mid: 300–999
Upper mid: 1,000–3,000
Large: >3,000

Not surprisingly, most pop bands and performers start at the lower end of the scale. At the bottom of the small-capacity (small-cap) category are what this text will (affectionately) call "bars"; "bar bands" are the professionals of this domain. This is not to say that sometimes bar bands don't play at high school dances or other private parties, because they do. But for a long time, everyone who wanted to be a rock and roll "star" started out by playing cover songs in bars.

In terms of size, a bar will rarely approach a capacity of three hundred. More often a bar semi-comfortably holds 100 to 150 people, sometimes fewer than that. Since a typical bar is a smaller venue that holds smaller crowds, it usually provides lower pay. The functional utilities of the audience experience—that is, why they're in the bar—are primarily socializing, dancing, and drinking, not necessarily in that order. For the venue, the primary income generation comes from the bar and food (if any.) The band represents a short-term, low-risk investment to attract patrons for a night and make them thirsty. Essentially bar bands sell beer and liquor.

Bar bands provide more than income opportunities for musicians; they are a professional proving ground. For a long time, individual musicians and bands learned their trade in bars: how to build a set that keeps people dancing (and dancing = thirsty); how to play different musical styles and master techniques by imitating more successful bands; and how to deal with adversity in the moment, whether it's a dead cable, a broken string, or a drunk grabbing at the mic to sing "Creep."[45]

At this level, musician payment structures range from a flat, often nominal fee (sometimes as nominal as a pitcher of beer), a percentage of the "door" if there is a cover charge for admission, or (this is the "holy grail" of bar bands) a percentage of bar sales. Getting a piece of the bar requires a position of leverage. It is, for example, possible for a demonstrably popular band to get a slice of bar sales, but often, even successful bands don't think to ask (but they should). Playing in bars as an education includes learning about the business.

The transition to larger (but still small-cap) venues—that is, from bar to "club"—involves developing an audience that is loyal to the band—a following. In other words, people have to be coming out not just to *a club,* but rather to hear a particular artist or group, regardless of where they are playing.

At clubs, there is typically an expectation for greater professionalism and for more expensive equipment on the part of both the band and the house. Clubs that emphasize music typically have in-house sound systems and lighting, and may provide a soundman and/or DJ to play music when the band is on break.

In clubs, though playing conditions and audiences sizes may be better, compensation may not increase very much. At this level (really, at all levels), compensation is still based on value production; that is, whether the band is capable of a significant audience draw based on its name. Every band playing in a rotating weeknight and weekend lineup is expected to draw a crowd. If they don't, they don't get booked again.

In order to be able to get a fee that exceeds the house "norm" requires an artist or band to be able to consistently bring in larger-than-usual crowds. To get there, to develop a following, a band usually has to have an active audience development strategy. Today, that is typically done via social media, but in years gone by, bands ran mailing lists, stuck fly-ers under car windshields advertising upcoming gigs, and so forth. Regardless of the tool, the goal is to make connections between the performers and the listeners—to create a social network and, by adding value for the audience, eventually extracting value for the artist.

In addition, somewhere along the arc of moving from smaller/lower paying clubs to the larger/better paying opportunities, a band must begin developing and refining original material to help define its brand and deepen audience loyalty. Artists that never transition from covers to originals stall out somewhere in the small-cap, cover band club scene.

If all of these things are done effectively—increasing professionalism, building and managing a core audience, defining an original approach—then a band can move to touring regionally (playing clubs in other cit-ies), advancing to lower mid-cap venues, and so on. At each step along the way, the size (and often, but not always, quality) of venues and audiences increases.

This type of work can produce a living income, but more realisti-cally, most of the proceeds must be reinvested into the venture. As such, it must be viewed as an investment in brand and audience development, as well as an opportunity to refine how one's performance and material play to a live audience. At the lower levels, band members can supple-ment their income by doing other musical or nonmusical work. At even the most basic touring stage, the logistics of keeping local jobs becomes more problematic, and capitalizing the band becomes a potential stick-ing point in a group's development.

In the mid- to late twentieth century, this is the point at which having a contract with a record label became a critical component of career development. Advances from labels capitalized both recording and touring projects as well as providing income for rising artists. In addi-tion, having a record on the radio while touring created a synergy that boosted album and ticket sales, as well as enhancing the artist's brand recognition. During most of the twentieth century, this is where the promotional resources of major labels became critical for bands to advance to the highest level of touring.

Large-Scale Tours and Shows

The most successful and well-known touring artists have reached the part of the business with the greatest potential economic success and cultural impact. This is a level that the great majority of professional artists never achieve. Those that do, however, have been the backbone of the music industry since the rock era began. These are the stars whose hits drove the "blockbuster economics" that kept the machine running throughout the twentieth century.

The same rationale leads to classical music presenters hiring well-known and extremely expensive soloists. In the classical sector, however, audiences and revenues are considerably smaller. As a result, the scale that makes "blockbuster economics" work in popular music rarely translates to the classical sector.[46]

In contrast, the scale of rock and other pop music shows grew relatively consistently until late in the century. At the high end of the spectrum, "big" was very big. As noted in chapter 1, U2's 360° Tour (2009–2011) presented 110 shows, producing revenue of over $700 million.[47] Live Nation's costs were estimated at $150 million.[48] The Rolling Stones's Steel Wheels tour (1989) grossed $260+ million globally, including tickets, merchandise, and sponsorship monies from Anheuser-Busch.[49]

Earlier still, the Beatles grossed $304,000 for their 1965 Shea Stadium concert (worth nearly $2.3 million in 2015 dollars) and over $1 million (at $50,000+ per night) in a nineteen-show tour the year before.[50] For all of these acts, ticket sales were only a part of the revenue generated by touring. In addition to boosting record sales, the sale of merchandise at the shows became increasingly significant (see chapter 9, "Artists, Audiences, and Brands").

Growth trends for live shows have not, however, been free of interruption. Summer tours, for example, can be especially vulnerable to broader economic and social concerns.[51] Individual artists can also cycle from successful to marginal from one tour to the next, depending on a variety of factors, including the recorded material they have in the marketplace or available via social media. Overall, live shows are still a vital part of the music business and will likely remain so in one form or another.

Success in the music marketplace always favors the creative, adaptable, and socially interconnected. There is no reason to think that this will not apply to the ongoing viability of live performance as a way for musicians to make music and money. There is also no reason to assume that what, at any point, represents "business as usual" will continue to apply for long.

That has certainly proven to be true thus far into the twenty-first century. More recent developments in live concert promotion are discussed in chapter 11, "State of the Art."

CORE PRINCIPLES

In a market-based context, scaling a concert is inseparable from selling it.

There is inherent danger in disconnecting from the marketplace because that is where the public both gains access to and demonstrates the value it places on musical experience.

KEY CONCEPTS

Ford Foundation

Matching funds grants

Package shows and tours

Touring festivals

Alan Freed

Murray "The K"

Chet Helms

Bill Graham

Barry Fey

C3

AEG Live

Live Nation

Scale and scalability

Venue sizes

EXPLORATION

On-Demand Touring

G. M., "On-demand Touring," *Economist* (07–12–2013), http://www.economist.com/blogs/prospero/2013/06/music-industry.

Survival Strategies

David Byrne, "David Byrne's Survival Strategies for Emerging Artists—and Megastars," *Wired Magazine* 16.1 (12–18–2007), http://archive.wired.com/entertainment/music/magazine/16–01 /ff_byrne?currentPage = all.

Ticketing Software: Enhancing the Ticket-Buying Experience

Kyle Russell, "YC-Backed TicketLabs Helps Small Music Venues Get More Fans through the Door," *TechCrunch* (08–12–2014), http://techcrunch.com/2014/08/12/yc-backed-ticket-labs-helps-small-music-venues-get-more-fans-through-the-door/.

Changing the Economics of Touring

John Jurgensen, "Kid Rock's Plan to Change the Economics of Touring," *Wall Street Journal* (6–6–2013), http://online.wsj.com /news/articles/SB10001424127887324063304578523523231085836.

Visual Media

Whenever I make music, I always have a visual in my mind.
I always see things.

—Dan Reynolds

Music is an art form in sound, and the musical experience is based on hearing. Yet prior to the development of recording and radio broadcast technologies, live performance was the only way to access musical experience. Consequently, seeing the performers was integral to hearing the music. During the twentieth century, even as media technologies began to provide visual access to musical performers, live shows retained a privileged position in the value "map" of the music industry. The live show remained vital for two reasons. One—the shared social experience of being at a concert with others. Two—you could see the artists live, and that matters to people. Simple as that.

It might be argued that the pervasiveness of music in visual media—particularly the opportunity to see performers and performances—reduced demand for live concerts. Any shrinkage in the concert sector that can be attributed to visual media, though, must be balanced with the new means of access, forms of creative expression, and revenue-generating opportunities created. Just as the recording studio developed from a place to simply "capture" live performance to become a complex tool for creating a new musical form, so visual media and music evolved together creatively and commercially.

TRANSLATION AND TRANSFERENCE

As any new media technology emerges, its earliest content tends to be adopted from previous platforms in relatively unchanged form. Then, as technologies and the skills of the people using them evolve, content gradually changes to reflect the possibilities inherent in the medium itself. Thus, in the multitrack recording era, record production came to be less about documenting live performance and more about creating a complex recorded sound artifact: the album.

Visual media follow the same pattern in regard to music. The first music on film was "captured" live performance, or performances onstage in the live theatre. Over time, the changing camera perspectives, close-ups on performers at critical moments in the music (during a guitar solo, for example), and even film of the audience's reaction produced a new form that is both musical and cinematic in character. Televised music was a hybrid of live performance and some film techniques at first, but then the music video appeared as a form more perfectly suited to the screen size and attention span of televisions and television viewers.

This process—replication of content from earlier media followed by modifications to suit the opportunities and constraints of the new environment—is a recognized component of media theory.[1] At each step of the way—for records, radio, film, television, and Internet—patterns of production changed, as did consumption, and then finally creation adapted to optimize new opportunities.

When visual media feature musical performances and recordings as the primary content (rather than in the background), they extend the performer's brand (in addition to her music) more than any previous technology. In addition, there are a number of potentially lucrative opportunities to license music in relationship to visual content that is not in and of itself musical. This includes background music, theme songs, and closing credit music.

Then there is advertising.

In music, advertising is multifaceted. Any musical performance can and does serve as advertising for the performer and the music itself. For example, playing a record on the radio may advertise that the record is for sale and/or the artist is in town to play a concert. Music also has a long history of being used to draw attention to and set an emotional mood for other kinds of content, including advertisements.

Though the particulars have changed over the years, television and Internet-based video ads almost always include a musical element, which generates revenue for composers, publishers, performers, publishers, and labels. The synergy between TV commercials and popular songs led to the development of the music video form, a critical component of music production, promotion, and consumption today.

In this chapter we explore how music presented in and used by visual media has engendered new creative and economic opportunities. We will also examine how the principles of convergence and aggregation play out in the realm of music and media. But we begin by looking at the basic framework of copyright law that protects ownership and facilitates access to music in the visual media environment.

LEGAL ISSUES IN VISUAL MEDIA

The incorporation of music into visual media involves four basic legal considerations: *performing rights, dramatic rights, synchronization rights,* and *master use rights.* When a song is performed via a visual medium—whether "live" on film or video or a previously recorded version is used—it is covered by the same performance right as in-person and radio broadcasts. The publisher and songwriter receive royalties as monitored and distributed by a performing rights organization (PRO) (ASCAP, BMI, or SESAC in the US).

If that song is included in a visual (or nonmediated dramatic) entertainment, not as a performance per se, but specifically to advance the plot or narrative, then a dramatic right becomes involved. Dramatic rights are not licensed by PROs, but instead must be negotiated with the composer and/or publisher of the work.

If a music recording is placed into a "timed relationship" with action in a visual medium—that is, synchronized—then synchronization rights come into play. A synchronization license is required for any use of copyrighted recordings in an audiovisual medium whether or not it is for a dramatic purpose.

Clearing—obtaining permission for—a synchronization license can be a complex process. A number of variables will be used by the publisher and/or master recording owner (typically a record label) to determine licensing fees. These variables include the following:

How long the permitted use lasts

Geographical limits, if any

Type of use

Featured means a song is performed over a title sequence or becomes an important part of the narrative. Featured use typically requires a more significant fee.

Foreground and *background* uses are licensed at progressively lower rates.

> *Broad rights* cover licensing for use of the song for all media,
> including DVDs and Internet streaming.[2]

Master use rights refer to incorporating a specific sound recording into a visual (or other) medium. This right is held by the owner of the master recording, typically a record label, and the license must be negotiated with the owner.

Using copyrighted and previously recorded music in film or video productions thus involves a number of rights, permissions, and copyright holders. Clearances can be complicated. As a result, a number of businesses have been established to facilitate the process. Music supervisors in film and television productions are responsible for music clearance and budgeting. As in all aspects of the music business, the use of music in visual media—whether film, television, or the Internet—involves finding an appropriate balance between creative and commercial opportunities and constraints.

FILM

From the beginning, music played an important role in the film business, despite a seemingly insurmountable technical obstacle: films lacked integrated sound until 1927. That did not mean, however, that music was not a part of the film experience for early audiences.

The first application of music to silent film was to have live performers accompany showings to cover the noise of the projector and to enhance the audience experience. The majority of this live music was performed by piano players, often improvising music as the film played. As the film business grew, demand for printed music for this purpose increased, and collections were published, for example, of "chase music," "love songs," and even music for "orgies, biblical or Roman."[3] Silent film music generated significant sheet music sales and performance royalties during the height of its popularity.

Silent film (and other visual media, such as slide shows) were often integrated into other theatrical presentations. The "illustrated song" is an excellent example of this practice. Beginning in the mid-1890s in vaudeville houses (and later in silent movie theatres), a live or recorded performance of a song was accompanied by a slide show illustrating the lyrics. Even after the film business was better established, illustrated songs were used as incidental entertainment preceding or between films. In addition, publishers considered illustrated songs to be an important advertising tool for the sale of sheet music.[4]

The film business fundamentally changed in 1926, "when Warner Brothers began the 'talking picture revolution' by screening *Don Juan*, the first full-length feature film using a synchronized musical score."[5] In 1927, the release of *The Jazz Singer* had an even greater impact on the public and therefore the business. By the end of the decade, with few exceptions, all films incorporated sound.

The impact of film sound on working musicians was catastrophic. Prior to the advent of sound in motion pictures, even mid-sized American cities employed full-time orchestras to work in theatres that presented films and live entertainment. "Talking pictures" devastated theatrical employment for these musicians. According to James Kraft, "By 1934, about 20,000 theater musicians, perhaps a quarter to a third of the nation's professional instrumentalists, had lost their jobs."[6] Coinciding as it did with the Depression, the advent of sound in film fundamentally and permanently changed the marketplace for working musicians.

While a different kind of opportunity was created for studio musicians who participated in the film production process, it was by no means on a scale approaching the number of theatre jobs that were lost. As for studio musicians in the record business, film score recording created opportunities for relatively few, highly skilled performers in specific cities. Los Angeles became a hub for both the recording and movie industries and thus became (and to a large extent remains) an important center for composers and performers of this kind.

Music Uses in Film

Theme Songs

Theme songs typically have the same title as the film or at least include the name of the film in the song's subtitle; for example, "Do Not Forsake Me, O My Darlin'" was also publicized as "The Ballad of *High Noon*." Early practice was to have the theme song play or be sung over the opening credits, but as film production techniques changed over time, theme songs were often placed elsewhere in the film. Regardless of placement, a theme song is used to promote the film and is, of course, included in any soundtrack album release.

The potential for the theme from a popular film to provide additional revenue was recognized very early in movie history. As noted in a *New York Times* review from 1929: "Boundless radio has found a common denominator with the audible cinema, the theme song; and already 'The

Pagan Love Song', 'Evangeline', 'Broadway Melody' and 'The Breakaway' are persisting through the tubes."[7]

In that unattributed article, the author observes how—since the 1910s and the silent film era—the popularity of a theme song could help promote the movie from which it came. Certainly, music publishers were willing and able to use popular films to promote the sale of sheet music, just as they used vaudeville. But moviemakers adopted an even more aggressive approach to music, not only using it to promote movies via publishing and radio but also buying publishing rights to prospective movie themes in order to control their use and monopolize any revenue generated by the song itself.

The 1928 film *Ramona* is a good example of the proactive, cross-promotional strategies of the early film business. The author of the 1929 *New York Times* article cited above discusses it this way:

> "Ramona" is really the progenitor of the modern theme song, although theme songs were composed and circulated vigorously as far back as "Mickey" and "Bluebird, Bring Back My Happiness . . ." Prior to the completion of the film "Ramona . . ." an astute sales manager named Emil Jensen summoned to his office at 729 Seventh Avenue in New York representatives of a music publishing house. He told them that he was anxious to exploit the new film in two ways: a Ramona rose, an artificial flower, would be manufactured and sold to film fans; and he wished a song composed, entitled "Ramona," and dedicated to the star.
>
> The company that was to manufacture the roses did not prosper, but out of the many songs submitted, one by Mabel Wayne and L. Wolfe Gilbert was selected. It achieved tremendous popularity and financial success, with royalties to the film producers from the song amounting to more than $25,000 [over $340,000 in 2015]. A picture that is not considered, either by its star or director, the finest work done by them, somehow attracted such numerous audiences that $1,500,000 was the gross business of that film in the United States and Canada alone—four times the normal gross of a feature film. Immediately after the success of the song, "Ramona," all was not quiet on the Western front. The supposition was that a song could establish the title of a film nationally, through radio and phonograph, and that the pleasant association of thought would conjure cordial visions of the film.[8]

The author of this article further observed that movie companies had not only embraced the potential of the theme song (as of 1929) but in several cases had also "purchased music publishing companies outright, or controlling interests in them."[9] In terms of optimizing the relationship between theme songs and radio, the author added: "Paramount has purchased a half interest in the Columbia Broadcasting System, and

Radio Pictures is a child of the Radio Corporation of America, thus achieving brotherhood with the National Broadcasting Company."[10]

The practice of using theme music to promote films was amped up in 1952 when Tex Ritter's performance of "Do Not Forsake Me, O My Darlin'" was used for the film *High Noon*. It was the first use of a song with lyrics for movie credits. Written by Dmitri Tiomkin, who also created the film score, it was praised for its value as a western song as well as for its integration into the film. It received the 1952 Academy Award for Best Original Song.

The cultural and economic impact of that song was not lost on other filmmakers. Deborah Allison states: "After the success of 'Do Not Forsake Me', there was a vast increase in the number of films, especially dramatic films, to open with a theme song during the credits. Between 1950 and 1954, only 13 percent of American feature films used this device. Over the next five years the percentage grew to 22 percent and by the late 1960s this figure had risen still further to 29 percent."[11]

Conversely, the potential of a film to make a pop song a hit was established in 1954, almost by accident. Bill Haley and His Comets released "Rock around the Clock" as the B-side to "Thirteen Women and Only One Man in Town" in May of that year. The record was modestly successful and reached #23 on the *Billboard* charts. That summer, a boy named Peter Ford kept playing the B-side of that record in his Beverly Hills home. His father, actor Glenn Ford, had signed to star in an upcoming film about juvenile delinquency, *Blackboard Jungle*. The production company was looking for music to represent what teenagers were listening to at the time. Perhaps because of repeated exposure, Ford brought his son's record of "Rock around the Clock" to the production company, and it was chosen to be played over the opening and closing credits of the film.

MGM purchased the rights to use the song for $5,000. It has been rumored that the publisher would have sold the song outright for $7,500. By the summer following the release of the movie in March 1955, "Rock around the Clock" had reached #1 on the charts, staying there for eight weeks and selling over 25 million copies.[12]

Once established, the practice of using a film to promote a song or album became standard. Virtually every film by Elvis Presley (1956–1969) was tied to an album release that included the songs in the film in addition to others. Since the 1950s the synergy between film and popular songs has been foundational to the business of producing and promoting film as well as promoting musical careers. Later developments deepened the relationship creatively and commercially.

Concert Films and Documentaries

Concert films and music festival documentaries provide a number of practical advantages to musical performers and film producers. First, a concert film provides several additional revenue streams from a concert or festival that has already been produced. The performers and concert/ event promoters do not need to re-create the event for the film, but only provide access to the filmmakers while it is happening.[13] Publishing income is also produced via performing rights and, since songs are performed on screen, they have "featured status" and are eligible for additional revenues from synchronization licensing.

Additionally, even performers without publishing credits would typically receive a payment for performing in the film based on the guidelines established by a variety of unions, including the American Federation of Musicians (AFM) for instrumentalists and, for vocalists, the American Federation of Television and Radio Artists, the American Guild of Musical Artists (AGMA), or the Screen Actors Guild (SAG).

Further, concert films and documentaries serve to advertise the products and services of the performing artists, both live and on recording. There were, for example, many people who had their first opportunity to experience Jimi Hendrix via the film *Woodstock* or *Monterey Pop*. The Who performed in the latter film, in which they destroyed their equipment at the end of a rave-up performance of "My Generation"; this appearance played a powerful role in jumpstarting US concert ticket and record sales for the band.

The type of concert film documenting an actual event rather than a "staged" production (like the musical shorts of the late 1920s and 1930s) began with classical concerts filmed in the 1930s (and continuing in the 1940s and 1950s). A rare exception to this classical music focus was the documentary *Jazz on a Summer Day,* filmed at the Newport Jazz Festival in 1958. But after the midpoint of the twentieth century, no musical genre was more adapted to film than rock and roll and other rock-era popular music.

Rock/pop concert films arguably begin with the *T.A.M.I. Show* in 1964, directed by Steve Binder.[14] It was followed by several more 1960s films that documented aspects of the pop music scene, including *The Beatles at Shea Stadium* and *The Big T.N.T. Show* (both 1966), *The Who in Finland* and *Don't Look Back* (both 1967), *Monterey Pop* (1968), and both *Woodstock* and *Gimme Shelter* (in 1970). Since then many hundreds of concert and festival films have been released, achieving varying degrees of success.[15]

The 1978 concert film *The Last Waltz,* directed by Martin Scorsese, is a benchmark in the music documentary genre for several reasons. First, it documents not just a concert or even a festival, but rather the final performance of the Band in 1976. The program featured many significant guest artists who had had relationships with the group over the years, including Bob Dylan, Van Morrison, Neil Diamond, and Muddy Waters.

Scorsese was already a major film director, acclaimed for his work in Hollywood. He became involved with the project as a result of his relationship with Robbie Robertson, guitarist, vocalist, and songwriter for the Band. For Scorsese, it was more than a movie about a band. He considered it a pastiche of American music and tried to bring all of the artists and performances together to tell a story.[16] The sophisticated filming and editing techniques Scorsese employed not only made *The Last Waltz* an outstanding (and successful) concert film but also redefined the genre and set the bar much higher for future films.

More recent concert films from popular artists include One Direction, *Where We Are* (2014); Muse, *Live at Rome Olympic Stadium* (2013); Justin Bieber, *Never Say Never* (2011); and Michael Jackson, *This Is It* (2009).

In terms of earning power, according the website Box Office Mojo, Bieber's *Never Say Never* grossed over $73 million, followed by Jackson's *This Is It* at $72 million.[17] The impact of concert films on the downstream sale of recordings and live shows is more difficult to estimate, but the common assumption is that a successful film ultimately boosts sales in all media.

Soundtrack Albums

Originally, the term *soundtrack* referred to the audio portion of a film, including the dialogue, sound effects, and music. The commercial music term came into use in relationship to album compilations of music from a movie. The practice of marketing the musical highlights of a film in album format began with the 1938 release of *Songs from "Snow White and the Seven Dwarfs"* (1937).

There are several varieties of the soundtrack album, including those that focus only on the songs as well those that also include selections from the film's incidental music. The latter tend to be specialty releases, primarily targeting film buffs and others with a particular interest in film scores. By contrast, song-oriented soundtracks have greater potential to generate revenue and promote both films and artists.

By the 1990s, there was a clear trend toward making soundtrack albums that included songs not heard in the movie. The trend toward inclusion of these "inspired by" songs was driven to a large extent by 1997's *Men in Black: The Album.* In July of that year the album was released along with the film and entered the charts at #2, with sales in excess of 177,000 units. That success marked the beginning of an era in which labels began to bid significant amounts of money for the rights to release a soundtrack (up to $1 million), while studios used them to build advance publicity for films.

In the case of *Men In Black,* star Will Smith's original video, "Men in Black"—produced independently from the film (with all original content) at a cost of about $1 million—was estimated to generate millions in free publicity due to its heavy rotation on MTV.[18]

According to a 1997 article in the *Los Angeles Times:* "'We started with Will's single and video and built a very good album around it,' says Glen Brunman, executive vice president of Sony Music *Soundtrax.* The newly formed division is releasing 'Men in Black' in conjunction with sister company Columbia Records. Both are owned by Sony, whose Columbia Pictures is releasing the movie."[19] The value potential of such collaborative relationships among media partners should be obvious. As noted in previous chapters, the capacity to aggregate creativity and distribution always provides a competitive advantage. And, as discussed previously in this chapter, the film industry was very quick to recognize the importance of the connections between film promotion, music publishing, and recordings.

In response to those in the film and music industries who have expressed distaste for the "inspired by" trend in soundtrack albums, Brunman states: "We're giving people an album that really holds together, that they will really like. The vibe of the movie is carried throughout the album."[20] It is clear that Brunman, among others, sees the soundtrack album not only as a revenue source but also as a way to extend the audience experience across both film and audio platforms.

The final value created by a successful soundtrack album is the capacity of music to expand or refocus the audience for a film and the music itself. In Marla Matzer's analysis of the soundtrack business in the 1990s, she states: "Five years ago this summer, a trio of movie soundtracks re-energized the soundtrack business, which has gone in cycles since the 1950s. 'Singles,' 'Boomerang' and 'Honeymoon in Vegas' were all pictures with somewhat limited niche appeal at the box office. That was their soundtracks' strength: They appealed to a young, record-buying audience."[21]

In addition to generating buzz within a desirable market segment in advance of a film release, revenue from soundtrack albums—though nominal in the context of feature film budgets—can help recoup music production costs from licensing the music used in the film. Licensing music for such placement has in recent years become an important avenue both for promotion and revenue generation in the music business.[22]

Music Supervisors

As the uses of music in film became more complicated and more dependent on music written independently of the film, it became increasingly necessary to have someone who could oversee all of the musical and licensing aspects of film (also television, advertising, games, and so forth). The role of *music supervisor* evolved to encompass working with the creative, technical, and legal issues attendant on using music in connection with virtually every visual medium.

According to the Guild of Music Supervisors, critical responsibilities for the music supervisor include acting to "secure and supervise any and all music related talent, which includes composers, songwriters, recording artists, on-camera performers, musicians, orchestrators, arrangers, copyists, contractors, music producers, engineers, etc.: liaise and negotiate with talent representation, including legal, label, talent management, agency, business management, etc."[23]

In addition, the music supervisor is expected to be able to coordinate efforts with other creative staff as well as management. Above all, the music supervisor must be able to make accurate projections as to licensing costs and manage the film's music budget. The role of the music supervisor in television is discussed in more detail below.

TELEVISION

Much as it was for film and radio, music was a natural fit for television. In part, this was due to early television programming being based on radio, film, and theatrical entertainments that used music. But it also became quickly apparent that by appearing on a television program such as the *Louisiana Hayride,* a performer could boost record and ticket sales. Further, television programs that focused on live music had lower production costs than did conventional dramatic productions.[24]

The ways music is used on television both reflect and extend film practice. Theme songs, featured performances, background music, and song placements have been common elements of television production from its earliest days. In addition, television commercials rely heavily on musical content, as do the transitions from the show to commercial and back again.

In this section we will examine several categories of television music, emphasizing those that have the greatest potential for economic impact for the show itself, for artists whose music is included, and for advertisers. These include concert performance shows, theme songs, diegetic music, musical montages, and closing credit music.

Concert/Performance Shows

In most ways, *concert/performance* television shows worked like radio for artists and record labels. Being on the show promoted their records, their upcoming tours, and their name recognition with fans. *American Bandstand* and *Soul Train* are early examples of popular music "performed"—but often with the performers lip-synching to recordings—on television. There were a number of other popular shows in the UK and Europe as well. Some of these also emphasized lip-synching to records, while others were committed to live performances in front of live audiences in the studio.

Theme Songs

Television theme songs work, in the broadest sense, the way theme songs work in film: they establish a mood at the beginning of visual content. By being played at the start of every episode of a recurring program, television theme songs also enhance brand recognition and encourage a sense of familiarity with the product. Because music can be so effectively embedded in memory, just hearing a few seconds of a familiar theme can evoke detailed memories of (and feelings about) the show itself. In addition, television music serves to bridge in and out of commercials and provides a transition from one show to the next.

For many years, television music, including theme songs, was written specifically for individual shows. But, as with film, there was a gradual progression in approach and application. First, theme songs were originally longer and often included lyrics that provided a narrative overview of the show's premise and introduced the main characters. Classic examples of this include the themes from *Gilligan's Island, The Beverly Hillbillies,* and *The Brady Bunch.*

Beginning in the 1970s—notably with the NBC show *Cheers* (1982–1993)—theme songs became less descriptive of the show itself. Some musical themes from the 1970s, such as the theme from *MASH,* were purely instrumental, used to accompany a montage of action clips and featured characters.

In the 1990s there was another shift, this time toward using independently created popular songs as themes for television shows. A famous example was the use of "I'll Be There for You," written by the Rembrandts and released on their third studio album, *LP* (1995). The song was adopted as the theme for the NBC comedy *Friends* from 1994 to 2004.

Though it has today become a common practice for pop bands to place songs in television, film, or advertising, twenty years ago it was not. The Rembrandts lost a great deal of credibility with their fans for their decision. Singer Danny Wilde recalls that "we went from being the darlings of the alternative scene to a proper mainstream band. I think we lost a lot of our original fans at that point, and many people stopped taking us seriously."[25]

The band became wealthy because of the licensing deal—the show had a lengthy run and endless reruns—but they were never able to recover their "alternative scene" credibility with their fans. Other 1990s shows that used pop artist songs include *Dawson's Creek* and *Ally McBeal,* among many others. From the last years of the twentieth century to the present, television shows have typically been represented by a combination of licensed and originally composed themes.

Diegetic Music on TV

In a broad sense, music can be part of a television (or for that matter, a film) production in two ways. The music can be playing in the background of the action on screen or it can be part of the story line. For example, if music is being played on the radio in a scene and the characters can hear it as part of the story, it is called "diegetic" music.

The diegetic use of music on TV can be traced back to *I Love Lucy* (1951–1957) and *The Adventures of Ozzy and Harriet* (1952–1966). In the latter, the actor playing the son, Ricky, was actually Rick Nelson, the real-life son of Ozzy and Harriet Nelson, the actors playing his parents on the show. Ricky Nelson's career as a popular singer was launched through an on-air performance of Fats Domino's "I'm Walkin'" in the episode "Ricky the Drummer," which aired April 10, 1957. Rick Nelson went on to establish a significant career as a songwriter, performer, and actor.

Another example of using a television program to create a musical career is *The Monkees* (1966–1970). The show was a calculated attempt to create a band from a group of actors and sell original music created for them by professional writers and producers. Each week's show featured the four young men's antics and a musical number. As was the case for Rick Nelson, song placements on *The Monkees* led to significant record sales. Eventually the band sold over 60 million records internationally.

Montage and Closing Credit Music

The practice of using a popular song—one written independently of the show—to accompany a dramatic "montage" during the course of an episode became popular in the 1990s. *Miami Vice* is an early example that used both original music (composed by Jan Hammer) and music from outside sources; the show spent some $10,000 per episode to license music, often to accompany an action montage.[26]

In addition, the show directly commissioned successful pop performers /songwriters to write songs for specific plotlines. Several of these—Glenn Frey's "You Belong to the City" and Andy Taylor's "When the Rain Comes Down"—were only released as part of *Miami Vice* soundtracks. Since then, television soundtracks have become an important source of revenue and an opportunity for brand expansion, much as they are for theatrical films.

Closing credit music has been an important part of film for decades. In television, the practice has been modified in two ways. First, for traditional network or basic cable programming, when commercial interruptions are present, the closing credit music is often played at a reduced volume in order to allow other programming to be promoted. In addition, television credits are often compressed and/or displayed at high speed in order to allow commercial advertising to be played between programs. In those contexts, the significance of closing credit music is vastly reduced.

Premium cable, however, operates differently in that there are no ads and no time constraints between shows. Consequently, using music to accompany closing credits or, more specifically, to accompany a closing montage that presents all of the characters engaged in some reaction to the events of that episode began on premium cable with shows like *The Sopranos, The Wire,* and others. It later spread to network television as well as independently produced shows. Today, the closing credit /montage song is a standard trope in the television industry.

ADVERTISING

As soon as broadcast and film media made the integration of music into advertising possible, it was rapidly adopted. As we examine advertising music we need to consider *branding, brand synergies,* and the progressive *convergence* of programming and advertising content.

Branding and Brand Synergy

The use of music to brand products dates from the beginning of the radio era. When a song is specifically composed for product advertisements, it is called a "jingle." Jingles began in the 1920s on radio; one of the earliest was "Have You Tried Wheaties?" The song was performed by the Wheaties Quartet, a group of amateur singers from Minneapolis. In test markets where the song was played, the company saw increases in sales in the tens of thousands of boxes.[27] Other businesses soon followed suit. In addition, radio stations began to commission jingles to brand the stations themselves while complying with the federal requirement that stations periodically self-identify on the air.

Television advertising adopted the original jingle approach over several decades, but in the 1980s, advertisers and advertising agencies began to explore original song placements. According to Timothy Taylor in *The Sounds of Capitalism,* advertisers began to use "oldies" in order to connect to the positive feelings songs could generate as potential customers listened to them:

> An early campaign that made use of rock music to attract nostalgic baby boomers was for Ford's Lincoln-Mercury division in 1984, which employed 17 classic rock hits underlying "witty mini-scenarios of baby boomer lifestyles." According to the advertising director at the advertising agency that produced the commercials ... "Research showed that they were reading a variety of positive things into the spot, recalling all kinds of wonderful moments from their college days, and attributing those moments to the brand name Mercury."[28]

Such song placements have come to be the definitive technique for television commercials, especially auto advertisements. But the strategy is by no means confined to using oldies. New music from relatively unknown bands is often used to announce a new auto model and, incidentally, help break a band into public awareness—an example of a brand synergy between the auto maker and musical artist.

In recent years, "what's that song in the Honda commercial" searches have become a common feature on the Internet. Sites specifically designed to answer that question have appeared.[29] Some have argued that licensing music to help brand and advertise products brands is becoming the new "album release" strategy and that advertisers and ad agencies are the new record labels.

Along those lines, companies now not only license a song for use in their ads but also provide tour and promotional support for young artists. Music supervisors at ad agencies are becoming the A&R players in this emerging music scene. In addition, branding agencies may represent not just companies but also musical artists in the various domains of branding, including song placements.[30]

Taken altogether, the opportunity for companies to associate their brand with music that connects to potential customers and for artists to reach a larger audience creates new commercial and creative synergies. This framework has emerged at a critical time in the post-Napster era. Traditional labels have less money for development and promotion of new artists. Brand-based licensing has proved so effective that many emerging artists do not sign with a record label at all, but rather work with publishers and other agencies to develop their licensing opportunities.[31] See chapter 11, "State of the Art," for a more in-depth discussion of modern promotional strategies.

Convergence of Content and Advertising

By the late twentieth century, particularly on television, there was an increasing overlap between program content and the advertising used to support it. And music was at the center of both.

For example, while a product-specific jingle (such as the one sung by the Wheaties Quartet in the 1920s) was specifically created to advertise the product, the Lincoln-Mercury "Big Chill" campaign or the Raisin Bran "I Heard It through the Grapevine" spots used music originally created as entertainment. It became clear that commercials were increasingly intended to entertain and make broader cultural connections as well as to sell cars or cereal.

As the second half of the twentieth century progressed, many wondered whether it was appropriate to see ads as merely an economic necessity to keep programming on the air; or were the shows simply the pretext for presenting the increasingly expensive and elaborate commercial spots? Consider, for example, the cultural significance of Super Bowl commercials. Such spots are expensive and can have a massive impact on a company's profitability, but they also generate discussion, conversation, articles, and blog content. As a result, the ads for a given Super Bowl may serve as a measure of the nation's mood and values at a particular time. Many people only watch the game to see the commercials, or don't bother to tune in at all but find the "best of" postings the next day for Super Bowl ads.

The convergence of art and advertising is ongoing, but it is nowhere more evident than in the music video, as defined in the MTV era.

MUSIC VIDEO

MTV began on August 1, 1981, with the video for the song "Video Killed the Radio Star," by the Buggles. The format was basically that of pop music radio. There were a limited number of songs played in rotation, introduced by "VJs" instead of DJs. Although MTV was not available in every cable market, the places where it was began to demonstrate its potential in terms of record sales. Within a few years, MTV was airing in virtually every US city, and even artists who had sworn they would never make a video were doing so.

The practice of creating what were then called "promotional clips" for songs and artists dates back to the late 1950s and 1960s. These were considered to be advertisements and not entertainment content. They were typically produced either to air as commercials for an upcoming concert or to be inserted into a television show when it was not possible for the artist to appear in person.

Promotional clips are an example of how it can be difficult to distinguish between advertising and short musical films as creative expression. For example, the only way that promotional clips worked was by capturing something about the artist to which the audience could relate and by being entertaining. Both factors apply equally to art and ads.

For many in the recording industry, the idea of MTV—a cable station that only played promotional clips—seemed irrational. But as the potential of music videos to increase album sales was proven, within a just a few years, record label budgets for music video production increased dramatically.

Though video singles were sold, they never became the source of revenue that 45-rpm singles had been. Part of the issue was timing. As home computing became increasingly popular, it changed how people stored and played music. Playback media formats—videotape, DVDs, and laser discs—were in flux. During the same period, MTV changed owners (a controlling interest was acquired by Viacom in 1986), and the channel changed its programming focus.

While the early years of MTV defined what a music video looked like, the form continued to evolve. The emergence of YouTube in 2005 provided the next platform for the music video as well as the next step of convergence: that of audience and artist roles. YouTube and its impact on the music business are discussed in more detail in chapter 11.

MUSIC IS ALWAYS ADVERTISING

Certainly the evolution of music promotional clips into the programming content of MTV is the story of the emergence of a new art form and cultural touchstone. This progression from ad to creative activity is also a reflection of multiple forms of convergence in advertising and entertainment. But was the resulting form—music as advertising and art—in any sense new? It can be argued that there is no public presentation of music—whatever its nominal motivation—that is not also a form of advertising.

Consequently, regardless of the medium in which music is expressed—live, print, broadcast, or visually mediated—music publicly performed both creates value in the experience itself and advertises the artist and his music. There are no exceptions.

Music is always advertising.

CORE PRINCIPLES

Music is always advertising.

KEY CONCEPTS

Music copyright and visual media

Performing rights

Dramatic rights

Synchronization rights

Master use rights

Silent and "talking" film

Theme songs

Soundtrack albums

Music supervisor

Concert/performance TV shows

Television theme, montage, and closing credit songs

Promotional clips and music videos

Convergence of advertising and content

EXPLORATION

Nelson George, "Leaping off the Screen: Nelson George Talks about 'Soul Train,'" *New York Times* (4–16–2014), http://article .wn.com/view/2014/04/16/leaping_off_the_screen_nelson_george _talks_about_8216soul_tr/.

"15 Songs Forever Linked with Popular TV Shows and Movies," *Fox News Magazine* (10–1–13), http://magazine.foxnews.com /celebrity/15-songs-forever-linked-popular-tv-shows-and-movies.

Brian Petchers, "Anthony Mandler on the State of Music Videos," *Forbes* (5–1–2013), http://www.forbes.com/sites/brianpetchers/2013 /05/01/anthony-mandler-on-the-state-of-music-videos/.

Mitchell Peters, "Angels and Airwaves Plans Free Digital Album Release," Reuters (1–22–2010), http://www.reuters.com/article/2010 /01/23/us-delonge-idUSTRE60M0BR20100123.

Shelley DuBois, "Are Advertisers the New Record Labels?" *Fortune* (3–14–2012), http://fortune.com/2012/03/14/are-advertisers-the-new -record-labels/.

CHAPTER 9

Artists, Audiences, and Brands

We essentially take these sound waves, this sound, and we
organize it into emotion, and that's how we connect with
our audiences.

—Stefon Harris

Musicians by and large make a living with a relationship
with an audience that is economically harnessed through
performance and ticket sales.

—John Perry Barlow

Regardless of the connecting medium, it is the relationship between artist and audience that generates all forms of value in music. It is difficult
to separate the music and—in particular, our experience of music—
from the person performing it. Even in the world of classical music, a
milieu in which "pure" aesthetic merit is most highly valued, there is an
ongoing fascination with not only the musical work but also the lives of
the great composers.

It is possible to value the compositions of Beethoven without knowing anything about the man, but even casual fans of classical music may
know that Beethoven's encroaching deafness shaped his life and work
and, in so knowing, their assessment and appreciation of his work
changes. Even removed by nearly two centuries, they may feel a wonder
at his accomplishment and perhaps sympathy for what must surely have
been a horrible circumstance for the man.

When the artist is living and is, as a person, accessible to the audience, it is virtually impossible to distinguish between the two—art and
artist. Beethoven was extremely well known in Vienna, arguably as recognized for his hair and imperious demeanor as for his musical genius.

Then as now, the composer/performer's identity is inextricably part of his music's value to society. Though fashions have changed and the media for connecting audience to artist have evolved, there is not much difference between Beethoven's hair, Elvis Presley's sideburns, James Brown's cape (and pompadour), Slash's top hat, or Lady Gaga's "meat dress" in terms of the capacity of those symbols to enhance the connection between artist and audience.

Though this connection creates value, it is not without cost. Being a celebrity performer adds value to music enterprise. It can also negatively impact the artist and human being. Many performers—from Elvis Presley to Kurt Cobain to Justin Bieber—have found that achieving the success that they once imagined came at the expense of their privacy, their artistic and personal autonomy, their physical and mental health, and even their lives.

When the artist becomes the product, there is a risk of being consumed.

ARTIST AS BRAND

It was clear to earlier promoters like P. T. Barnum and Colonel Tom Parker that publicity was built by piquing public interest in the artist as person as much as—if not more than—the music or musical event being promoted. The "face" of musical ventures from popular bands to opera productions (almost always the "lead" singer) and even symphony orchestras (typically the conductor) becomes the brand for the audience/customer. Musical ensembles and genres that did not have such a "face"—string quartets, instrumental bands, or symphony orchestras without charismatic conductors—tended not to be as successful in the marketplace as the twentieth century progressed.

The idea of personal branding dates back to the 1930s and began to be more widely applied as a business model in the 1980s and 1990s. By then, however, it was an already long-established practice in music. Much as "experiential branding"—treating business transactions as performances experienced by customers—drew on music and entertainment practices, personal branding was a concept adopted from entertainment and applied to business generally.[1] These practices not only demonstrate how much art and commerce overlap in the music marketplace but also how the creative sector—beyond adding value to society and the economy directly—has a lot to teach the commercial sector: from the power of celebrity to the experience economy to the socially mediated "sharing" economy (see chapter 11).

The Celebrity Economy

The concept at the heart of this chapter is what we will call the *celebrity economy*. Barnum understood that established celebrity could be enhanced and leveraged by carefully calibrated press releases. Jenny Lind was known for her charitable gifts, but Barnum aggressively advanced that narrative—even making donations in her name, but using his own money—to generate interest in her US tour. Colonel Parker understood that the public's fascination with Elvis Presley as a person could build demand for his music and movies.

Celebrity optimization became—quite early—a standard practice in the music business. A major factor in artist "discovery"—finding new artists to promote—was based on their potential for developing such celebrity. As such, the music business focused not just on finding talent but also on "engineering" celebrity. Consequently, music enterprise can be called a "celebrity industry" almost regardless of era and musical genre.

As celebrity became a more and more important product of the entertainment business, it impacted how music (as well as film, television, and other performing arts) was discussed in the press and in society generally. Entire sectors of broadcast and online media developed to track, document, and dissect the personal lives of performers.

Early forms of this kind of public coverage of celebrities include the gossip magazines and tabloids, including *Hollywood Confidential* in the 1950s. Since then the form has proliferated across broadcast and online media to the point where even nominally serious journalistic platforms include a component of celebrity gossip. These outlets frequently publish photos of celebrities, not only onstage or at public events, but quite often in their private lives.

Bemoaned as intrusive, this type of coverage undoubtedly enhances celebrity and, consequently, the value of celebrity brands. Not only are personal lives the subject of such journalistic inquiry, but embarrassing events are accorded particular importance. As a result, there is a growing willingness for artists and management not to just make the best of such difficult situations as divorce, arrests, lawsuits, or substance abuse, but to engineer embarrassments in order to garner the attention.

One (relatively) innocuous example of what we might call "planned celebrity misfortune events" are so-called wardrobe malfunctions. Janet Jackson's well-documented "slip" at the Super Bowl in 2004 was immediately characterized as "a malfunction of the wardrobe" by a Jackson spokesperson.[2] But the legitimacy of the event's accidental nature was almost immediately questioned. Within a week, FCC chairman Michael Powell characterized it as "a classless, crass, and deplorable stunt."[3]

Though the exposure—inadvertent or otherwise—led to hundreds of thousands of viewer complaints and heightened FCC restrictions on live broadcasts, it produced at least one positive result. Jackson's new album, *Danita Jo,* released five weeks after the Super Bowl—though building more slowly than her previous release, perhaps due to television and radio boycotts—opened at #2 on the Billboard 200 and ultimately sold enough to achieve multi-platinum status.[4]

The marketability of celebrity misfortune—engineered or otherwise—is a manifestation of a larger shift. To return to the discussion of convergence (chapters 5 and 8), we can see that there has been a progressive blurring of the performing and personal activities of musical artists. The distinction between what happens onstage as the primary focus—with the business mechanics and logistics of production kept "backstage" because they are presumably not interesting or relevant to audiences—has broken down. Opening chart positions, sales figures, contractual disputes, and personnel changes—once the domain of managers and industry analysts—are all now routinely covered by multiple media platforms.

The late twentieth-century convergence of onstage/backstage distinctions and of public/private life is in part a logical consequence of a century driven by advertising and marketing. But there is another axis of convergence: the roles of artist and audience.

With the advent of social media, the distinction between artist and audience roles—who was onstage and who was sitting in the audience—became, to an unprecedented extent, permeable. User-driven video archive sites such as YouTube, whose motto is Broadcast Yourself, were a revolutionary phenomenon, the implications of which are still unfolding.

The aggregate impact of these multiple forms of convergence is the overarching topic of this chapter. How did the evolving nature of celebrity and celebrity value, the merging of onstage and backstage content and processes, and the convergence of artist/audience and producer/consumer roles change musical production and reception in the marketplace and the culture?

We begin with another look at the value of celebrity.

Celebrity Capital Revisited

In an environment of blurred edges early in the twenty-first century, celebrity value was more complex and more leveraged than ever before.

If we conceptualize celebrity value as "capital," we might describe it, following Olivier Driessens, "as accumulated media visibility that results from recurrent media representations."[5] In other words, appearing in the media generates celebrity and being a celebrity increases opportunity for media appearances, producing a self-reinforcing process. Consequently, in an entertainment marketplace where "being known" drives value as much as being talented, the creation and expansion of celebrity becomes a primary rather than a secondary goal.

Many have observed that contemporary society and culture have become increasingly "celebritized." This is arguably a result of an entertainment industry devoted to cultivating celebrity, along with the increasing pervasiveness of media in everyday life. Increasingly, people expect not just celebrity performers, athletes, politicians, chefs, designers, economists, home remodelers, and so forth; anyone and everyone is, at least potentially, a "star."[6]

One might think that the unprecedented expansion of celebrity status—everyone actually getting her "fifteen minutes" or more—would diminish its value.[7] In some ways, perhaps it does. But new stars in popular music appear every year, even as talent search television programs continue to popularize (and monetize) the dream of universal celebrity. Anyone can broadcast himself to the world via YouTube, yet YouTube "stars" rise above the rest. Consequently, despite an economically reasonable expectation that the proliferation of celebrity would reduce the value of celebrity capital, the opposite seems to be occurring.

An answer to that apparent contradiction may be found in Driessen's theory that celebrity capital may result from either the intrinsic qualities and efforts of the individual or be an artifact "which is co-produced by the celebrity industry."[8] Thus celebrity status can derive simply from the public pursuit of celebrity—for example, via talent shows, video sites, and social media. In this context and for as long as there is an active celebrity industry to support it, the market value of celebrity will not be exhausted until everyone gets his fifteen minutes.

Driessen's operational theory is that "it could be argued that the building blocks of the celebrity apparatus are the celebrity, the media, the public, and the celebrity industry."[9] Manipulating those four elements and their interrelationships might also be described as the process of branding. The next section explores several examples of celebrity-driven brand management in music.

BRAND-DRIVEN BUSINESS MODELS

Rolling Stones

One of the possibilities supported by a celebrity economy is that music is only one of several avenues for value creation for musicians. One of the first bands of the rock era to develop an integrated business model based on who they are as well as what they do is the Rolling Stones. Though their economic model is not as diverse as that of some later artists, the Stones have fully exploited the revenue streams from touring, recording, licensing, and merchandise. In addition, they have structured different business models and benchmarks for each revenue sector and developed strategies to make sure that all of their initiatives remain in alignment.[10] Mick Jagger described the individual elements of the band's brand enterprise: "They all have income streams like any other company. They have different business models; they have different delegated people that look after them. And they have to interlock. That's my biggest problem."[11]

The Rolling Stones enterprise is structured as a partnership of the four performers, with four subsidiary companies: Promotour, Promopub, Promotone, and Musidor. According to Andy Serwer, in *Fortune* magazine: "This family of companies is based in the Netherlands, which has tax advantages for foreign bands. When the group isn't touring, these companies employ only a few dozen employees. At the high-water mark of a tour, on the night the band is playing, say, Giants Stadium, the Stones may employ more than 350."[12]

Between 1989 and 2002, the band made over $1 billion on the road. The *Steel Wheels* tour (1989) was a milestone in that it grossed $260+ million globally, including tickets, merchandise, and sponsorship monies from Anheuser-Busch. In the late 1990s and early 2000s the Stones cut costs by playing fewer stadiums, thus carrying a smaller crew and physical setup with them. In addition, the band maximized merchandising by going well beyond T-shirts, selling "some 50 products–such as underwear by Britain's Agent Provocateur and new, expensive items like shirts, jackets, and, yes, dresses."[13]

In 1970, early in their brand development, the band's "lips and tongue" logo cost them £50. It has since become one of the most recognizable trademarks in the world. They were originally cast as the "bad boys" (compared to the Beatles being "nice boys"), which was an idea they embraced and cultivated. Even as older musicians, they have thus far been able to play against type with the "too old to rock and roll" meme and generate press and public interest in all of their more recent tours.[14]

Madonna

One might argue that irrespective of her musical talents, Madonna has consistently displayed genius in branding and rebranding herself. Madonna Louise Ciccone began her career as a dancer but soon moved to music, signing with Sire Records in 1982 and releasing her self-titled debut in 1983. She quickly became an iconic, single-name star in music, as well as in music video and fashion, releasing commercially successful, Grammy-winning albums in the 1980s and 1990s.

Along the way, Madonna not only successfully kept her music current and relevant to new audiences, but also leveraged her personal charisma and style. Rachel Johnson observed about Madonna's cultural and economic impact that

> her constant revolutionizing sexiness is her brand—a form of artistic self-expression. In the 1990s, she wore the infamous Jean Paul Gaultier cone bra with the dizzying spirals to emphasize sexuality, juxtaposing it with her Catholic upbringing (all while seducing a chair) during her Blonde Ambition tour. She reportedly grossed nearly $63 million which made her most successful tour at the time. A decade later, her Confessions tour, during which she sang *Live to Tell* hanging from a cross, earned her $194.7 million.[15]

In addition to extending her career as a performing and recording artist into the twenty-first century—her 2013 MDNA tour, for example, grossed $305 million, and Madonna was listed by *Forbes* magazine as the highest-earning musician of the year—she pioneered other, more extended brand management strategies.[16] Like a number of other late twentieth- and early twenty-first-century artists, Madonna supplements her music income with extended brand offerings, most notably "her Material Girl clothing line and Truth or Dare fragrance."[17] An even more significant decision—and one with far-reaching influence—was to leave Warner Brothers to sign a comprehensive deal with concert promoter Live Nation in 2007.[18]

As reported by the *Wall Street Journal,* the ten-year, $120 million cash and stock deal gave the promoter the rights to "sell three studio albums, promote concert tours, sell merchandise, and license her name."[19] Although such "360-degree deals" were already becoming common, they were initially used for new artists in order to increase opportunities to recoup initial investments in unproven talent. Using them with established, "superstar" acts was seen as less desirable because the financial scale of a "big name" deal substantially increased the amount of support necessary, as well as the financial risk.

360-Degree Deals

As a response to declining record sales and an increasing dependence on alternate revenue streams, a number of labels, promoters, and management companies began to explore the idea of managing and sharing in the profits from all sources of revenue that the brand of a musical artist could generate. These kinds of multi-rights arrangements came to be called 360-degree deals because they covered the entire span of productivity in "all directions."

There were multi-rights contracts long before the term came into use in the 2000s.[20] Motown in the 1960s was one of the first labels to control all aspects of its performing artists' careers. Sonicbids CEO Panos Panay describes the Motown version of the comprehensive deal this way: "If you were [an artist] signed to Motown in the late 60s, they owned your likeness, your touring, publishing, record royalties, made the record deal, told you what to wear, they told you how to walk."[21] Concert promoter Live Nation was an early adopter of this type of deal in the twenty-first century.[22] Initially, the company formed a label, Live Nation Music, and signed emerging artists like Zac Brown, later entering into comprehensive deals with more established acts.

Rather than assuming the traditional record label role of discovering, developing, and promoting talent, "superstar" deals are joint ventures in which well-established artists (who don't need to be discovered, developed, and so on) can continue running aspects of their own enterprise while using the Live Nation infrastructure.[23] For the sponsoring company, such deals allow diversification of risk and revenue opportunities. The net assessment is that these deals, like traditional record label contracts, are skewed in favor of the managing company rather than the artist. As we will explore below (and in chapter 11), there are alternative means of optimizing multiple forms of productivity that give artists more autonomy and control.

Brand Synergies

Jay-Z

In some ways, Jay-Z's career epitomizes what Live Nation (or any other organization interested in a 360-degree deal) is looking for in an artist/

partner. After overcoming a poverty-ridden upbringing, Shawn Carter built a successful career in music, becoming one of the best-known names in hip-hop. As NPR's Joel Rose notes, Jay-Z's 2007 appearance at the Hammerstain Ballroom in New York City

> was just the beginning. Jay-Z then launched his own record label, his own clothing line, and his own nightclubs—basically, his own lifestyle brand. Jupiter Research analyst Michael Green says that's what concert promotion agency Live Nation is after.
>
> "They know it's not just music that's making money for these superstars," Green says. "It's their movies, apparel—all the other things they can market in addition to what made them famous to begin with."[24]

Hip-hop artists generally were among the first to aggressively exploit the synergy between the celebrity brand of the performer and nonmusical merchandise. Zack O'Malley of *Forbes* observed that several musicians on the magazine's 2013 list of top-earning musicians attribute "nearly all their income to sources other than music sales, record labels and touring. Sean 'Diddy' Combs, who ranks No. 12 with $50 million (making him Hip-Hop's highest-paid act), earns the bulk of his bucks from his wildly successful Ciroc vodka deal. His Revolt TV network, launched in October, should provide a big boost to future earnings."[25]

Toby Keith

Artists in other genres have also explored the potential of extended brand relationships. Performers like Toby Keith are not only leveraging their music careers to support merchandise sales but also optimizing the synergy among their brands. Having been invited onto Toby Keith's tour bus and invited to "swallow the worm" by the star, Zack O'Malley discusses the Keith business model this way:

> There's little about Toby Keith . . . that isn't calibrated for maximum synergy. The mezcal–and the worm–were from the 52-year-old's own liquor label, Wild Shot. His road trip to the stage is part of a multimillion-dollar endorsement deal with Ford, whose executives had filled his preshow tour bus, and once he's up there, he makes sure to play "I Love This Bar," a song after which he's named his restaurant chain. The teens down in front with the Taylor Swift shirts? Keith owns a piece of her, too. The $1 million or so he'll earn for the 90-minute concert itself feels almost incidental.

Toby Keith is a one-man 360-degree deal whose opening song on tour is "American Ride," which sets the mood for the audience and supports the Ford sponsorship of the tour. According to O'Malley: "Keith pulled in $65 million over the last 12 months–more than any musician not named Madonna, Lady Gaga or Bon Jovi, and easily outpacing masters of product extension like Jay-Z ($42 million), Beyoncé ($53 million) and Jennifer Lopez ($45 million)."[26]

Scalable Brand Extension

It is easy to see how, in an era of declining sales for recorded music, record labels would want to access additional revenue streams generated by artists. Since concert ticket sales and concert merchandise are robust components of music revenue today, this empowers promoters—particularly large-scale promoters like Live Nation. For artists, the situation is less clear in many ways.

Obviously established brands—particularly those of artists who have already created a reputation in nonrecording, nonconcert markets—are in a position to improve their business opportunities by establishing joint ventures with large-scale entertainment organizations. For new and emerging artists, though, the situation is much riskier. No one can predict the scale of value that the "points" in a 360-degree deal may represent as a career evolves over time, and sponsors are averse to high-risk deals.

The self-represented 360-degree deal epitomized by Toby Keith brings the greatest workload and responsibility to the artist in exchange for the greatest control and potential profitability. It also means that a fully self-directed 360-degree enterprise puts all the risk on the artist himself.

On the plus side, self-direction is also the most scalable brand extension model. Even local startup bands, using freely available social media tools, can grow and leverage their popularity while they are honing their musical product. It may not be possible to earn $500 million "Toby Keith" money without the number one singles, but it is possible to optimize brand recognition and income on a much smaller scale.

Pomplamoose

The duo Pomplamoose epitomizes the DIY branding approach. Jack Conte and Nataly Dawn began recording covers and original tunes in a spare bedroom in their San Francisco home and posting them on YouTube in 2008. Their version of Beyoncé's "All the Single Ladies" was viewed over 4 million times. Hundreds of thousands of their songs have been sold on their own site and via iTunes. A Patreon campaign (a crowdfunding company launched by Conte) has demonstrated that there is a growing grassroots fan base willing to invest in the band financially. In addition, they still sell their homemade grapefruit soap on their website. They have no record or promotion deal.[27]

AUDIENCE TO ARTIST, CONSUMER TO PRODUCER

The Pomplamoose enterprise suggests how powerfully the use of digital recording technologies and social media can connect "homemade" music to large national and international audiences. And to do so without the resources of traditional gatekeepers and nurturers like labels, promoters, and broadcast media.

It is a significant concept. Game-changing.

Without a record deal, it was once impossible to have a large-scale music career. Artist/entrepreneurs like Dawn and Conte demonstrate—via Pomplamoose—that today you can be your own nurturer and gate-keeper (or gate jumper). Not everyone, however, has the combination of talent, enterprise, and persistence necessary for success in the DIY music world. For many, making the leap from being in the audience to standing onstage takes a bigger push. This is where the celebrity industry comes in: selling the dream of celebrity, via the celebrity experience.

Talent Shows: Selling Artist Discovery

There has always been a certain fascination with the idea of moving from a seat in the audience to stand in the lights onstage. To no small degree, the dream of seeing one's "name in lights" has been a motivating factor for many musical careers, successful and otherwise. But it has also supported the idea of the amateur talent show. On rare occasions, such talent shows may actually serve as a discovery tool for new talent. That is not, however, their primary purpose.

The rationale for the modern talent show is to provide three interrelated opportunities. First, talent shows represent a chance for members of the audience to cross over the line to performance territory and be—however poorly or briefly—an artist looking outward at the people in the seats. Second, they provide the opportunity for people in the audience to see and hear how well or, more often, how horribly their peers perform. No small part of the experience is the painful pleasure of watching someone else's disastrous performance and feeling pity, relief (that you're not up there doing that), or even a kind of sadistic amusement. Third, they transform the discovery phase of the A&R process into a marketable product paid for by advertisers and watched by millions.

Talent shows have been around for a long time. They predate broadcast media, but were subsequently threaded through all forms, including more recent shows such as *American Idol* (Fox, 2002–2016), *America's Got Talent* (CBS, 2006–present), *The X-Factor* (CBS, 2011–2013), and *The Voice* (NBC, 2011–present).

These shows are in the business of presenting amateur performers to build the brand of the show itself and of the contestants. There's not much difference between signing onto *American Idol* and signing a record deal. The show, like the label, owns your creative productivity for a period of some years. Where they differ is that a record label may invest more money in development and promotion and be much more dependent upon producing a commercially viable product at the end of the process.

Shows like *American Idol,* though they provide some limited mentoring, make their money and develop their own brands by showing the public and often painful struggles of untrained and sometimes minimally talented artists. The shows make their money every week independent of whether or not the performances are good. In fact, sometimes truly terrible performances are better for business than merely competent ones.

While the *American Idol* approach does not fundamentally change the show's role as a label-like gatekeeper, it does utterly disrupt the idea that finding, selecting/rejecting talent, and preparing performers is all "backstage" stuff—to be done before a product is offered to the public. All of that, including the most disastrously embarrassing preliminaries, is put on the air as product. Things traditionally kept off-stage—rejections handled with few people in the room, personal details about catastrophic private lives, contestants' hopes, dreams, and fears—are all there, onstage, integrated into, and constitutive of, the program itself.

Showing backstage, production, and rehearsal content (like the "making of" phenomenon in film) and even painful personal issues are now essential components of content and are currently built into the production process for film, television, tours, and recordings. The approach takes the viewer behind the scenes, backstage and into personal lives, and allows for the personality of the artists—the personal brand—to be enhanced. It is a scalable idea and one that would apply across many musical genres, including DIY production and promotional models.

> Every aspect of the discovery, development, and production process, as well as the personal life of the performer, is potentially marketable content.

In addition to the nominal "talent" content and on-screen branding, talent shows also embody fairly traditional artist-management relationships. Before contestants participate in a show like *American Idol*, for example, they sign contracts putting the production company of the show (19 Entertainment in the case of *American Idol*) in charge of their management, merchandising, publishing, and recording. It is, in other words, a compulsory 360-degree deal. Winners are held to a multiyear contract that controls all of their productivity.[28]

These contractual arrangements are among the few things that are not fodder for the show itself. Public revelations of these contracts—typically as the result of a successful contestant suing the production company—underscore how heavily they favor management over the artist. The usual justifications apply. Certainly 19 Entertainment assumes virtually all of the financial risk and provides most of the resources so that contestants can compete. At the same time, the terms, including the required performing engagements for friends of executives, have a definite exploitive vibe reminiscent of the old-school artist management approach of Colonel Tom Parker and others.

ARTIST-MANAGEMENT PARADIGMS

Thanks to new and emerging media, as well as changing social and economic structures, artists can now bypass some aspects of the traditional structures of record labels and legacy broadcast media. In addition, long-established beliefs about the roles and relationship between artist and management have begun to shift. Perhaps the most significant shift comes as a convergence. Where once it was believed that there was an unbridgeable gap between creativity and commerce—artist and management—they are increasingly seen as two aspects of the same process.

A Parable: Elvis and the Colonel

No professional relationship in music more dramatically demonstrates the gulf between creativity and commerce than that of Elvis Presley and

Colonel Tom Parker. It has been reported that following Presley's death in 1977, Parker stated, "I had his whole career mapped out from the start—the Rebel, the G.I., the Eunuch, followed by the Raunchy Rhinestone Messiah."[29]

Those terms and his description of the career/brand phases they represent may be the result of hindsight or simply of Parker's characteristic boastful style. Regardless, Parker evidently had a vision for managing Elvis's public image and connecting it to the marketability of his records, films, and public appearances.

Many have argued that Parker's control over all aspects of Elvis's productivity stifled the performer creatively and ultimately contributed to his demise. It is clear, however, that Elvis benefited financially from the relationship and was worth some $4.9 million at the end of his life. His estate is worth much more today, with annual earnings in the range of $40 to $55 million per year throughout the 2000s.[30]

That said, the Colonel's financial relationship with Elvis has been the subject of much fascination and disapproval. Its framework was simple: as the Colonel's only client, Elvis gave 50 percent of all earnings to the Colonel, who made virtually all creative and business decisions on behalf of his client. Parker was the quintessential paternalistic manager who removes not only business, legal, and logistical problems from the life of his performer, but also the need to make choices of any kind. Within this relationship, Elvis became a childlike figure, abdicating all responsibility for his own brand and enterprise, as well as for much of his personal life.

The facts and mythology of the Elvis-Colonel relationship are so vivid and so extensively documented that it has become an iconic model of manager-artist deals, as well as a symbol of "disastrous celebrity." John Lennon reflected on "what it was to be Elvis Beatle, surrounded by slaves and sycophants who were only interested in keeping the situation as it was."[31] Kurt Cobain wrote in his journal about his desire to achieve the popular recognition of Elvis without sharing his personal fate. Presley's mainstream popularity remained a charged image for Cobain and Nirvana, referenced as a bitter joke and perhaps as a cautionary tale.[32]

The extreme nature and widely discussed details of the Elvis Presley–Tom Parker relationship makes it a useful benchmark for assessing management-artist collaborations generally. It is an interesting exercise to examine the career progression of various musical artists and their management/production teams to see who is playing "Elvis" and who is "the Colonel."

Fusion Entrepreneurship

One possible response to the artist-manager dichotomy and the dangers it represents is to fuse the roles. Madonna is an obvious example of an artist who is also an entrepreneur. She has been able to be both "Elvis" and "Colonel" as necessary. The Rolling Stones also demonstrate an integration of creative and commercial talent across all of the band's ventures. Both cases show how creative entrepreneurship was entirely possible—though not necessarily common—even in the major label era of the latter twentieth century. Clearly, there are other examples that refute the naive artist–predatory manager dyad.

One common problem is that many artists are poorly informed about how the business side of music works. Practically speaking, with few exceptions, musicians start out passionate about music and come to learn about the business only later in their professional lives—a basic lack of knowledge that has often been used to the advantage of management. This is especially true early in musical careers, when performers haven't had much validation, economic or otherwise. This is not necessarily an indicator of "bad" intentions—though, of course, it can be. More often, it has to do with the realities of risk management in the recorded music business. Attempts at risk mitigation, including accounting practices that heavily favor labels over artists, have historically been the cause of a great deal of artist-management frustration and resentment.

In the post-Napster digital era, from the final year of the twentieth and well into the twenty-first century, two new models for managing musical creativity have developed. The first is the DIY approach. Aspiring artists no longer assume they must have a record label deal to move forward. DIY models do not, however, eliminate risk; they relocate it.

DIY artists capitalize their own ventures, buy performance and recording equipment, and produce their own records. They market their brand and distribute their product using the free or low-cost services provided by the Internet. It is now well established that artists can achieve a significant measure of success using these means and make that the basis for signing a promotional or distribution deal with a label or other management company. On that footing, it is easier for artists to negotiate a deal that is smaller in the sense that they don't need start-up capital, and less risky in the sense that prospective managers/optimizers/

distributors can see how the band works with audiences and supports its own brand.

This brings us to the second model: collaborative artist-management ventures. Many record labels, both large and small, have begun to systematically scan the DIY universe, especially the YouTube content created by unsigned bands, as a kind of unfunded A&R department. In this way, labels can preselect performers not only for potential but also for audience appeal as demonstrated online. But in and of itself, this does not necessarily lead to a collaborative relationship.

Smaller management companies and labels often collaborate with emerging artists to optimize their brand and their music using a combination of tools and relationship structures that include artists self-publishing and retaining master rights for recordings and licensing distribution deals to larger labels. One of the primary differences between collaborative ventures and traditional label deals is that—in the absence of significant up-front investment—collaborative models can emphasize long-term success as opposed to short-term returns from hit singles.

On the surface, this new environment seems better for both artists and music fans. It does not, however, resolve the issue of risk versus reward. It shifts risk downstream to smaller ventures and individual artists, even as profits shift upstream to Internet-based music service aggregators. Streaming services provide access on a massive scale, but both labels and artists get fractional (and increasingly smaller) shares of revenue (see chapter 11).

An excellent example of collaborative artist-management relationships can be seen in the career of 21 Pilots, currently managed by independent producer Chris Woltman of Element 1. The band's recordings are licensed to Fueled By Ramen, a subsidiary of Warner Music Group that is distributed by Atlantic Records.

At the ground level, 21 Pilots developed a local and then regional reputation in Columbus and central Ohio by playing live shows and leveraging an engaged approach to social media. Thus, their brand and market potential were well established and were a major component of getting signed. Woltman sees the deal as a joint venture in which the band's talents and business savvy are fused with his management expertise and industry connections. The scalability of their creative product is supported by a major label subsidiary. In many ways, this represents the state of the art in twenty-first-century deal making in music.

Discover, Promote, Broadcast Yourself

The most transformational aspect of contemporary, Internet-based media has been to make traditional media and entertainment companies increasingly irrelevant in terms of discovery and distribution. One media entity that opened the gate wide, offering individual music creators access to viewers and listeners on a global scale, is YouTube. The mechanisms for promotion and, later, monetization provided by YouTube are discussed in more detail in chapter 11. For the purposes of the present discussion, no media platform has ever done more to democratize production and distribution or more directly facilitate the transition from audience to artist.

An early example of a YouTube star was Gary Brolsma, creator of "The Numa Numa Dance." This 2004 clip was a lip-synched, webcam-recorded cover (with web-cam choreography) of "Dragostea Din Tei" ("Under the Lindens") by the Romanian band O-Zone. Originally submitted to a YouTube predecessor, Newgrounds.com, the video ultimately garnered over 15 million views on that site alone. Once uploaded to YouTube it reached views in the hundreds of millions, and Brolsma was a featured guest on *Good Morning America*, CNN, CBS, MSNBC, and VH1. Brolsma notes on his own site that his video helped propel sales of the original song. Today, at peace with his then-unexpected and somewhat disturbing celebrity, Brolsma is pursuing a career in music.[33]

Another early example of creating an inadvertent international Internet sensation comes from China. Wei Wei and Wang Yixin, students at the Guangzhou Arts Institute, made their first video for reasons similar to Brolsma: to amuse their friends. They posted it on their college intranet in January 2005. That first effort was a webcam-recorded, lip-synched, and choreographed version of the Back Street Boys song "I Want It That Way."

In relatively short order, after their videos reached YouTube, Wei and Wang, soon called the "Back Dorm Boys," accepted offers to represent Pepsi and Motorola in China. Since graduation, the two have added spokesperson deals to their portfolio and are currently completing "a five-year contract with Beijing media company Taihe Rye that has made them full-fledged TV stars, including appearances in commercials for major vendors such as Pepsi."[34]

While the talent levels involved in both the Brolsma and Back Dorm Boys videos are more typical of private jokes than commercial products, the social, cultural, and even economic consequences suggest otherwise.

These Internet stars also appear to indicate the potential of online video and social utilities to democratize production and distribution on a large and economically significant scale.

While YouTube, as a company, created no videos and generated little revenue by providing access, it did redefine cultural consumption and artistic production by aggregating not only millions of audience member/viewers but also hundreds of thousands of consumer/producers. This sparked a disruption on a global scale in the music, entertainment, and information sectors of the economy as the audience became the artists and broadcast their own brands across the globe.

CORE PRINCIPLES

Every aspect of the discovery, development, and production process, as well as the personal life of the performer, is potentially marketable content.

KEY CONCEPTS

Celebrity economy

Celebrity capital

Rolling Stones

Madonna

Toby Keith

360-degree deal

Brand extension and synergy

Talent shows

Fusion entrepreneurship

Discover, promote, broadcast yourself

FOR FURTHER CONSIDERATION

Elvis or the Colonel: Analyzing Artist-Management Dynamics

When Tom Parker signed on as manager for Elvis Presley, he took over more than just the management of the business side of the performer's life. Parker became a parental figure, removing all responsibility from Presley not only for business but also for creative and personal decisions. Ultimately, Parker came to stand for the manager who exploits an artist financially without protecting him creatively or personally. Elvis symbolizes the tragically self-indulgent and self-destructive artist without any business sense.

In terms of this symbolic relationship, it is important to consider how much is truth and how much is myth. The reason it matters is that the Parker-Presley dynamic is often considered a template for manager-artist relationships.

Consider this book review by John G. Nettles: "The Curious Life of Elvis Presley's Eccentric Manager by James L. Dickerson," *Pop Matters,* http://www.popmatters.com/review/colonel-tom-parker/.

Then answer the following questions:

Are the roles of Elvis and the Colonel oversimplified? In what way?

Did Parker bring value to the relationship with Presley? If so, what was it?

Did Presley take enough responsibility for his own creativity? How could he have taken more responsibility?

We tend to see the dichotomy as: Elvis = Good and Parker = Bad. But is there evidence of a "bad Elvis" and a "good Colonel"? What is it?

EXPLORATION

Brand Extension

Dalia Fahmy, "Madonna to Debut New Collection of Sunglasses, Teen Fashion," *ABC News,* (3–31–2010), http://abcnews.go.com /Business/madonna-debut-collection-sunglasses-teen-fashion /story?id = 10242440.

Jon Freeman, "John Rich Launches Redneck Riviera Lifestyle Brand," *Country Weekly* (3–18–2014), http://www.countryweekly .com/news/john-rich-launches-redneck-riviera-lifestyle-brand.

OK Go

Tim Walker, "OK Go: How Video Saved the Radio Stars," *Independent* (2–14–2012), http://www.independent.co.uk/arts-entertainment/music/features/ok-go-how-video-saved-the-radio-stars-6896560.html.

Amos Barshad, "OK Go's Damian Kulash Talks about the Band's Split with EMI," *Vulture* (3–10–2010), http://www.vulture .com/2010/03/ok_gos_damian_kulash_talks_abo.html.

YouTube and Blockbuster Economics

David Lowery, "Only 0.33% of YouTube Videos Generate 1 Million or More Views . . . #SXSW," *Trichordist* (3–12–2014), http://thetrichordist.com/tag/audiam/.

CHAPTER 10

Digitization

One of my few shortcomings is that I can't predict the future.
—Lars Ulrich

As the second millennium approached, the worlds of music production, distribution, and consumption were about to be disrupted and, in some sectors, destroyed. No period, with the possible exception of the advent of recorded sound and radio between 1877 and 1925, approaches the impact of the digitization of music on commerce and society in the years between the late 1980s and 2000.

At the beginning of the 1980s, analog sound-recording technology was the established basis of a massive, billion-dollar-a-year music-recording industry and had been so for decades. While innovations like 8-tracks, cassettes, and various portable devices for playing them changed the consumer experience, the production side of the music industry itself was based on a stable recording/production platform. The primary vehicle for record sales was the vinyl LP and few, if any, predicted that the business of creating and consuming music would change very much, let alone be fundamentally transformed—some might say, "blown up"—in less than twenty years.

But that is exactly what happened.

DIGITAL SOUND

Early in the 1980s a multitrack digital recorder for studio use and the compact disc (CD) for consumer playback both entered the market. Around this time, the personal computer was also being introduced to consumers by IBM (1981) and Apple (1984). In 1986 consumer digital audiotape (DAT) recorders were introduced in Japan and in 1987, Digidesign launched a program called "Sound Tools," a digital audio workstation (DAW) for the Macintosh computer.[1]

The digital era had begun, though its implications were not yet clear. Those inventions, which were met with varying degrees of interest and disdain by professionals and consumers, contained within them the raw materials for the end of an era in music.

Analog recording technology replicates the frequency and pressure fluctuations of sound waves with analogous voltage fluctuations and imprints them on a physical medium. Digital audio is based on taking a large number of discrete samples of a sound wave. A detailed discussion of digital (or analog) technology is beyond the scope and purposes of this text, but the critical factors to understand are that the sampling rate is very important for audio quality, which also determines the size of the resulting digital audio file.[2]

There was and continues to be a debate about the relative quality of analog versus digital recording and playback. But it is indisputable that transforming an analog sound wave into digital data opened up a world of possibilities for storage, compression, transmission, and creative manipulation, providing options that were simply impossible before. As a result the science, practice, and art of audio recording and production were profoundly changed.

Compact Discs

On the consumer front of the digital revolution, the first product on the market was the compact disc, introduced in 1982. Public adoption was relatively slow due primarily to the high price of the first CD players (over $2,000 on average). In addition, the relatively high price of CDs, at $12 to $16 (LPs were then $8 to $10) did not encourage consumption by any but the most committed early adopters of technology.[3] Within a few years, however, player prices dropped to 15 to 20 percent of the initial offerings.

Even with more affordable players, consumer adoption of CDs was still slow. Many were resistant to abandoning their vinyl record collections and to buying the same music content again on a new playback medium. Gradually, however, consumers began to accept the CD. In 1999, total US music sales (and licensing) totaled $14.6 billion. Many analysts believed that number was largely the result of wide-scale replacement of LPs and cassettes with CDs rather than purchases of new music. The year is often used as a benchmark, however, from which to measure the decline in album sales from 2000 to 2009.[4]

When combined with widespread social diffusion of the personal computer (PC), the adoption of digital media for music playback had another far-reaching effect. By the late 1990s, computer users were not only moving away from vinyl but also beginning to question the necessity of physical media of any kind. The practice of ripping CDs and storing the music as digital files on personal computers was spreading.

MP3s

The MP3 has become the most common digital file format for music. Like so many transformative digital technologies, MP3s were developed in the 1980s. In 1982 Karlheinz Brandenburg was a doctoral student whose dissertation advisor posed a question about data transfer and "noise" on digital phone lines. The search for an answer led Brandenburg to develop a technology that could separate a digital signal into layers "which could each be saved or discarded depending on relative significance."[5]

Brandenburg's further breakthrough was to tailor the technology to the characteristics of human hearing. This process not only improved quality but also could "reduce bitrates of music."[6] Reduced bitrates affected audio quality to some extent, but the more important effect was to drastically reduce the size of the file containing the music, making it more easily transferable. By 1992 his research team, the Moving Picture Experts Group (MPEG), released the MPEG Audio Layer III format, the process for encoding and decoding digital music. The MP3 became a reality.

The business model for the MP3 was that the encoding technology would be expensive and relatively complex, but the decoding/playback technologies would be inexpensive and easy to use. Still, adoption of the MP3 format was not rapid. The earliest commercial uses reflected the original purposes of Brandenburg's research: sending music files via ISDN phone lines. It was not until the mid-1990s, when the Internet was recognized as the logical "home" for MP3 music applications, that diffusion of the MP3 began to accelerate.

The history of the MP3's social acceptance reveals a critical principle concerning the diffusion and adoption of technically complex innovations:

synergy. Without the widespread digitization of music by producers and consumers, the expanding popularity of home computing, progressive increases in home computer speed and storage capacities, and the social adoption of Internet-based services (also fueled by improvements in home computing), the music MP3 would have had no popular utility and no market.

> The value of a complex innovation rarely stands alone. Its potential for creating a culture-changing innovation wave often depends on synergy with interrelating technologies, processes, and behaviors.

The MP3 was facilitated by all of these digital innovations, and in aggregate all of those elements produced the transformative and disruptive innovation of Internet-based music file sharing. That synergy was not only responsible for the success of the MP3; it ultimately transformed first public consumption and soon afterward music production.

Well, almost. There was still one missing piece.

File-Sharing Networks

The final piece was a method that enabled music fans not only to rip CDs or share individual MP3 copies with friends, but also to share them across Internet-based networks. File sharing is an immensely complicated topic. In the 1970s, data file sharing required physical media, such as the 3.5-inch floppy disk. The practice of file sharing became significant in the modern sense first through institutional intranets and then the Internet. Initially the tools for this kind of sharing were network structures like Usenet, which allowed users to receive and distribute files among themselves. Each decade after the 1970s brought new protocols and network structures.

One feature these applications had in common is that they were relatively complicated and were used primarily by the technically sophisticated. One of the things that made Napster groundbreaking was not that it was a Peer-to-Peer (P2P) file-sharing network, but rather, that it was relatively easy to download the Napster software and then upload your own and download music from other users.[7]

Napster brought file sharing to the masses.

NAPSTER

When Napster went live in the spring of 1999, it wasn't even a real P2P network. The database of music files was located on a central server rather than on the "peer" computers. But Shawn Fanning's software, developed with online help at hacker message boards (including help from cofounder Sean Parker), still proved to be the perfect idea at the perfect time. At its peak, Napster had over 70 million users. It is still listed in the *Guinness Book of World Records* as the "fastest growing business of all time."

One of the great ironies of the Napster startup was not that its founders were too young or naive to understand that it was an infringement of copyright. Fanning was quite aware of the probable illegality of the venture, but saw that as a short-term problem in light of future potential.

According to Ali Aydaar, Napster senior director of technology:

> [Shawn] felt pretty strongly that if he built something really good and really cool, that the artists and record labels would appreciate the distribution mechanism and the amount of data you could pull from it—understanding who's listening to what, who's engaged with what content. He wasn't focused on the legality. He felt like once he built something really good, any issues would solve themselves.[8]

In other words, Fanning and Parker thought they were building something that would help the music industry, anticipate the importance of data analytics in music, and encourage a buyout of their company and/or its technology. Their problem wasn't that Napster and its technology didn't do what they hoped. It did. Their problem was the music industry's decision to try to destroy, rather than adopt and assimilate, the concept.

Napster's impact on the established music industry was perceived by most insiders to be catastrophic rather than transformational. Fanning and Parker met with many record executives to explain the potential benefits of their compay. Some, like Jay Samit of EMI, recall that "Shawn and Sean came in, and they didn't have a model. Their model was: Somebody other than them makes money. Somebody has to pay. I said, 'Come back, and tell me how someone is going to get paid.' And they never came back."[9] Interestingly, many label representatives were not so much hostile to the idea of Napster as such, but simply not clear on how to monetize the music file sharing it represented. Others were concerned that distributing online via Napster would harm relationships with traditional retailers like Tower Records. Elizabeth Brooks, Napster's vice president of marketing, remembers some of those early meetings this way: "They [the record labels] thought, we do a deal with Napster, we won't be able to distribute to Tower Records anymore. Now you can see that worrying about alienating Tower Records was a shortsighted concern."[10] Tower Records went out of business in 2006.[11] They were not the only company considered a pillar of the record business in 2000 to be washed away by the digital deluge. Ultimately, despite some interest at labels about doing business with Napster and a lot of genuine confusion about what kind of business opportunity Napster actually represented, on December 6, 1999, the RIAA filed a lawsuit on behalf of five labels.

Napster's explosive growth caused alarm because of the numbers of songs downloaded, instead of—at least hypothetically—being purchased through traditional means. One of the more pressing concerns in those early months leading up to the RIAA-led lawsuit, however, was the amount of press and media attention that Napster was getting. Their head start gave them a competitive advantage over other emerging online music companies, including those more willing to sign licensing agreements and pay royalties.[12]

The major labels included in the RIAA suit (Sony, Warner, BMG, EMI, and Universal) saw Napster as a pirate company, one that facilitated the theft of major label, big star releases. Even independent entrepreneurial artists tended to see Napster as a threat to their foundational business practice—selling records—and the value of their back catalogs.

Sean Combs was quoted in an RIAA press release as an artist and industry executive who supported the lawsuit:

> I couldn't believe it when I found out that this Napster was linking thousands of people to the new Notorious BIG album "Born Again," a week before it even hit the streets. This album is a labor of love from Notorious BIG's friends to the man, his kids, the rest of his family and everyone else whose lives will never be the same since BIG passed. BIG and every other artist Napster abuses deserve respect for what they give us.[13]

Reaction to the lawsuit against Napster was mixed. Some saw it as a necessary response to a flagrant violation of copyright law: the right to make and distribute copies. Others saw the issue in terms of fair use. Once you own a copy of a song, legally purchased, are you not entitled to share it with a friend, or several? The answer to that question hinged largely on the issue of scale—when "several" became "several million" friends.

Scale was the basis of the legal decision handed down on February 12, 2001, by the Ninth Circuit Court of Appeals in San Francisco. The court ruled that by facilitating widespread sharing of copies, Napster was infringing on the rights of the copyright owners.[14] RIAA president Hilary Rosen spiked the ball a bit by announcing that "it's time for Napster to stand down and build their business the old-fashioned way—they must get permission first."[15]

The court issued an injunction preventing Napster from continuing business as usual. "The judges ruled that not only does the evidence show that Napster abets copyright infringement but that individual Napster users are infringing copyrights. 'Repeated and exploitative unauthorized copies of copyrighted works were made to save the expense of purchasing authorized copies,' the panel said."[16]

From late 1999 through 2001, only one major label, Bertelsmann, attempted to create a fee-based online music service with Napster. Even after the ruling in February 2001, Bertelsmann and Napster announced plans to move forward with a subscription model for the fall of that year. In November of 2000, ASCAP also indicated a willingness to license the music distributed via Napster. President Marilyn Bergman reiterated in a press release that the organization had no desire to shut Napster down. "Indeed, we would be happy to see it grow and prosper."[17]

Many legal authorities predicted—incorrectly—that these overtures by Bertelsmann and a leading PRO would lead to agreements with other labels. What actually happened was that Bertelsmann became embroiled in Napster's legal difficulties. In 2002, as the lawsuit continued, a court ruled that "Napster was liable for contributory or vicarious copyright violations because it was allowing millions of users to download music for free."[18] Napster was unable to pay the financial damages, and the RIAA and others shifted their attention to Bertelsmann on the rationale that by loaning Napster some $85 million, Bertelsmann had facilitated ongoing damage to the value of copyrights owned by other labels and publishing companies.[19]

At the time the loans were made, Thomas Middelhoff, Bertelsmann CEO, stated: "Napster has pointed the way for a new direction for music distribution, and we believe it will form the basis of important and exciting new business models for the future of the music industry."[20] Though his remarks were remarkably forward-looking and would eventually prove to be correct, the court did not agree. Damages claimed in the original suit were billions of dollars and the settlements in 2006 and 2007 were distributed as follows:

National Music Publisher Association, $130 million

Universal Music Group, $60 million

Warner Music Group, $110 million

EMI, undisclosed amount[21]

Almost immediately following the ruling in 2001, many saw it as one that would ultimately damage the recording industry. Intellectual property law expert Lawrence Lessig stated, "My view is that the R.I.A.A. loses the battle and loses the war, because they become the bad guys."[22] Becoming the "bad guys" is what happened to print music publishers in 1900 when they aggressively attacked pirated copies, and it is exactly what happened to the RIAA and the labels in 2000 and after.

Ultimately, other file-sharing services took over when Napster was forced out of the marketplace. Though initially less easy to use, companies like Grokster, Freenet, and Gnutella became very attractive to millions of former Napster users, if for no other reason than that they filled a void.

Gene Kan, a Gnutella developer, put the injunctions against Napster into context in this way: "This is going to make life difficult for a lot of music-swapping fans out there. But maybe the larger concern should be that there's no above-ground alternative for Napster users, in the sense that the music industry has not come forward with their own version of Napster to allow people to swap files on line, which is something they obviously want to do."[23] The need for an "above-ground alternative" was not addressed until 2003, when Apple launched the iTunes store.

For the first few years of the twenty-first century, the majority of record labels (with the notable exception of Bertelsmann) opted to use the legal system to stop Napster and work to redefine music copyright for the Internet era. But the Napster ruling and its legal ramifications, though important, were only part of a broader shift in intellectual property law in the digital era.

DIGITAL TECHNOLOGY AND THE LAW

Concern for the legal implications of digital technology began before Napster. In the mid-1990s the US Copyright Office took the position that "digital transmission of sound recordings [was] likely to become a very important outlet for the performance of recorded music" and that "these new technologies also may lead to new systems for the electronic distribution of phonorecords with the authorization of the affected copyright owners."[24]

Further, the Register of Copyrights stated that "[digital] music services could offer options for the enjoyment of music in digital formats either by providing the public an opportunity to hear any sound recording it wanted on-demand or by delivering a digital version of the work directly to a consumer's computer."[25] It is a strikingly prescient statement that describes the music business of the future: digital downloads and streaming music services. It also addressed a more specific legal concern: the relevance and suitability of existing mechanical license regulations for the digital age, if "mechanical" copies were going to become obsolete. Such concerns led to a series of significant revisions to copyright law for the emergent digital age.

Digital Performance Right in Sound Recordings Act

The Digital Performance Right in Sound Recordings Act of 1995 (DPRA) was the first effort to comprehensively adjust copyright law to cover digital delivery of music. The DPRA updated the scope of compulsory mechanical licensing to include a newly defined category, "digital phonorecord delivery" (DPD). The DPRA established three tiers of digital transmission. Each tier was defined by its potential to facilitate copyright violation with a fee and licensing structure reflective of that potential. The tiers were nonsubscription broadcast transmissions, non-interactive Internet transmissions, and interactive Internet transmissions.[26]

The first tier, *nonsubscription broadcast,* is (or was, see DMCA, below) exempt from the provisions of the DPRA and simply extended the long-standing exemption afforded to broadcast radio from paying for the use of copyrighted sound recordings. The second tier, *non-interactive Internet transmission,* is subject to compulsory license fees for the use of sound recordings. The logic is that because listeners can't choose specific music on demand, the experience is similar to broadcast radio. But services like Pandora do allow a degree of choice—building personalized playlists ("stations") based on specific songs or styles, for example. Because of that, the DPRA considers Pandora's potential to infringe the rights of sound-recording copyrights to be greater, and the license and statutory payments are compulsory. The third tier, *interactive Internet transmission,* is the least like traditional radio in that it facilitates on-demand listening to specific songs. As a result, it is also the most restricted under the DPRA, requiring service providers to negotiate permissions and fees directly with all copyright holders. Because this is a noncompulsory category, the owners are free to set any price they wish or refuse permission entirely.

Though some of its provisions were changed by later laws, the DPRA was a critical step toward the future of digital music law. Most significant was its recognition that digital transmissions of any kind involve mechanical licensing and public performance rights for both the musical composition (traditional publishing) and the sound recording. Thus, for the first time, labels and performers were in a position to be compensated for the "broadcast" of recordings.[27]

Despite continued lobbying from performing and recording artist groups such as the American Federation of Musicians (AFM), American Film, Television, and Radio Artists (AFTRA), and record label representatives like the RIAA, the performance right exemption for broadcast radio's use of sound recordings remains in effect. In May 2009, a bill removing the exemption for terrestrial radio left committee in the US Congress but was not brought to a vote.

Further negotiations between the National Association of Broadcasters (NAB) and musicFIRST (established in 2007 as a coalition of artists and labels to address the terrestrial radio exemption) stalled over disagreements about terms. Some privately negotiated arrangements have been made (for example, Clear Channel's 2013 agreement to pay Big Machine Music and Warner Brothers terrestrial royalties), but a change to federal law still appears to be out of reach.[28] To date, broadcast radio still pays performance royalties only to composers and publishers and not to labels or performers.[29]

Digital Millennium Copyright Act

In 1998, the US Congress enacted the Digital Millennium Copyright Act to bring US law in line with the World Intellectual Property Organization (WIPO) copyright treaties of 1996. A more critical factor in the revision, however, was the rapid growth in music streaming sites. Internet-based streaming was a major point of contention between the RIAA and sites that streamed Internet "radio."

The DPRA had included an exemption for nonsubscription broadcasts. As a result of pressure from the RIAA, the DMCA removed that exemption. Under the new law, anyone digitally retransmitting an AM/FM radio broadcast is required to pay statutory licensing fees for the use of sound recordings. In addition, the DMCA established a complicated list of requirements for licensing as a webcaster.

Radio stations challenged the requirement, claiming that music programming that was exempt when broadcast should also be exempt when identically transmitted digitally, and that the complex licensing requirements and new fees would make it impossible for either public access or commercial radio stations to continue webcasting. The case of *Bonneville International Corp. v. Peters* (2001) settled the legal question by specifically stating that digital rebroadcasts of terrestrial radio were also required to pay royalties to labels and performers.[30]

The disagreement between Internet radio stations and the RIAA was not resolved, however, and in an attempt to facilitate a resolution, the US Copyright Office gave permission for webcasters and the RIAA to establish royalty rates themselves. Those negotiations were extraordinarily complex and unsuccessful. The US Copyright Office then established the Copyright Arbitration Royalty Panel (CARP), which set a statutory rate for digital transmissions.

While the RIAA and larger Internet radio providers were ultimately satisfied, small webcasters felt disadvantaged by the terms, asserting that the proposed statutory rates would require them to pay more in royalties than they received in revenue. In response, Congress passed the Small Webcaster Amendments Act of 2002 (SWAA).[31] The SWAA reintroduced the idea of allowing private negotiations between webcasters and copyright holders and empowered a division of the RIAA—SoundExchange—to negotiate and collect royalties.

SoundExchange

SoundExchange was established in 2001 as an "unincorporated division" of the RIAA to track and distribute digital royalties; it distributed $4 million that year to artists and labels.[32] In 2003, the organization became an independent nonprofit entity and in 2007 it was designated by the Copyright Royalty Board (CRB) as the sole collective "to collect and distribute royalties paid by webcasters and Internet simulcasters."[33] Through 2013, SoundExchange distributed almost $2 billion in royalties.[34] Currently the organization collects and distributes royalties in almost twenty countries.[35]

SoundExchange versus Direct Licensing

The collection and distribution of digital royalties remains a source of legal and business controversy. For example, in 2011, SiriusXM radio began negotiations to license music directly from labels rather than paying the statutory rate via SoundExchange. By using the music rights administration service Music Reports Inc. (MRI), SiriusXM was attempting to gain a competitive advantage over other services by being able to allow its customers to record, rewind, and fast-forward programming, making SiriusXM less like "radio" and more like on-demand streaming competitors such as Spotify or Rhapsody.[36]

This strategy was a concern to SoundExchange in that being taken out of the loop would diminish the organization's influence and ability to deduct costs from royalties paid. For artists, the concern was even greater because under the statutory provisions governing SoundExchange, 50 percent of the royalties go to the sound-recording copyright owner (typically the label), 45 percent to featured artists, and 5 percent to nonfeatured artists. SoundExchange made those payments simultaneously, but under the licensing agreement, SiriusXM would make all payments to the label, which would then distribute the artist share. In addition, the SoundExchange board consists of nine artist representatives and an equal number of label representatives, assuring a voice in decision making for all stakeholders. Label licenses would afford no such balance.

From another perspective, independent artists who owned their own labels could potentially benefit from direct licensing rather than using SoundExchange. Jeff Price, cofounder of TuneCore, summarized the alternatives as follows: "SoundExchange takes around 6.7% of the money it collects to cover its administrative costs (they need to pay people to do this). This comes off the top of the amount owed . . . After SoundExchange takes its around 6.7% from the money it collects, 50% goes to the 'label,' 45% goes to the lead performer, and 5% goes to musician unions." Price contrasted that structure with the direct licensing approach. If SiriusXM, to use his example, directly licenses music from a label, SiriusXM pays the label directly, not SoundExchange. When the label receives royalty payments from anyone other than SoundExchange, it is not obligated to pay the "lead performer" or the musicians' union. The label is free to apply those moneys toward recoupment of costs and pay the artists only the percentage of royalties specified in the label-artist contract.[37]

For well-established major label artists, direct licensing to the record label would eliminate the SoundExchange deduction, but increase the risk of delayed payment and deductions by the label. For independent artists who own their own labels, however, revenue under direct licensing could actually increase due to the reduction in SoundExchange processing costs and, potentially, musicians' union fees.

Complicated? Yes.

As we move more deeply into the digital era and opportunities for monetization diversify, finding the optimal choice for a given musical enterprise becomes more and more information dependent and situational. As noted by Price in the conclusion to his article, this is "why it's so important to have all the information before reaching a conclusion as to what position you would like to support."[38]

Pre-1972 Recordings

As noted briefly in chapter 6, the Copyright Act of 1976 marked the first time that sound recordings were covered under federal law. Prior to that, recordings were only protected under assorted state laws. The 1976 revision established federal protection for sound recordings made from 1972 forward, but recordings older than that remained under the law of the relevant state. As a result of that decision, all states are eligible to keep pre-1972 works under copyright protection until 2067.

There was a tremendous amount of popular music recorded before 1972 that is still culturally relevant and commercially viable. Since performing and mechanical protections have existed since 1909 for composers and publishers, they were largely unaffected by this lack of federal protection. There is, however, a significant window of vulnerability—or at least ambiguity—for labels and performers whose work was recorded prior to 1972.[39]

This was not a particularly significant issue for much of the twentieth century because broadcast radio was already exempt from paying performance royalties for records. The introduction of Internet radio and other forms of digital transmission changed the royalty equation, and the pre-1972 recording issue made an already complicated situation even more complex. Pandora and SiriusXM, as examples, play quite a few songs from the pre-1972 era. In the case of SiriusXM, such music represents 10 to 15 percent of total airplay. According to the royalty rate established by federal law for 2012 to 2017, service providers like Sirius must pay 8 percent of "gross revenues," which are based on subscriptions and advertising. For failing to include pre-1972 recordings in their revenue calculation, SoundExchange sued SiriusXM in 2013.

SiriusXM asserted that in the absence of federal protection, they are free to use the sound recordings. In fact, the rules that apply to such broadcasts from 2013 to 2017 specifically allow SiriusXM to deduct revenues from pre-1972 recordings. SoundExchange argued that because such permission did not exist prior to 2013, they should collect between $50 and $100 million for payments not made by SiriusXM between 2007 and 2012.[40] By the end of 2013, SiriusXM was being sued by SoundExchange, Sony Music Entertainment, Warner Music Group, and UMG Recordings, as well as the 1960s band the Turtles, for roughly $500 million in various state courts.[41]

Pandora has been sued for similar reasons: failure to report revenues from pre-1972 sound recordings. Spotify is not likely to be directly affected by these legal actions because as an on-demand streaming service, the company must license directly from music publishers and labels regardless of the era in which the music in question was produced.

In June 2015, SiriusXM agreed to pay $215 million for pre-1972 records, and in October of the same year, Pandora agreed to a $90 million settlement.[42]

DIGITAL CAPITALISM

There was no legitimate "above-ground" alternative to Napster and other file-sharing sites in the first several years of the twenty-first century. While the lawsuits against Napster and individual downloaders provided a "stick" for the RIAA and the Music Publishers Association (MPA) to use against what they saw as piracy, there was no "carrot" for consumers; there was little incentive to make legal purchases of digital music. The question was how to make a huge song catalog available on demand cheaply enough to lure listeners away from the "pirates."

iTunes

Ultimately, the answer—an above-ground alternative for the digital music era—came from Steve Jobs and Apple in the form of the iTunes store, an innovative solution for an emergent problem. iTunes was actually based on the adaptation of old ideas—music "stores" and single "record" sales—to the new online context. Apple provided the large on-demand catalog of songs that listeners were coming to expect at a price point close enough to "free" to convert sharers to customers.

As he often did, Jobs not only grasped the big picture—the cultural frame—but also the operative details: people no longer wanted to buy entire albums; they wanted individual songs. This was among a number of things that record labels resisted. "When we first approached the labels, the online music business was a disaster," Jobs told Steven Levy, author of *The Perfect Thing*. "Nobody had ever sold a song for 99 cents. Nobody really ever sold a song. And we walked in, and we said, 'We want to sell songs a la carte. We want to sell albums, too, but we want to sell songs individually.' They thought that would be the death of the album."[43]

In addition, Apple provided real protection for copyright holders in the form of Digital Rights Management (DRM) copy protection software and, in the beginning, limiting playback to Apple devices.[44] Putting the store inside the Apple operating system universe put a "fence" around it. Apple became an aggregator, distributor, retailer, and gatekeeper with a single initiative: the iTunes store.

Negotiations with Warner and Universal were resolved primarily via digital rights management limitations: iTunes purchases were playable on only three "authorized" computers and could only be burned to a physical medium seven times.[45] BMG, Sony, and EMI soon followed.

Once Jobs had major label buy-in for the iTunes concept, he was able to establish an online digital "record store" and on April 28, 2003, the Apple iTunes music store opened with a catalog of some two hundred thousand songs priced at ninety-nine cents each. At the same time, Apple released the generation three iPod player. One million songs were purchased in the first week. Within six months, Apple convinced the labels to extend availability to Windows device users.

Impressive enough, but Jobs's real innovation was more profound. By creating and integrating the software and hardware for both listening to and purchasing music, he transformed the relationship between distribution and consumption, placing Apple in a position of dominance in the music download market that remained unchallenged for years.[46]

The main limitations to Apple's dominance were consumer frustration with DRM restrictions and that the iTunes software worked perfectly on Apple operating systems but caused problems for Windows users. iTunes never worked well on Windows devices, but from Apple's perspective that only encouraged more people to by a Mac. DRM was more problematic, and when Amazon entered the online music store marketplace in 2007, it was able to immediately gain market share by offering DRM-free MP3s. Just over a year later, in early 2009, Apple announced DRM-free songs as well.

No other online music store based on downloads offered serious competition to iTunes in the post-Napster world. It was not until the second decade of the twenty-first century and the launch of a number of music streaming services such as Spotify that Apple's dominance in music sales was challenged. We will examine streaming music business models in more detail in chapter 11, but it is worth observing here that it wasn't so much Apple's business model that was outmatched by streaming services, but rather, the cultural shift away from buying "things" of any kind, even if those things only occupied hard drive space.

IN RAINBOWS EFFECT

Another result of the file-sharing revolution and Internet-based networks generally was the empowerment of independent artists and small labels to reach large, global audiences. With surprising speed and user-friendly simplicity, video-sharing platforms like YouTube made international exposure and promotion accessible to virtually anyone. But, while the capacity to reach a vast audience was undeniable, independent artists and labels had the same problems as the majors in the online environment. However much people might view, "like," or download your music for free, they were not necessarily willing to pay for it.

Despite many innovative software tools and platforms for selling/sharing music online developed in the late 2000s, many began to wonder if the practice of paying for recorded music might actually be coming to an end.[47] Some asked, what if the future of music were free? That question was met with a mixture of denial, continuing lawsuits, and even a few creative responses.

One of the most widely recognized and discussed initiatives in the post-Napster world was the release, in the fall of 2007, of *In Rainbows*, the seventh studio album by Radiohead. After completing their multi-year contract with EMI, they recorded and produced *In Rainbows* without a record label. What made the album noteworthy was not the absence of a label or even the fact that it had been four years since their previous album was released. What was unusual was the distribution and pricing structure. Josh Tyrangiel described it this way in *Time Magazine*:

> *In Rainbows* will be released as a digital download available only via the band's web site, Radiohead.com. There's no label or distribution partner to cut into the band's profits—but then there may not be any profits. Drop *In Rainbows'* 15 songs into the online checkout basket and a question mark pops up where the price would normally be. Click it, and the prompt "It's Up To You" appears. Click again and it refreshes with the words "It's Really Up

To You"—and really, it is. It's the first major album whose price is determined by what individual consumers want to pay for it. And it's perfectly
acceptable to pay nothing at all.[48]

That was not the entire distribution and pricing story, but it was the part
that got people talking. The "pay as you like" rollout on October 10
was followed by an $80 box set release (online only) on December 4. On
January 1, 2008, the physical CDs and digital albums were released at
retailers.

All of this got a lot of press, but opinions about what it meant varied
considerably. NPR's Eric Garland covered the press coverage:

> From the start, journalists couldn't make up their minds. There were plenty
> of articles anointing this "new model" as the best path forward for the whole
> industry. *The New York Times* wrote, "For the beleaguered recording busi-
> ness, Radiohead has put in motion the most audacious experiment in years."
>
> But the skeptics were equally vocal. Nicky Wire of the band Manic Street
> Preachers said flatly that the offer "demeans music." *Fortune* magazine listed
> the *In Rainbows* experiment in its article, "101 Dumbest Moments in Busi-
> ness." (A sample: "Can't wait for the follow-up album, 'In Debt.'")
>
> *The Los Angeles Times* ran an editorial titled "Enough Radiohead
> Already!" (and, yes, the exclamation point was theirs).[49]

At minimum, in terms of generating buzz for its first release in years, the
release/pricing strategy was a success for Radiohead. But did it make
money? Did it have an impact on "pirate" downloads?

Although the majority of people who downloaded the "pay as you
like" version chose to pay nothing, *In Rainbows* still generated more
revenue before the January 1 CD/digital release than their previous
release, *Hail to the Thief* (2003), sold in total. The *In Rainbows* sales
figures include the $80 box set, which sold approximately one hundred
thousand copies.[50] By more conventional metrics, *In Rainbows* entered
both the US and UK charts at #1 in January 2008 and went on to sell
millions more copies.

In terms of impact on piracy, the results are counterintuitive according
to Garland: "Despite the fact that the band offered a legal free and low-
cost option to obtain the album from its Web site, piracy was up. Way,
way up. In fact, *In Rainbows* was downloaded from unauthorized
sources at 10 times the rate of new releases from other top artists. On
file-sharing networks, 400,000 copies of *In Rainbows* were swapped in a
week. By the end of the month, the number was more than 2 million."[51]

So, yes, *In Rainbows* made money. But no, it did not discourage
piracy; it boosted it. While many bands have since tinkered with price

points, "pay what you like" releases, and so forth, no one—including Radiohead—has replicated this strategy.

The digital revolution in music was the result of the synergy among new technologies, changing social behaviors, and emerging economic opportunities. Considered as an "innovation wave," the digitization of the music experience profoundly disrupted business and creative models. It also provides us an opportunity to revisit and propose some new core principles.

First, as introduced in chapter 4, *access and convenience trump everything else.* As Frederic Dannen observed, "Consumers of recorded music will always embrace the format that provides the greatest convenience."[52] Digital delivery brought access to an entirely new level of convenience and appears to underscore the importance of this concept. Second, a new principle: *punitive legal action cannot stop an innovation wave and most often brings negative consequences upon those who initiate it.* None of the litigants in the Napster and other file-sharing lawsuits came out of the experience unscathed in terms of economic, social, or cultural capital. Third—also new—*times of disruption favor the adaptable.* Any number of record labels could have embraced the potential represented by Napster. Almost none did. Instead, they "doubled down" on established business and legal practice. Steve Jobs and Apple created a new, adaptive solution that benefited everyone. Finally, based on the impact of the iTunes store: *on a large enough scale, aggregating technologies, artistic product, and audiences not only optimizes market position but also changes social behavior and culture.*

At least for a while.

CORE PRINCIPLES

The value of a complex innovation rarely stands alone. Its potential for creating a culture-changing innovation wave often depends on synergy with interrelating technologies, processes, and behaviors.

KEY CONCEPTS

Digital audio

MP3

P2P

Digital Performance Right in Sound Recordings Act of 1995 (DPRA)

Digital Millennium Copyright Act (DMCA)

Digital phonorecord delivery (DPD)

SoundExchange

Pre-1972 sound recordings

iTunes

"Pay what you like" pricing

FURTHER CONSIDERATION

Consider the following proposed core principles. Are they worth incorporating into a music enterprise analysis/framework, or will it take more time for them to prove persistent and adaptable to new situations? Why do you think so? Choose specific examples to support your position.

Punitive legal action cannot stop an innovation wave and most often brings negative consequences upon those who initiate it.

Times of disruption favor the adaptable.

On a large enough scale, aggregating technologies, artistic product, and audiences not only optimizes market position; it also changes social behavior and culture.

EXPLORATION

David Kravets, "10 Years Later, Misunderstood DMCA Is the Law That Saved the Web," *Wired* (10–27–2008), http://www.wired.com/2008/10/ten-years-later/.

Ron Harris, "Napster Offers $1 Billion Settlement," *ABC News* (2–20–2001), http://abcnews.go.com/Technology/story?id=98832&page=1.

Mitchell Peters, "Angels and Airwaves Plans Free Digital Album Release," Reuters (1–22–2010), http://www.reuters.com/article/2010/01/23/us-delonge-idUSTRE60M0BR20100123.

CHAPTER 11

State of the Art

Making money is art and working is art and good business
is the best art.

—Andy Warhol

The digitization of musical experience transformed the creation, production, distribution, and consumption of music. Naturally, businesses
were disrupted and in some cases destroyed. But the transformations
didn't stop with production and distribution structures. The ways that
audiences experienced music, decided how much to pay for it, and even
whether music should be owned or only shared—all changed.

New models for business, based on these new behaviors and values,
appeared and thrived. The iTunes store, YouTube, and Spotify became
the new aggregators of creativity. Entertainment businesses that had
been at the top of the twentieth-century food chain—major record
labels and music groups, for example—began to be consumed (aggregated) by these new Internet-based companies.

Emerging artists, once dependent upon gatekeepers like record labels,
were largely abandoned as the sale of recorded product declined. At the
same time, they were empowered to become their own labels—producing,
promoting, distributing, and selling their own creativity via the Internet.

The dynamic tension between major labels and independents also
changed. Even as major labels were being absorbed into massive online
aggregators, independent labels began to dissolve outward into a complex and interconnected web of DIY artist/entrepreneurs and the per-
service businesses created to support them.

Despite the apparent chaos, music enterprise persists as a framework of
relationships among artists, aggregators, and audiences. That structure,

however technologically or economically framed, always rests upon the foundational connection between artist and audience: the transactional music experience.

This chapter focuses on two domains of contemporary music enterprise: new forms of large-scale aggregation and independent artist/entrepreneurship. Both facilitate artist-audience relationships in different ways, creating musical experiences based on everything from streaming media to live shows and on scales ranging from global to the living room. Both also depend heavily on digital media and the social networks and capital they facilitate.

There has never been greater or more widely diffused opportunity to make music accessible to a global audience. There has also never been less certainty that money can be made doing it.

This is the state of the art.

THE NEW AGGREGATION

Regardless of the era, the music business must aggregate artists in order to benefit from their collective creativity. In addition, in order to realize the economic advantage from taking a business to scale, audiences must also be aggregated. This is a core principle of the music business as an industry: aggregation of creativity plus aggregation of audiences equals large-scale economic success and cultural influence.

> Aggregation of both artists and audiences is the foundation of music business as industry.

YouTube

YouTube began in February 2005 when three former PayPal employees began developing the idea for a website where people could share and rate videos. A dating website provided early design inspiration for one of the founders, Jawed Karim: "I was incredibly impressed with HOTorNOT, because it was the first time that someone had designed a website where anyone could upload content that everyone else could view. That was a new concept because up until that point, it was always the people who owned the website who would provide the content."[1] YouTube was not the first video-sharing site—there were many ahead of it; its success was inarguably a result of its convenience to users. Since users were the content providers and audience, convenience was obviously a critical factor in its growth. Their ease-of-use playbook remains the basic template for user utility and convenience: video format flexibility, simple cut-and-paste of video URLs for sharing purposes, ease of embedding videos on social media sites, and, critically, view counts, comments, and thumbs up/thumbs down voting. Engaging the public and providing metrics of that engagement has become a critical feature of building online brands in music as well.[2]

YouTube uploads and views grew slowly at first, but consistently. Capital investment followed. Early content included home movies, entertainment clips from television shows, and music videos, both commercial and DIY. It was the convergence of the music video and a broadcast television clip that revealed the true potential of YouTube. On December 17, 2005, NBC's *Saturday Night Live* aired the music video "Lazy Sunday." Created and performed by cast members Chris Parnell and Andy Samberg, it was a satire featuring two "nerdy" white performers "rapping" to a hip-hop beat about a relaxing Sunday trip to the movies. Soon after that broadcast, it was uploaded to YouTube, and ten days later it had been viewed 1.2 million times—very big numbers for 2005.[3]

The views soon surpassed 5 million, and NBC requested that YouTube take the clips down, citing copyright infringement. Similar to the RIAA and major label attempts to stop Napster a few years earlier, NBC's efforts did nothing to stop the viral spread of the original and response mashups, which ultimately boosted the popularity of SNL, ironically, the intended purpose of creating "digital shorts" like "Lazy Sunday."

While a legacy media company like NBC may have initially missed the significance of the event, others did not. Google's acquisition of YouTube in 2006 for $1.65 billion was noteworthy for a number of reasons, not least because the video company had not yet turned a profit.[4] In addition, the purchase triggered a series of lawsuits by record labels and media companies against YouTube and its parent company, Google, for copyright infringement. The massive billion-dollar lawsuit brought by film and television producer/distributor Viacom against Google in 2007 was finally settled in March 2014.[5]

Despite the litigation, it was increasingly apparent that Google, via the purchase of YouTube, had become one of the most—if not *the* most—important aggregators of artists and audiences. As a result, labels were compelled to look for ways to either compete or, failing that, collaborate with the aggregative giant.

VEVO

In the fall of 2008, Universal Music Group (UMG) leaked plans to establish a "Hulu-like" website featuring commercial music videos. The release referenced the company launched a year earlier by NBC Universal, Hulu, to provide broadcast television content online. Insider reports revealed that UMG was particularly interested in the advertising-based model used by Hulu, in which 100 percent of videos sold advertising; only 3 percent of YouTube videos were then sponsored by ads.[6]

This news story also triggered discussion about the future of the existing deal between UMG and YouTube, as well as other major content providers. YouTube remained confident in the future of its relationship with record labels: "We have great partnerships with major music labels all over world that understand the benefit of using YouTube as another way to communicate with their fans."[7] But despite the evident and increasing importance of YouTube to reach music fans, there were concerns. According to music industry insiders, these included potential monetization of music videos, the low-resolution quality on YouTube, and the persistent presence of copyright infringement on the site.[8]

In early 2009 it was revealed that "a new premium music video Web site," tentatively called "Vevo," would be a joint venture between UMG and YouTube, with other major labels (Sony Music Entertainment [SME], Warner Music Group, and EMI) in negotiations as well.[9] Nine months after that, on December 7, 2009, Vevo launched as a partnership between UMG, SME, EMI, and Google/YouTube, with all partners sharing advertising revenues.[10] It was a groundbreaking agreement and a recognition that labels needed to adapt to survive in the new century.

In July 2013, it was announced that the contracts between Google/YouTube and the record label (and capital investment firm) owners of Vevo would be renewed. A compelling factor was undoubtedly Vevo's "50.2 million unique viewers," making it "the top channel partner on YouTube."[11] Though not part of the Vevo deal, Warner Music Group established its own YouTube channel.

One of the most interesting aspects of the relationship between YouTube and Vevo (as well as other label "channels") is not how "new" it was, but how much it reflected the conflicts and struggles of the older radio/label model of promotion and distribution. The basic point of contention was the advertising revenue split between Google/YouTube and the label that owned the content. Google argued that the exposure provided by YouTube was a significant value in and of itself. Labels argued that as the content developer and producer, their contribution was being undervalued. As in the "old school" model, artists were excluded from this larger value discussion, and artist shares of revenue were handled via their individual contract with the label.

The mechanisms that artists used—collectively and individually—to respond to these large-scale label/YouTube partnerships are discussed in more detail below. But, it is critical to note that these new business structures were designed at the corporate level and favored the major labels (as well as large entertainment content providers in other media) above the independent labels and producers.

In 2014, for example, YouTube's announcement of a new premium service allowing users to pay a fee to skip ads triggered a new round of negotiations with labels. The first deals were struck with the three majors (Universal Music Group, Warner Music, and Sony Music Entertainment). Negotiations with independent labels and artists began later. The problem from the perspective of the independent labels was twofold.

First, although independents represent a 32.6 percent market share of recorded music sales and streams—via their licensing agency, Merlin, and the Worldwide Independent Network (WIN)—they felt the deal offered to them was vastly inferior to that offered to the majors.[12] "We have tried and will continue to try to help YouTube understand just how important independent music is to any streaming service and why it should be valued accordingly," said WIN chief executive Alison Wenham.[13]

Second, because the YouTube subscription service was based on an overall reorganization of fee and licensing structures, independents that did not sign under the new subscription service terms would be dropped from YouTube altogether. According to the *Financial Times,* "YouTube is about to begin a mass cull of music videos by artists including Adele and the Arctic Monkeys, after a number of independent record labels refused to sign up to the licensing terms for its new subscription service."[14]

This tendency to privilege major labels over independents created a complex dynamic. On one level, even the majors were reluctant participants in a model where they were compelled to negotiate with limited leverage against media giants like Google. They had learned, however, that the alternative—wide-open file sharing and piracy—was cata-strophic. A controlled environment that reduced infringement and gen-erated some revenue was clearly the better alternative. In addition, even if they were no longer at the top of the power structure, the majors definitely received preferential treatment in it.

Independent labels, on the other hand, lost even more ground. Because they also needed access to YouTube viewers, they had to nego-tiate the terms of their own aggregation. But because the majors were the preferred partners, independents struggled for viability in the new model.

One consequence of this power and influence dynamic was that the gap between majors and independents widened. As independents strug-gled for access and economic viability, the difference between what a smaller label could accomplish versus what an individual musician/entrepreneur could do using emerging web-based DIY resources grew smaller. These two interrelated tendencies—aggregating the major pro-viders upward and pushing the independents outward—were amplified by the increasing popularity of streaming music services.

Brief History of Streaming

The idea of streaming music online dates back to 1999, a pivotal year in the digital music revolution. Even before Napster came online, one of the first online streaming audio platforms was launched. TuneTo.com functioned as a kind of Internet radio. Perhaps the most significant thing about TuneTo was its proprietary player and sound file distribu-tion system. TuneTo was purchased by Listen.com in 2001.[15] Later that year, the service was relaunched as Rhapsody and began months of negotiations with major labels, while Napster, the RIAA, and the majors were still locked in a series of lawsuits.

The Rhapsody negotiations came to fruition on July 1, 2002: "Today, Universal Music Group, the world's biggest label, is expected to announce it has licensed music from its roster of stars—including Eminem, Sheryl Crow, Beck, Jay-Z and U2—to the online music sub-scription service offered by Listen.com Inc. of San Francisco."[16] That announcement meant that Rhapsody was the only service—including two run by labels themselves—to offer music from all five major labels. Those five plus another fifty independents meant that Rhapsody made roughly 90 percent of all recorded music available to its subscribers. Users paid a monthly subscription fee and songs were not downloadable. But because Rhapsody had negotiated all necessary permissions and payments under the DPRA tier system, listeners could select specific songs.

Unlike most companies that entered the streaming music field in its first decade, Rhapsody never offered a "freemium" version of the service. When Rhapsody CEO John Irwin was asked in an *Xconomy* interview about the possibility, he "didn't dismiss a freemium model as something that would never happen at Rhapsody. But he labeled it a kind of gimmicky move to grow users, basically 'a gamble based on venture capital.'"[17] Irwin asserted that time-limited free trials provided a better value to shareholders than freemium models: "We have the ability to pivot to that if we want. But I'm about creating shareholder value, which means I'm going to continue to grow my base as sustainably as possible," he said.[18] Rhapsody purchased and reconfigured Napster in 2012. Today the paired streaming services have over 2.5 million subscribers globally. But the "gimmicky" competitors noted by Rhapsody CEO Irwin, gambling on venture capital and free, paid, and "freemium" models, continue to grow, attracting attention and consumers.

Pandora

In 1999, Savage Beast Technologies (SBT) was founded to allow the creation of individualized radio "stations" that matched individual users' music preferences. The technology that underpinned this concept was called the "Music Genome Project," a system of categorization for songs based on some four hundred key indices. The idea was that once a user had indicated a few songs he liked, the genome could predict others that would match the user's musical taste.

For several years, the company tried to do business by licensing the technology to third parties, music retailers in particular, but was unable to make the strategy work economically. In 2005, SBT returned to the original concept of individualized radio, got funding from private venture capitalists, and went public in 2011.

One of the most significant aspects of Pandora Internet radio is the integration of its own Music Genome Project (MGP) data.[19] Launched in 2000, the Music Genome Project had a central goal: "to create a database of discrete musical characteristics for a given song in order to identify other songs with similar qualities."[20] Company cofounder (and musician) Tim Westergren wanted human beings to analyze the songs that went into his database, so MGP was actually implemented as a collaboration of software designers and musicologists, and as many as 450 attributes are rated on a ten-point scale for every song.

Unlike virtually every other web-based music service, Pandora does not depend upon user recommendations or social media components.[21] It is entirely the result of human experts tagging songs and individual users indicating whether they want to hear or skip a song on their personalized radio station.

Westergren observed of the MGP model: "It's profoundly unscalable. Our method is really absurd in that regard. That was the VCs' [venture capitalists'] biggest objection: How could you use this approach given how much music is out there? In the end, the only way to answer that question is to look at the experience itself and to ask, does this approach give you noticeably better results?"[22] Pandora's numbers answer that question. In 2013, Pandora announced that it had 72.7 million registered users listening some 1.36 billion hours of music per month.[23] Pandora's competitive advantage over Internet radio competitors such as Apple's iTunes radio involves more than being first to the market.

The eight years of user data Pandora has collected since launching the Music Genome Project—including thumbs up and thumbs down on individual songs, correlated with MGP data, along with where and when users are listening and on which devices—not only adds value for advertisers but also enhances the accuracy of MGP predictions, improving the listening experience.

In October 2014, Pandora launched Pandora AMP, a "suite of tools . . . intended to provide artists with the data for such tasks as picking singles, crafting set lists and routing tours."[24] Pandora AMP lets artists played on Pandora see how many listeners they have, how many streams, where those streams originate, how many unique users have created a personal station based on the artist, and how many "thumbs up" they have received. In addition, "an interactive heat map breaks down the audience by region within the United States."[25]

Altogether, Pandora's collected data and data analytics capacity amount to a significant advantage in an era when more and more music business decisions are based on "big data."[26]

Spotify

The Swedish streaming music service Spotify was launched on October 7, 2008, with an announcement on its blog that the company had signed deals with a number of major labels and music groups, including

Universal Music Group, Sony BMG, EMI Music, Warner Music Group, Merlin, the Orchard, and Bonnier Amigo.[27] The context for those deals is that 2008 was a particularly dismal year for the recording industry. From a peak of $27 billion in 1999, income from recordings had dropped nearly 50 percent by 2008 to $14 million, according to the International Federation of the Phonographic Industry (IFPI).[28]

That was the year the labels agreed to give their catalogs to a startup company in Sweden. Led by Daniel Ek, a programmer and website builder with no experience in the music business, Spotify launched in seven European countries by offering free access to 13 million songs.[29] By 2011, Spotify was serving 1.5 million subscribers in seven European countries. Subscribers paid roughly $15 per month. Later that year the service was introduced to the US with a planned three-tier system: up to ten hours per month, free; unlimited ad-free listening for $5 per month; mobile devices included for $10.[30]

Early predictions about the company's future in the US varied from the euphoric to the dismal. One observer was quoted as saying, "Spotify is going to be a great resource for artists and the music industry. It's refreshing to finally see emerging companies get a chance to change a broken playing field."[31] Another said, "I would rather be raped by Pirate Bay than . . . by (Sony boss) Hasse Breitholtz and Sony Music and will remove all of my songs from Spotify pending an honest service."[32]

Divergent opinion remains a defining feature of discourse concerning Spotify. Fans love the access and freemium option. Big labels value the scale and scope of the exposure it provides for their artists. Artists are displeased by what they see as miniscule per-stream payment rates. Independents feel even more at a disadvantage because it is so easy to disappear into the millions of tracks on the service, spawning a new term (and business model): "Forgotify."[33]

Like Pandora, Spotify is driven by data. According to Spotify engineer and engineering lead for monetization Jason Palmer, "At the heart of Spotify lives a massive and growing data-set. Most data is user-centric and allows us to provide music recommendations, choose the next song you hear on radio and many other things. We do our best to base every decision, programmatic and managerial, on data and this extends into the culture."[34]

Unlike Pandora, data at Spotify drives every decision, from internal emails to listener programming, including using algorithms to make recommendations on Spotify radio. Measures of the effectiveness of being a data-centric company include a reported $1 billion in revenue for 2013, with 36 million users. In response to artist complaints about per-stream royalty rates, CEO Daniel Ek "said that the company had paid a total of $2 billion in music royalties since it began in 2008, and argued that 'our free service drives our paid service.'"[35]

Despite its persistent failure to turn a profit (the company lost $197 million in 2014), Spotify was valued $8.4 billion by investors in April 2014, while Pandora was valued at $3.6 billion. Investor numbers do not necessarily reflect a company's practical worth, but rather its' potential to shape the market in its favor.[36]

In addition, according to Andrew Sheehy, chief analyst at Generator Research, given the scale on which it operates, "Spotify could get to the point in the future where the very small amount of profits it's making per user would be enough to cover the costs."[37] Plus, because it seems clear that the future of music will inevitably include streaming access, it is hard for most to imagine a music marketplace without Spotify. While that may seem more wishful thinking than business plan, it would be possible for investors to recoup and even increase their capital through a strategic buy-out of Spotify.

Again, Andrew Sheehy: "Spotify wouldn't necessarily need to be profitable as long as it isn't losing too much money. Samsung, being Apple's major competitor, is going to be de-positioned because they don't have a music service after Beats launches. I wouldn't be surprised if they're considering a move on Spotify." There is another aspect of aggregation: services. In addition to musical creativity and audiences, large companies like Spotify and Google can aggregate services that expand the user experience and the company's brand.

For example:

> Spotify could use some of its cash to start introducing new services, such as interviews with artists, livestreams of shows, instrumental music written by robots, or playlists created by an AI. (The latter of which doesn't seem all that crazy considering Spotify acquired music intelligence platform The Echo Nest last year.) Users might pay more for extras like these, meaning one day Spotify may profit from cheaply produced premium services.[38]

While some of these ideas may be more imaginative than profitable, they reflect practices already integral to the digital marketplace. Amazon, for example, began as an online bookstore but has expanded into a wide array of products (physical and digital) and services. The Amazon music store was an early and effective DRM-free competitor to iTunes. Amazon's Prime Music service, launched in June 2014, made the company a competitor in the streaming marketplace. Prime Music was an extension of an earlier initiative, Amazon Prime, which began as a free and reduced shipping premium service and subsequently aggregated access to first video, then reading, and finally music.[39]

Aggregating additional services may be the result of a company's internal development, or a result of the acquisition of an innovation created by a startup company. A third path is something we might call "collaborative aggregation." The leader in this area is unquestionably Apple, but apps for all smartphone operating systems provide an opportunity for enterprising designers with a narrow focus to reach a very large audience.

Shazam

Shazam launched in the UK in 2002, several years before Apple, via the iPhone, created the "app economy."[40] Shazam began with a simple premise: to solve the perennial problem of hearing music and wondering, what's that song? Now, using the Shazam app, your phone can "listen" to the music and tell you the name of the song and the artist. It was introduced to the US market in July 2008, when Apple made it a free download from the iTunes store. By September, 1.5 million had downloaded the app.[41] By the end of 2008, 35 million people had "Shazamed" a song.[42]

By August 2014, Shazam had had 100 million users and over a half a billion downloads. Its integration into download and streaming services—collaborative aggregation—is where Shazam really excels. When users Shazam a song, they're taken to iTunes, Google Play, or Amazon to download it, or to music streaming services such as Spotify. Shazam takes a cut of these revenues, but recently the company's advertising business has surpassed what it makes from music sales and even licensing deals with partners like Apple, which integrated Shazam's service into Siri for iOS 8.[43]

Shazam continues to further aggregate services for its users and advertisers by pivoting to television programming and ads. The idea is that when users "tag" broadcasting content they can "unlock bonus videos, discount offers and other goodies."[44] According to Shazam CEO Andrew Fisher, advertising is "a $300 million market opportunity . . . and if they can incentivize you to Shazam an advert by giving you a voucher or some other incentive, then they can build a relationship with you."[45]

Many of Shazam's external relationships are based on data about users, the songs they tag, and where they tag them. Shazam provides this information, for example, to record labels every Monday. Labels can use the data for artist discovery and repertoire development. Combined with Shazam's increasing interconnectivity with advertising, it has broadened a pathway for artists to reach audiences: song placement in television ads.

> In 2005, for instance, Volkswagen ran an ad in Europe for the Golf GTI that featured a remixed version of "Singin' in the Rain" by Mint Royale. The song inspired a lot of searching on Shazam—and prompted the band's label to release the track, which then shot to the top of the European charts. "We probably see that at least once a month around the world," [Shazam CEO] Fisher says. In other words, Shazam doesn't only help an audience find music. Sometimes it helps music find an audience.[46]

Data-driven companies like Shazam and Spotify offer another potential value: prediction. Before the 2013 Grammy Award broadcast, both companies predicted the winners based on their own data.[47] Spotify used total streams for each nominee and song. Shazam based its predictions on the total number of tagged songs between February and December of 2013. Spotify correctly predicted four out of six categories (67 percent) and Shazam eleven out of sixteen (69 percent).[48] That year and in the years since, the two services have been more accurate than almost any other source, including *Billboard* magazine.[49]

Shazam's integration into the Grammy broadcast provides a live data dimension as well. The most "Shazam-ed" moment of 2015 was the performance "Evil Woman" by members of the Electric Light Orchestra reprising their 1978 hit. Because Shazam allows users to click through to buy a song they have tagged, the company also provided that data for the show.[50]

Big Data

As companies like Shazam, Spotify, Pandora, and others increasingly demonstrate the value of the data they collect, data analytics—"big data"—is becoming more and more important to music enterprise. In one sense, it is simply an aspect of audience aggregation, one that allows producers and distributors to understand their listeners and customers. This is the functionality that the founders of Napster thought that record labels and artists would appreciate about their service.

In this sense, big data would be situated on the record label process map (figure 8, chapter 6) on the bottom arc, as an enhanced version of monitoring. This is what Shazam's weekly data figures provide to record labels. Spotify Artists, launched in 2013, also provides analytics on performers' streams on the site, as well as education about how the company distributes royalties—a critical factor given the increasingly severe criticisms made by artists about Spotify's business model.[51]

Ghosts in the Machine

For artists, streaming distribution and enhanced audience data have been mixed blessings. New businesses like Spotify and Shazam provide unprecedented access to and information about a global audience of music listeners. But per-stream revenues are far lower than those from physical sales or downloads. Further, typical revenue-sharing formulas privilege major labels and artists with large, well-established catalogs. New artists tend to get lost in the machinery of the streaming business.

Radiohead's Nigel Godrich and Thom Yorke expressed concern about the potential impact of new economic models on creative innovation:

> Some records can be made in a laptop, but some need musicians and skilled technicians. These things cost money. Pink Floyd's catalogue has already generated billions of dollars for someone (not necessarily the band), so putting it on a streaming site makes total sense. But if people had been listening to Spotify instead of buying records in 1973, I doubt very much if "Dark Side" would have been made. It would just be too expensive.[52]

In addition, royalty payments for streams are a fraction of those for physical product sales. Songwriter Damon Krukowski explained how it worked for him in 2012. After noting that he was happy that his music was being heard on Pandora and Spotify, he explained his concerns about the per-stream compensation. For 7,800 plays on Pandora, the three songwriters for "Tugboat" were paid, collectively, twenty-one cents. For 5,960 streams on Spotify, royalties came to a total of $1.35. Krukowski concluded that "it would take songwriting royalties for roughly 312,000 plays on Pandora to earn us the profit of one—*one*—LP sale. (On Spotify, one LP is equivalent to 47,680 plays.)"[53]

It should be clear from those numbers that the revenue from streaming cannot replace the sale of LPs or other physical product. On the other hand, because of its promotional value, traditional radio was also completely exempt from paying royalties to labels and performers. Spotify and other Internet-based music services advance the same rationale: being streamed worldwide has a massive promotional value for live concerts, merchandise, and other brand-affiliated products and services that can drive revenue to artists.

There are two issues with that logic as applied to the twenty-first-century streaming marketplace: *access* and *developmental support.* Prior to the digitization of music and online access, a major reason to own a physical copy of a song was to have access to it on demand, which radio did not provide. Streaming services, however, do provide such access to millions of songs for a nominal fee, or even offer free, advertising-based alternatives.

In this context Spotify is both the radio station and the record store. Unfortunately for artists and labels, it is a store where revenue for forty-seven thousand–plus streams equals the sale of one LP. Labels can profit, to an extent, from having many artists and large catalogs represented. In contrast, most artists—constrained by their individual productivity—simply cannot generate enough total streams to achieve any comparable profitability.

In addition, since the large aggregators have stopped (or never started) investing in artist and music discovery, development, and production, those functions have been pushed outward, not only to independent labels that have traditionally excelled in those aspects of A&R and production, but even further, to the independent artist.

Ironically, an era of big data and big aggregation has also been a time of unprecedented opportunity for the artist/entrepreneur. That's the good news. The bad news is that such entrepreneurship is increasingly mandatory. So if every artist and every song are going to be aggregated in order to reach listeners and create value, the question is simple: are you a consumable product or a collaborative partner?

Collaborative Aggregation: The DIY Entrepreneur

Collaborative aggregation is a process that connects individual entrepreneurs with networked support structures through which value is exchanged and multiplied. In this environment it is possible to emphasize individual creativity while still optimizing access to your music by a large audience.

Thus, instead of depending on labels, artists outsource, network, and DIY all the functions necessary to create and bring new music to the public: discovery, development, production, promotion, distribution, sales, data analysis, accounting, and royalty collection. In effect, this replicates all the stages of the record label process map (chapter 6, figure 8) but distributed across a network of both commercial and open-source vendors and services.

As a result, even the lone DIY musician can compete on virtually the same basis as an independent label, distributing and monetizing her music across multiple platforms: iTunes, YouTube, Spotify, and many more. In addition, a number of companies provide resources for licensing, live performance booking, and capitalization. The following sections explore a small sample of the available DIY entrepreneurship support options; the traditional record label process components addressed by each one are listed in parentheses.

TuneCore (Distribution, Sales, Monitoring, Royalty Collection)

When Jeff Price and partners launched TuneCore in 2005, it was to empower artists to be their own distributors in the digital download and streaming marketplaces. Price had been a musician and run a record label since the 1990s. He recognized that the missing ingredient in a product-rich digital market with a global reach was distribution.

His take in 2011:

> For the past century, artists could record, manufacture, market, and, to some degree, promote their own music, but no matter if they were The Beatles, Elvis or Led Zeppelin, they could not distribute it and get in placed on the shelves of the stores across the country; the required costs and infrastructure of the physical world were just too massive—a 500,00 square foot warehouse staffed with 30 people, trucks and inventory systems, insurance, a field staff of 30 people walking to music stores leveraging, begging, pleading and paying to get the CD, album, 8-track, wax spool, etc., on the precious shelves of the retail stores—and checking up afterwards. Distribution was out of the hands of any one person, no matter how dedicated or wealthy. Without the music available to buy, there was no way for it to sell.[54]

That was the conceptual basis for establishing TuneCore, a service designed to empower bands to manage their own distribution. Price continues:

> With the launch of TuneCore (full disclosure here, I am the CEO and founder), for the cost of a six pack and a pizza (around $30), anyone can now be his own record label and have the same distribution as any "signed" artist. But this new model allows artists to keep all their rights and receive all the money from the sale of their music via a non-exclusive agreement that can be canceled at any time, all while having infinite inventory with no upfront cost or risk.[55]

TuneCore operates as a distribution company to all major online digital music stores. For a fee of $9.99 per single or $29.99 per album (plus $49.99 per year), artists retain all of their publishing rights and royalties.[56] TuneCore paid out over $300 million to artists between 2006 and 2014.[57]

By 2012, TuneCore represented approximately 10 percent of the 20 million songs in the iTunes store and some 4 percent of digital sales as a whole.[58]

Audiam (Monitoring, Royalty Collection)

After leaving TuneCore, Price and Peter Wells went on to found Audiam, a business designed to identify and collect royalties from both artist- and user-generated content (lip-synch and mashup videos, for example) on YouTube. In an interview about the launch with *Billboard*, Price advanced a familiar concept for the company: "The music business has come to YouTube, and Audiam is going to democratize it."[59]

For a 25 percent administrative fee, Audiam handles licensing and collection for artists. Unlike TuneCore, the new company has signed both independent and major label artists.[60] Price estimates that "every month for almost 12 years, somewhere between 10%–30% of the money owed to songwriters/publishers is not paid by many streaming services,"[61] a total he estimates to be approximately $100 million.

Audiam represents a critical resource for the independent artist/ entrepreneur. YouTube has proven its value not only for music discovery and artist-audience connection, but also as a monetization platform via Vevo, other label channels, and its own YouTube Partner Program.[62] But with the exception of the partner program, the monetization opportunities have been heavily tilted toward major labels and content aggregators. Audiam fills a niche that is characteristic of all of the artist/ entrepreneur support companies: empowerment of artists to aggregate their own services and productivity laterally across a collaborative network.

Next Big Sound (Development, Promotion, Monitoring)

Next Big Sound (NBS) was established in 2009 as a startup that grew from an assignment in an entrepreneurship course. The company was named by *Billboard* as one of the thirty best digital music startups of 2010 and one of its founders, CEO Alex White, as one of the "executive stars to watch."[63]

Created by musicians and music fans, Next Big Sound was initially inspired by a desire to figure out how bands and artists became famous.

Then they realized that what they really wanted was to be able to identify "the next Lady Gaga."[64] They recognized that for the music industry of the twentieth century, the main tools for tracking popularity were record sales, ticket sales, and radio requests. With the advent of downloading (legal and illegal), streaming, setting songs as ringtones, "friending" artists on Facebook, following them on Twitter, or editing a *Wikipedia* page, fans had many portals of engagement with artists and their music, and all of those activities were trackable data.[65]

But how significant might that data turn out to be?

"The idea is that lying in these massive, massive data sets are untapped correlations and value that can be harnessed," says White. "If you can sift through and track and filter this data in meaningful ways, there is a huge opportunity in identifying the next big sound and understanding how markets and bands grow in popularity and spread."[66]

Next Big Sound currently tracks twenty metrics: Facebook, Facebook Insights, Google Analytics, Instagram, Last.fm, Purevolume, Rdio, ReverbNation, SoundCloud, Tumblr, Twitter, Vevo, Vimeo, Vimeo Custom Video Tracking, Vine, Wikipedia, YouTube, YouTube Analytics, YouTube Custom Video, and YouTube Detections. Most of these are further divided into subcategories. The YouTube metric, for example, is segmented by subscribers, likes, video favorites, and video raters. In aggregate, these numbers form a composite picture of online fan engagement—social, sharing, and purchases—for every artist in the NBS database.

Those functions—understanding how markets and bands grow and how relationships with listeners develop—are (or were) the role of A&R and marketing departments, but with the human intuition largely replaced by hard data.

As a component of the collaborative network resources available to the DIY artist/entrepreneur, Next Big Sound is a powerful A&R and marketing tool. The weekly email reports are customizable and free. For labels and other aggregators, the company provides that functionality on a broader and more comprehensive scale and at a lower price point than SoundScan or PollStar. NBS also provides data-driven information on branding and "music-related partnership decisions" based on "5 years of historical data, 500 thousand artists & brands, 100 million songs & videos, and 1.5 trillion interactions in 2014."[67]

Because the music industry was one of the first to move fully online, data from every phase of the transactional music experience—from artist to audience—is potentially available. As Next Big Sound states,

"Measurability from awareness to engagement and ultimately revenue can be realized."[68] Since the company tracks listener behaviors "from social to sales, from purchases to plays," it does more than help artists and managers make decisions.[69] NBS is actually building a composite image of musical culture and, potentially, changing it.[70]

Sonicbids (Promotion, Sales, Licensing, Live Performance)

Sonicbids is a Boston-based company founded in 2000 by Panos Panay, an alumnus of Berklee College of Music, "so that emerging bands could use the Web to connect with music promoters."[71] Panay states, "Sonicbids has grown into the industry standard for connecting bands and music promoters, contributing to the booking of nearly one million shows. It has democratized the process of musicians gaining access to diverse audiences, enabling people from over 100 countries to cross borders and touch audiences from different cultures to which they never would have had access otherwise."[72]

In addition, Sonicbids has aggregated its services to include brand partnerships. According to Panay: "We find that bands are not just looking for gigs. They are also looking to connect with brands, to have their music in TV commercials, to have their music on Broadway and in film."[73] Like other companies in the artist/entrepreneur support network, Sonicbids recognizes that because there are multiple forms of artist-audience engagements and multiple revenue-generating possibilities, the functions of promotion, distribution, and sales must be defined more comprehensively than in traditional music business models.

In January 2013, Sonicbids was sold to Backstage, a print publication launched in 1960 to provide casting information for theatrical actors. The merger of the two companies is an example of service aggregation: print plus social mediation, music plus theatrical performance. In the press release announcing the acquisition, Backstage CEO John Amato stated:

> Backstage reaches thousands of professional performers who sing onstage and onscreen, who are trained musicians, and who are engaged in creating original content for live performance and digital media. By bringing Sonicbids into the Backstage fold, we can now offer those performers an even greater array of opportunities to find work, connect with other artists, and advance their careers in a diverse and evolving media world.[74]

The new company reflects the shared mission of both Backstage and Sonicbids: to empower artists to manage their own careers and monetize their own productivity across multiple channels. It also acknowledges the increasing convergence of those streams across concert and theatrical performance and multiple media platforms.

Kickstarter: The Crowdfunding Era (Capitalization, Promotion)

In response to declining financial support by record labels—especially for new artists—alternative funding methods have become necessary. While some opt to use personal resources to launch a startup enterprise, others have looked to the mediated community for capitalization.

Going to the public to find financial backers has a long history, dating to the classical period in music at least. The digital era and the mediated social networking it supports have amplified the speed, scale, and accessibility of that approach dramatically. It is, for example, possible to aggregate thousands of small financial gifts into a significant amount of capital. And, since production, promotion, distribution, sales, and noncommercial consumption of music are also threaded through social media, online crowdfunding leverages and optimizes existing social capital.

One of the best-known crowdfunding sites in the US is Kickstarter, founded in 2008. Since then, the company has raised over $775 million for some forty-eight thousand projects.[75] In addition to dozens of other sites specifically devoted to musical projects, YouTube announced in the summer of 2014 a crowdfunding option as part of its long-planned subscription music service, partially in response to criticisms from independent labels and artists.[76]

A more recent music-specific site, Patreon, was launched by Jack Conte of the DIY band Pomplamoose (see chapter 9). Patreon was specifically designed to improve monetization opportunities for creators of digital media, including music. In 2013, Patreon began connecting musicians (and others) with people willing to provide startup and ongoing financial support for creative projects.

In just over a year, the company distributed over $1 million to artists, some earning as much as $100,000 during that period, based on fifteen thousand content creators and fifty thousand patrons with an average monthly contribution of $9.80 ($117.60 annually). Thus an artist with a following of three hundred patrons making the minimum contribution could realize just over $35,000 a year from Patreon alone.[77]

Patreon is not only a crowdfunding business. It is a network that functions to connect artist-to-artist, business-to-artist, and patron-to-patron.

It is a good example of a networked community that aggregates and shares social, cultural, creative, and economic capital.

CULTURAL PRODUCTION AND AGGREGATION

The network of businesses supporting DIY production, promotion, and monetization by independent artist/entrepreneurs also exploits them. That is not a negative assessment. Even when the commitment to empowering artists is genuine, these entrepreneurship service providers must aggregate creative producers in order for their business models to work. The emergence of these providers is both a validation of the competitive advantage that accrues from aggregation and an indicator of a larger cultural shift.

The fundamental exchange between performer and listener must be between at least two people. That's theory. In practice, music business models have almost always been based on growing audience size in order to increase revenue opportunity. Once public concerts began to replace patronage, the first aggregation was simply the need for performers to "collect" audience members. As concert programming seasons evolved, artists could be aggregated by venues. Later, recording and media companies did the same. All of these aggregation models were based on the idea that creative productivity was the raw material for turning listeners into buyers.

With the advent of Internet-based platforms for social networking, content creation, and distribution, it became possible to aggregate new types of audiences and producers. YouTube, for example, produced no content in the traditional sense. Instead, it aggregated millions of DIY producers and connected them with hundreds of millions of viewers, also aggregated by the site. Although it initially may have appeared that YouTube's "product" was a large number of viewers, it was also—and even more critically—the amateur producers, who were themselves viewers.

One consequence of this structure and the diffusion of "user-produced" content across the web was a rise in what Alvin Toffler in 1970 called "prosumers" and what William Deresiewicz in 2015 called "producerism."[78] Toffler, a futurist, was anticipating how emerging media—long before the Internet or even personal computing—would empower people to increasingly produce the products they wished to consume. Deresiewicz was describing an already established trend in the culture and economy: "'Producerism,' we can call this, by analogy with consumerism. What we're now persuaded to consume, most conspicuously, are the means to create."[79]

In the realm of popular music enterprise, the shift toward producerism was simply an extension of the arc from labels aggregating songwriters and performers, to major labels aggregating independent ones, to digital music providers (downloads and streams) aggregating labels, to independent artists attempting to aggregate themselves.

This last stage creates an opportunity for both altruism—empowering artists to create and thrive—and opportunism—aggregating aspiring producers as consumers of services. The category of "aspiring" producers is important in a market sense because there are so many more of them than viable, professional producers of music. This is the market understanding that drives talent shows (chapter 9) and YouTube's Broadcast Yourself motto and business model.

Though worthwhile, catering to the interests of existing amateurs is not sufficient to maintain a massive customer base. In order to go to scale, DIY service providers must develop and foster a culture of "producerism" in which the public increasingly values and desires the experience of being a producer. That is important—vital, even—because even if many (or most) aspiring artists get few practical results from the purchase of production support services, they will continue to buy if the production experience is sufficiently enjoyable.

An interactive network of service providers is thus marketing not only practical support tools but also an experiential product: the opportunity to be a creative rather than simply a consumer. On a large enough scale, producerism begins to become a personal brand and lifestyle. Because the majority of the consumers are members of a generation that is networked across both professional and personal life, that experience is "networked, curated, publicized, fetishized, tweeted, catered, and anything but solitary, anything but private."[80]

The consumers of the production experience aggregate themselves, reshaping the economy and the culture. As a result, the musical experience has never been more transactional, or more diversely produced, mediated, and consumed.

CONCLUSION: PUTTING IT TOGETHER

Early in this book, we examined the concept that music enterprise—in all of its varied forms—is about the places where musicians, audiences, and economic opportunity converge. As we moved through the history of this enterprise and tried out some structural concepts and analytical tools for understanding them, it became apparent that those who control opportunities for convergence—whether physical venues, broadcast media, physical recordings, and more recently, online "spaces"—have had tremendous opportunity not only to profit from but also to control who and what has access to convergent space.

From the perspective of the creative artist—the content creator—multiple factors constrain her capacity to monetize productivity. First, there is the necessity to make the public aware of the music and then provide access to it. On a small scale, this is not a necessarily burdensome or complex task. But as scale increases and revenue potential grows, so do the logistical, technical, and management demands.

Over the course of the twentieth century, a clear advantage emerged—one based on aggregation—for companies who could pull together the creativity of multiple artists and leverage them across various promotional and commercial platforms. Artists would sign over ownership of their work in exchange for production, promotion, and distribution expertise. This gave rise to the fundamental roles of the recording era: record label as both nurturer and gatekeeper of music, discovering new talent, shaping it, and providing or denying access to the places where audiences (and dollar amounts) measured in the millions.

As we saw at many points along the way, changes in technology, social behavior, or economic conditions can destabilize a business model. More important, however, is what happens when innovative technology, social adoption (and emerging new behaviors), and economic opportunity coincide, producing an *innovation wave*. The early years of the twentieth century brought such a wave as broadcasting, recording, social migration, and economic opportunities aligned, first disrupting and then rebuilding the music industry. It happened again at the end of the century, as the rise of digital audio, personal computing, and the Internet set the stage for the emergence of Napster in 1999.

What was striking about that later emergence was not the new technology or even the complex synergy among tools, people, and money. What was amazing was how long it took the music industry establishment to recognize that another large-scale shift in culture was already happening—a shift that would change more than business models.

In 2000, the file-sharing crisis was still unfolding in the courts and the media and industry talk was all about digital copyright protection. But that same year, Janelle Brown wrote the following statement in *Salon* magazine: "Record companies should stop worrying about

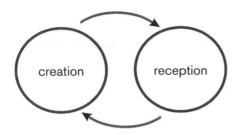

FIGURE 10. Music transaction diagram.

security and start giving people what they really want: Music, any-where, anytime."[81]

That's it . . . the whole map of music business for the next fifteen years and beyond in one sentence. Brown nailed it: *music, anywhere, anytime.*

In the first chapter, we looked at the diagram illustrating the concept of music as transaction, considering it as a template for all music enterprise, regardless of style, era, or technological means (see figure 10). While the basic diagram remains as relevant here as it was in the first chapter (and in the twenty-first century as in the nineteenth), the "box" around it has changed a lot. That box represents not just venue or social setting. It is the cultural context that frames everyone's experience, giving it meaning and value. That's what Brown is talking about: the "box" for the twenty-first century music experience is the "music, anywhere, anytime" box.

Brown's observation also comprises three of the four goals discussed in chapter 4: *describe, understand,* and *predict.* Had anyone taken her at her word and immediately moved to build a "music, anywhere, anytime" model, would it really have taken until 2008 to launch Spotify, the closest thing to achieving it so far?

But it's the fourth goal that matters: *control.* Understanding what to do and having the resources in the right place at the right time is critical because that is how you change the cultural framework and create a "new normal." That is how you aggregate people, products, services, values, and beliefs to produce culture. That is also how you define your own creative experience, productivity, and ability to bring value into the world.

Music is an art in the medium of sound capable of producing multiple forms of value that can only be fully realized in a social context—a space where musicians, audiences, and economic opportunity come together.

Music changes everything.

CORE PRINCIPLES

Aggregation of both artists and audiences is the foundation of music business as industry.

KEY CONCEPTS

Aggregation of services

Collaborative aggregation

Rise of streaming music services

Pandora

Music Genome Project

Spotify

TuneCore

Audiam

Crowdfunding

Fusion entrepreneurship

Producerism

FURTHER CONSIDERATION

New Aggregation Process Map

Consider the role of new aggregators in the music marketplace today, including those who stream content and provide DIY services to small-scale producers. If you were to create a process model to reflect how these twenty-first-century aggregators operate, what would it look like? Would the start and endpoint circles still be "artist" and "audience," as in the model shown in figure 8 (chapter 6) or figure 9 (chapter 7)? Would the connecting steps largely remain the same, change somewhat, or need to be revamped entirely? In terms of the top arc: what content is being delivered? And in terms of the bottom arc: what value is being produced? And for whom?

Big Data: Who Writes the Songs?

While the traditional quarterly profit and loss report remains a staple of the business, labels and management companies can now look at data based on customer behavior as it happens. A few decades ago, music producers used weekly sales figures to make decisions. Later, entities like PollStar provided overnight details on concert performances. Both Spotify and YouTube, to name two platforms, provide ongoing analytic data to content providers/channel owners. Data aggregators like Next Big Sound do so across multiple platforms and levels of engagement. As a result, more decisions about production and distribution, at least, can be based on real-time data about consumer behavior.

Further, much as Pandora's music genome aspired to create a predictive database for listener song preferences, tools to use data analytics to make creative decisions began to emerge in the second decade of the twenty-first century.

Consider the articles below. Do you think that big data can help musicians write "better" songs? Will this become a new norm for the music business? What are the opportunities and consequences of data-driven creativity in music?

Eric Chemi, "Can Big Data Help Music Labels Find That Perfect Backbeat?" *Business Week* (3–7–2014), http://www.businessweek.com/articles/2014–03–07/can-big-data-help-labels-find-that-perfect-back-beat.

Kadhim Shubber, "Music Analytics Is Helping the Music Industry See into the Future," *Guardian* (4–9–2014), http://www.theguardian.com/technology/2014/apr/09/music-analytics-is-helping-the-music-industry-see-into-the-future.

Stuart Dredge, "Spotify Opens up Analytics in Effort to Prove Its Worth to Doubting Musicians," *Guardian* (3–12–2013), http://www.theguardian.com/technology/2013/dec/03/spotify-analytics-musicians-streaming-music-artists-earn.

Adam Bychawski, "Most-Shazamed Rock and Indie Songs of 2014 So Far Revealed," NME (5–22–2014), http://www.nme.com/news/coldplay/77454.

EXPLORATION

How Weird Al Subverted the Aggregational Hegemony of Social Media Giants

Robinson Meyer, "The Surprisingly Savvy Weird Al Internet Machine," *Atlantic* (7–19–2014), http://www.theatlantic.com/technology/archive/2014/07/the-surprisingly-savvy-weird-al-internet-machine/374649/.

Keith Erickson, "5 Things 'Weird Al' Yankovic Can Teach Us about the Music Biz, Future of Music Coalition (7–25–2014), http:// futureofmusic.org/blog/2014/07/25/five-things-weird-al-yankovic-can-teach-us-about-music-biz.

Amazon Prime Music—Convergence of Streaming and Downloading?

Chris Welch, "Amazon Prime Music Is No Spotify Killer, but It Doesn't Need to Be," *Verge* (6–12–2014), http://www.theverge .com/2014/6/12/5802810/amazon-prime-music-hands-on.

Jilian D'Onfro, "I'm Obsessed with a Music Streaming Service Millions of People Probably Don't Know They Can Use for Free," *Business Insider* (5–16–2015), http://www.businessinsider.com /why-i-love-amazon-prime-music-2015-5.

Stuart Dredge, "Which Is the Best Music Streaming Service?" *Guardian* (2–16–2016), https://www.theguardian.com/technology /2016/feb/16/which-is-the-best-music-streaming-service-spotify-apple-music.

Notes

INTRODUCTION

1. Definition adapted from the following sources: "About Complex Systems," New England Complex System Institute, http://necsi.edu/guide/; "Definitions of Complexity," http://serc.carleton.edu/NAGTWorkshops/complexsystems /definitions.html; "Complex Systems Modeling: Using Metaphors from Nature in Simulation and Scientific Models," http://www.informatics.indiana.edu/rocha /complex/csm.html.

2. Deborah Tussey, "Music at the Edge of Chaos: A Complex Systems Perspective on File Sharing," *Loyola University Chicago Law Journal* 37 (2005), 105. http://www1.it.luc.edu/media/lucedu/law/students/publications/llj /pdfs/tussey.pdf.

CHAPTER 1. MUSICAL EXPERIENCE AS TRANSACTION

1. Definitions for *aesthetic* in this paragraph come from www.merriam-webster.com/dictionary/aesthetic.

2. "Live Nation Entertainment Announces New Touring Record: U2 360 Is the Most Successful Tour of All Time," Live Nation Entertainment (4-11-2011), http://www.prnewswire.com/news-releases/live-nation-entertainment-announces-new-touring-record-u2–360-is-the-most-successful-tour-of-all-time-119587979 .html.

3. See also http://www.billboard.com/biz/articles/news/touring/1176894/u2s-360-tour-gross-736137344.

4. See http://www.cbsnews.com/stories/2010/07/01/entertainment/main6636986 .shtml for details.

5. Michael Carroll, "The Struggle for Music Copyright" (Working Paper No. 2005-7), Villanova University School of Law, Public Law and Legal

Theory, http://www.floridalawreview.com/wp-content/uploads/2010/01/Carroll-BOOK.pdf.

6. Pierre Bourdieu, "The Forms of Capital," in *Handbook of Theory and Research for the Sociology of Education,* ed. J. Richardson, Greenwood (1986).

7. For more details, see, for example, Gavin Edwards, "'We Are the World': A Minute-by-Minute Breakdown on Its 30th Anniversary," *Rolling Stone* (3–6–2015), http://www.rollingstone.com/music/features/we-are-the-world-a-minute-by-minute-breakdown-30th-anniversary-20150306.

8. See "On Music Row: McBride to Feature in SunnyD Campaign," *Nashville Post* (3–14–2010), http://nashvillepost.com/news/2010/3/14/on_music_row_mcbride_to_feature_in_sunnyd_campaign.

9. https://www.youtube.com/user/TroyeSivan18; Benjamin Law, "Troye Sivan, the Most Famous Teenager You've Never Heard of," *Sydney Morning Herald* (2–27–2015), http://www.smh.com.au/good-weekend/troye-sivan-the-most-famous-teenager-youve-never-heard-of-20150209-13a11r.html.

10. Reviews of *Artpop* from Alexis Petridis, "Lady Gaga: Artpop—Review," *Guardian* (11–7–2013), http://www.theguardian.com/music/2013/nov/07/lady-gaga-Artpop-review; Andy Gill, "Album Review: Lady Gaga, ARTPOP—It's Hard Not to Feel Underwhelmed," *Independent* (11–7–2013), http://www.independent.co.uk/arts-entertainment/music/reviews/album-review-lady-gaga-Artpop—its-hard-not-to-feel-underwhelmed-8926676.html; Caryn Ganz, "Lady Gaga 'Artpop' Review," *Rolling Stone* (7–13–2013), http://www.rollingstone.com/music/albumreviews/artpop-20131113.

11. Kevin Rutherford, "Lady Gaga Discounts Rumors, Hints at Deception in Website Vent," *Billboard* (6–5–2014), http://www.billboard.com/articles/news/5862267/lady-gaga-discounts-rumors-hints-at-deception-in-website-vent.

12. Kevin Rutherford, "OneRepublic Extends Summer Tour, Talks 'Counting Stars' Success," *Billboard* (2–17–2014), http://www.billboard.com/articles/news/5900971/onerepublic-extends-summer-tour-talks-counting-stars-success.

CHAPTER 2. TRANSIENCE TO PERMANENCE

1. See, for example, Alexander Charchar, "Gutenberg and the Book That Changed the World," http://retinart.net/beautiful-things/gutenberg-book-changed-world/.

2. Andrew Lippman and David Reed, "Viral Communications," Media Laboratory Research (5–19–2003), http://dl.media.mit.edu/viral/viral.pdf.

3. See "Woodblock Printing," Music Printing History, http://musicprintinghistory.org/woodblock/woodblock-printing.html.

4. See "About Music Engraving," Music Printing History, http://musicprintinghistory.org/engraving/about-music-engraving.html.

5. See http://www.breitkopf.com/history.

6. See "Printing and Publishing of Music," Parlor Songs Academy, http://parlorsongs.com/insearch/printing/printing.php.

7. Ibid.

8. The references to the Breitkopf and Härtel Company in this and the following paragraphs are taken from "History of Breitkopf and Härtel," http://www.breitkopf.com/history.

9. "Beethoven's Correspondence with Gottfried Christoph Härtel and the Publishing House Breitkopf and Härtel (1808–1812)," http://www.raptusassociation.org/haertelbriefe_e.html.

10. Adrian Johns, *Piracy: The Intellectual Property Wars from Gutenberg to Gates,* University of Chicago Press (2009), 18.

11. Paul R. Paradise, *Trademark Counterfeiting, Product Piracy, and the Billion Dollar Threat to the U.S. Economy,* Greenwood (1999), 15.

12. Ibid., 16.

13. Johns, 331–332.

14. Ibid., 333.

15. Ibid., 334–335.

16. William F. Patry, "England and the Statute of Anne," in *Copyright Law and Practice,* Bureau of National Affairs (1994), http://digital-law-online.info/patry/patry2.html.

17. F.M. Scherer, "The Emergence of Musical Copyright in Europe from 1709 to 1850" (Faculty Research Working Papers Series), John F. Kennedy School of Government, Harvard University (2008).

18. Michael Carroll, "The Struggle for Music Copyright" (Working Paper No. 2005-7), Villanova University School of Law, Public Law and Legal Theory, http://www.floridalawreview.com/wp-content/uploads/2010/01/Carroll-BOOK.pdf, 915.

19. Ibid., 916.

20. Ibid., 31.

21. See, for example, Ed Christman, "U.S. Dept. of Justice to Review ASCAP and BMI Consent Decrees," *Billboard Biz* (6-4-2014), https://www.billboard.com/biz/articles/news/legal-and-management/6106492/us-dept-of-justice-to-review-ascap-and-bmi-consent. The issue of ASCAP, BMI, and the antitrust consent decree is discussed in more detail in chapter 6, "Massification."

22. "Copyright History," http://www.timetoast.com/timelines/60538.

23. "Copyright Timeline: A History of Copyright Law in the United States," Association of Research Libraries, citing "H.R. Rep. No. 2222, 60th Cong., 2nd Sess., p. 7" (1909), http://www.arl.org/focus-areas/copyright-ip/2486-copyright-timeline#.U8vMfEjD-00.

24. Much of the challenge of understanding music industry contracts has to do with the "assign-ability" of copyright. If, for example, as a songwriter or beat maker you sign a work-for-hire contract, you have already, and in advance, given away all publishing and performance rights for any musical work you produce under that agreement. For more information see "Works Made for Hire," Circular 9, US Copyright Office, http://copyright.gov/circs/circ09.pdf.

25. William Arms Fisher, *One Hundred and Fifty Years of Music Publishing in the United States,* Oliver Ditson (1933), 114.

26. Jody Rosen, "Oh! You Kid! How a Sexed-Up Viral Hit from the Summer of '09—1909—Changed American Pop Music Forever," *Slate* (6-2-2014),

http://www.slate.com/articles/arts/culturebox/2014/06/sex_and_pop_the_for-gotten_1909_hit_that_introduced_adultery_to_american.html.

27. Ibid.

CHAPTER 3. THE RISE OF COMMERCIAL MARKETS

1. Derek B. Scott, *Sounds of the Metropolis: The Nineteenth-Century Popular Music Revolution in London, New York, Paris, and Vienna,* Oxford University Press (2008), 4.

2. Such antipathy was by no means universal among the upper classes. Queen Victoria, for example, notoriously loved the sentimental popular song "Home, Sweet Home," by light opera composer Henry Bishop.

3. Hugh Arthur Scott, "London's Earliest Public Concerts," *Musical Quarterly* 22.4 (October 1936), 446–457.

4. W. E. Weber, ed., *The Musician as Entrepreneur, 1700–1914: Managers, Charlatans, and Idealists,* Indiana University Press (2004).

5. Gabriella Dideriksen and Matthew Ringel, "Frederick Gye and 'the Dreadful Business of Opera Management,'" *19th Century Music* 19.1 (Summer 1995), 6.

6. Ibid., 8–9. In 2014 dollars those figures are roughly $7,950,000, $1,136,000, and $4,440,000. Historical British pound and US dollar exchange rates were taken from http://www.measuringworth.com/datasets/exchangepound/result .php. US dollar inflation calculated using the data from the annual *Statistical Abstracts of the United States* and http://www.westegg.com/inflation/.

7. Weber, 175.

8. Robert Newman quoted in Weber, 179.

9. Robert Newman quoted by Ivan Hewett, "The Proms and the Promenerders," *Daily Telegraph* (London) (7–12–2007), http://www.telegraph.co.uk /culture/music/classicalmusic/3666494/The-Proms-and-the-Promenerders.html.

10. Weber quoted by Peter Mullen, "Everyone Knows Henry Wood Set Up the Proms: But Who Remembers the Man Who Hired Him to Do It?" *Independent* (London) (7–21–1995), http://www.independent.co.uk/arts-entertainment /music/everyone-knows-henry-wood-set-up-the-proms-but-who-remembers-the-man-who-hired-him-to-do-it-by-peter-mullen-1592519.html.

11. Ibid.

12. Paganini and other "star" performers, however, had managers much earlier than this to manage performance and touring logistics. It was the "ordinary" working-class musician and performer who remained unrepresented for many decades.

13. "The Story of Music Hall," Victoria and Albert Museum, http://www .vam.ac.uk/content/articles/t/the-story-of-music-halls/.

14. Hugh Cunningham, *Leisure in the Industrial Revolution, c. 1780-c. 1880,* Taylor and Francis (1980), 164–170.

15. In 1899,172,000 pianos were manufactured in the US alone. For a further discussion of the economics of the piano see Jeffrey A. Tucker, "The End of the US Piano Industry," *Mises Daily* (12–10–2008), https://mises.org/library /end-us-piano-industry.

16. "Showman," *The Oxford Pocket Dictionary of Current English* (2009).

17. Philip B. Kunhardt Jr., Philip B. Kunhardt III, and Peter W. Kunhardt, *P. T. Barnum: America's Greatest Showman,* Alfred A. Knopf (1995).

18. Vaudeville is beyond the scope of this book; a more detailed discussion of its orgins and characteristics can be found in S. D. Trav, *No Applause, Just Throw Money: The Book That Made Vaudeville Famous,* Macmillan (2005).

19. Francis Rogers, "Jenny Lind," *Musical Quarterly* 32.3 (July 1946), 437–448.

20. Barnum quoted in Kunhardt et al.

21. "The Visit of Jenny Lind to America," *Times* (London) (3–6–1850), 7.

22. P. T. Barnum, *The Life of P. T. Barnum,* American Museum/P. T Barnum (1855), 304.

23. Sherry Lee Linkon, "Reading Lind Mania: Print Culture and the Construction of Nineteenth-Century Audiences," *Book History* 1.1 (1998), 94–106.

24. In 1964, the Beatles were met by "only" 4,000 fans, 200 reporters, and 100+ police at JFK airport in New York. For more details see Jim Farber, "Beatles' Historic Arrival in New York City 50 Years Ago Gave Big Apple Unforgettable Lift," *New York Daily News* (01–24–2014), http://www.nydailynews.com /new-york/beatles-electrified-nyc-50-years-article-1.1590579.

25. "Stephen Foster," *American Experience,* PBS (2001), http://www.pbs .org/wgbh/amex/foster/index.html.

26. See chapter 12 of Adrian Johns, *Piracy: The Intellectual Property Wars from Gutenberg to Gates,* University of Chicago Press (2009).

27. John Tasker Howard, Ray Lev, and Dorothy B. Commins, *A Treasury of Stephen Foster,* Random House (1946), 107.

28. Center for American Music, the University of Pittsburgh, Stephen Foster biography, http://www.pitt.edu/~amerimus/Fosterbiography.htm.

29. Ibid. See also Aaron Skirboll, "The Next Page: Stephen Foster's Sad End," *Pittsburgh Post-Gazette* (3–1–2014), http://www.post-gazette.com /opinion/Op-Ed/2014/03/02/Next-Page-Stephen-Foster-s-sad-end/stories /201403020083.

30. Edward A. Berlin, "Scott Joplin Autobiography," Scott Joplin International Ragtime Foundation (1998), http://www.scottjoplin.org/biography.html.

31. Ibid.

32. Tucker.

33. See "Sears Roebuck Advertisements," http://antiquepianoshop.com /online-museum/sears-roebuck-company/. For more information about the player piano, see "History of the Pianola—An Overview," Pianola Institute, http://www.pianola.org/history/history.cfm.

34. Tucker.

35. Statement of Marybeth Peters, Register of Copyrights before the Subcommittee on Courts, the Internet and Intellectual Property of the House Committee on the Judiciary (2004), http://www.copyright.gov/docs/regstat031104 .html.

CHAPTER 4. MEDIA REVOLUTIONS

1. Stephen J. Dubner, "What's the Future of the Music Industry? A Freakonomics Quorum," *Freakonomics* (blog) (9–7–2007), http://freakonomics.com/2007/09/20/whats-the-future-of-the-music-industry-a-freakonomics-quorum/.

2. For contemporary trends in musical amateurism, see Douglas McClennan, "Hail the Amateur, Loved by the Crowd," *New York Times* (6–10–2011), http://www.nytimes.com/2011/06/12/arts/music/amateur-musicians-and-crowd-sourced-talent-competitions.html?pagewanted = all&_r = 0.

3. "Leon Scott and the Phonautograph," Audio Engineering Society, http://www.aes.org/aeshc/docs/recording.technology.history/scott.html.

4. The *first-mover advantage* (FMA) is usually defined as the advantage gained by the first significant participant in a market segment. One of the most common sources of FMA is technological leadership. For a deeper discussion of the topic, see Marvin B. Lieberman and David B. Montgomery, "First-Mover Advantages," *Strategic Management Journal* 9 (Summer 1988), 41–58.

5. Charles Cros's 1877 letter describing his Paleophone and his French patent for it are archived at http://www.phonozoic.net/wile.htm.

6. To hear one of the earliest extant Edison recordings and one of the few on tin foil cylinders see Lisa Brenner, "Hear Thomas Edison's Earliest Known Recording from 1878 for the First Time (Audio)," KPCC, http://www.scpr.org/blogs/news/2012/10/25/10712/hear-thomas-edison-sing-rare-1878-audio-restored-f/, and the associated Sound Cloud file, https://soundcloud.com/kpcc/foil-top-ewc?in = kpcc/sets/edison-1878-tin-foil. See also http://www.nps.gov/edis/photosmultimedia/very-early-recorded-sound.htm for mp3's of wax cylinders from the 1880s, the next generation of sound technology.

7. Edison's 1927 reenactment of his historic 1877 recording of "Mary Had a Little Lamb" is archived at http://www.pbs.org/wgbh/amex/edison/sfeature/songs.html.

8. Edison's first patent for his "Phonograph or Speaking Machine" is archived at http://edison.rutgers.edu/patents/00200521.PDF.

9. Gert J. Almind, "History of Coin-Operated Phonographs" (unpublished MS dated 2–23–2015), http://coin-o-phone.com/history.pdf.

10. See http://www.mainspringpress.com/studio_photos.html, which shows photo restorations by Allan Sutton (including photos showing arrangement of performers in relationship to the recording cone).

11. "The Recording Studio," chapter posted from Mike Thorne, "Music in the Machine" (unpublished MS), http://www.stereosociety.com/recordingstudio.shtml.

12. Scott Alexander, "The First Jazz Records," http://www.redhotjazz.com/jazz1917.html. For the 1917 recording of the song see http://www.loc.gov/jukebox/recordings/detail/id/5370/.

13. Ben Sisario, "From One Mine, the Gold of Pop History," *New York Times* (10–30–2012), http://www.nytimes.com/2012/10/31/books/360-sound-celebrates-columbia-records-125th-anniversary.html?_r = 0.

14. See http://www.billboard.com/articles/business/6875175/power-100-universal-lucian-grainge-columbia-rob-stringer-billboard-party.

15. "Historic RCA Studio B," http://studiob.org/.

16. Almind.

17. Almost certainly derived from the word *juke*, a term for the places where people went to hear music, drink, and otherwise recreate, especially in the South. Much of the performance history of the acoustic blues tradition, for example, occurred in "juke joints" in the Delta region of Mississippi.

18. Almind, 22.

19. Stanley Green, "Jukebox Piracy," *Atlantic* (April 1962), http://www.theatlantic.com/magazine/archive/1962/04/jukebox-piracy/305829/.

20. "Performance Rights in Sound Recordings," Subcommittee on Courts, Civil Liberties, and the Administration of Justice of the Committee on the Judiciary, H.R., 95th Congress, 2nd sess. (1978). See also chapter 6, "Massification."

21. Sound recordings did not exist when the Copyright Act of 1909 was enacted. It was not until the 1976 revision that sound recordings earned copyright protection. At that time, the radio industry was able to successfully lobby Congress to provide an exemption for the broadcast of musical recordings with the justification that the promotional value of airplay was adequate compensation for their use. Despite numerous attempts to change the law and remove the exemption, it continues to apply to all terrestrial (traditional broadcast) radio today. For an overview of the radio exemption see http://www.thembj.org/2008/03/the-last-hurrah-copyright-law-as-it-relates-to-performance-rights/.

22. John Philip Sousa, "The Menace of Mechanical Music," *Appleton's Magazine* 8 (1906), http://explorepahistory.com/odocument.php?docId = 1-4-1A1.

23. Alex Ross, "The Record Effect: How Technology Has Transformed the Sound of Music," *New Yorker* (6-6-2005), http://www.newyorker.com/archive/2005/06/06/050606crat_atlarge?currentPage = all.

24. Donna Miller and David Bruenger, "The Rise and Fall of YouTube: How Compressive Effects of Technology and Digital Capitalism Shape Social Media," paper presented at the International Association for Intercultural Communication Studies Conference, Harbin, China, 2007.

CHAPTER 5. CONVERGENCE AND CROSSOVER

1. For more information about the music industry in this era, see William H. Young and Nancy K. Young, *Music of the Great Depression*, Greenwood (2005).

2. Rogier Kappers, *Lomax, the Song Hunter*, PBS (8-22-2006), http://www.pbs.org/pov/lomax/.

3. From http://www.loc.gov/folklife/guide/folkmusicandsong.html.

4. See "Nashville Time Machine," http://nashvilletimemachine.com/about.html.

5. Ed Ward, "How the Bristol Sessions Changed Country Music," NPR (4-19-2011), http://www.npr.org/2011/04/19/134173199/how-the-bristol-sessions-changed-country-music. Johnny Cash quoted in Ben Wynne, *In Tune: Charley Patton, Jimmie Rodgers, and the Roots of American Music*, LSU Press (2014), 150.

6. See http://www.nps.gov/history/delta/blues/people/robert_johnson.htm.

7. For more information about Robert Johnson and the Delta blues, see Elijah Wald, *Escaping the Delta: Robert Johnson and the Invention of the Blues,* Amistad (2004).

8. See http://www.bluesworld.com/SpierOne.html.

9. Quoted by Pat Howse and Jimmy Phillips, "Godfather of Delta Blues: H. C. Speir," originally published in *Peavey Monitor Magazine* (1995), http://www.bluesworld.com/SpierIntro.html.

10. Wayne W. Daniel, "Charlie D. Tillman (1861–1943)," *New Georgia Encyclopedia* (11–15–2013), http://www.georgiaencyclopedia.org/articles/arts-culture/charlie-d-tillman-1861–1943.

11. Ibid.

12. "James David Vaughn," Southern Gospel Music Association (SGMA) Hall of Fame, http://sgma.org/james-david-vaughan/.

13. Ibid.

14. "The WLS National Barn Dance," http://www.wlshistory.com/NBD/.

15. Ibid.

16. "Will the Circle Be Unbroken," *Grand Ole Opry History,* http://www.opry.com/history.

17. See http://www.kingbiscuittime.com/?page_id = 7.

18. Gene Fowler and Bill Crawford, "Border Radio," *Handbook of Texas Online,* http://www.tshaonline.org/handbook/online/articles/ebb01.

19. For a historical overview of "clear channel" radio stations—not to be confused with the later twentieth-century media company Clear Channel Communications—see Mark Durenberger, "Behind the Clear-Channel Matter," http://www.oldradio.com/archives/general/clears.htm.

20. Richard Florida and Scott Jackson, "Sonic City: The Evolving Geography of the Music Industry" (Working Paper, January 2008), Martin Prosperity Institute, University of Toronto, http://www-2.rotman.utoronto.ca/userfiles/prosperity/File/Sonic%20City%20RF3.w.cover.pdf.

21. Ibid.

22. Richard Florida, Charlotta Mellander, and Kevin Solarik, "From Music Scenes to Music Clusters: The Economic Geography of Music in the U.S., 1970-2000" (Working Paper, June 2009), Martin Prosperity Institute, University of Toronto, http://martinprosperity.org/media/pdfs/Manuscript_Music_Scenes_to_Music_Clusters_June_2009.pdf.

23. For more information about *Billboard* magazine, see its corporate site at www.billboard.com. For early magazine history, see http://www.billboard.com/articles/columns/chart-beat/5777989/happy-birthday-billboard. For a more recent overview, see http://www.nytimes.com/2014/01/09/business/media/leadership-change-may-signal-new-start-for-billboard-magazine.html?_r=0 .

CHAPTER 6. MASSIFICATION

1. "Music Publishers Map Campaign to Revive Sheet Sales," *Variety* (5–18–1950), http://proxy.lib.ohio-state.edu/login?url=http://search.proquest.com/docview/1285965177?accountid=9783.

2. There are a number of fan sites, regional and otherwise, about garage bands during the 1960s. See, for example, Chris Bishop, *Garage Hangover* (2016), http://www.garagehangover.com.

3. In 2014, over $1.3 billion was spent in the US on guitars alone. "The 2014 NAMM Global Report," https://www.namm.org/files/ihdp-viewer/global-report-2014/A7352D4907B25A95B2CE27A075D3956F/2014MusicUSA_final.pdf.

4. AlvinToffler, *Future Shock*, Random House (1970).

5. John Broven, *Record Makers and Breakers: Voices of the Independent Rock 'n' Roll Pioneers*, University of Illinois (2009), 28–30, n. 15.

6. "Historic RCA Studio B," *Country Music Hall of Fame and Museum* (2016), http://studiob.org.

7. Daniel F. Cuff, "RCA Records Plans Bertelsmann Link," *New York Times* (6-13-1984), http://www.nytimes.com/1984/06/13/business/rca-records-plans-bertelsmann-link.html.

8. On RCA/Jive, see "Sony, BMG Agree on Music Merger," CNN (11-7-2003), http://edition.cnn.com/2003/BUSINESS/11/06/sony.bmg.reut/. On the shutdown, see Shirley Halperin, "RCA Execs Confirm Jive and Arista Labels Shut Down," *Hollywood Reporter* (10-7-2011), http://www.hollywoodreporter.com/news/rca-execs-confirm-jive-arista-245392.

9. Ben Sisario, "EMI Is Sold for $4.1 Billion in Combined Deals, Consolidating the Music Industry," *New York Times* (11-11-2011), http://www.nytimes.com/2011/11/12/business/media/emi-is-sold-for-4-1-billion-consolidating-the-music-industry.html?_r = 2&.

10. Ibid.

11. "About Sun Records," Sun Entertainment Corporation (2012), http://www.sunrecords.com/about.

12. "Elvis Presley," Sun Entertainment Corporation (2012), http://www.sunrecords.com/artists/elvis-presley.

13. "Sam Phillips: The Sound and Legacy of Sun Records," *Morning Edition*, NPR (11-28-2001), http://www.npr.org/programs/morning/features/2001/nov/phillips/011128.sam.phillips.html.

14. The practice of putting a white face on the "cover" of a record originally record by an African American artist began in the 1920s. These "white covers" were made in order to take advantage of racially segregated programming and retailing practices, often co-opting the commercial potential of the original. There are many, many instances of white cover versions commercially outperforming original recordings, not so much because of actual or perceived musical superiority, but because of access to the better promotion and distribution channels available to white performers and their labels.

For more information about and examples of white covers, see Norah Berlatsky, "Elvis Wasn't the First to Steal Black Music: 10 White Artists Who 'Borrowed' from R&B before the King," *Salon* (5-17-2014), http://www.salon.com/2014/05/17/elvis_wasnt_the_first/.

15. Mike Callahan and David Edwards, "The Chess Story," Both Sides Now (11-4-2005), http://www.bsnpubs.com/chess/chesscheck.html.

16. Joel Francis, "The True Story of Cadillac Records: The Final Days and Legacy of Chess Records," *Daily Record* (12-12-2008), http://joelfrancis.com/2008/12/08/the-real-cadillac-records-three/.

17. Ibid.

18. "The Rise and Fall of Vee-Jay Records," *Fresh Air*, NPR (1-15-2008), http://www.npr.org/templates/story/story.php?storyId = 18112344.

19. Ibid.

20. Derek Rath, "The Success and Undoing of Vee-Jay Records," *Day to Day,* NPR (8–21–2007), http://www.npr.org/templates/story/story.php?storyId =13774728.

21. The terms *commercially viable* and *master* have practical and legal implications. *Commercial viability* is the end goal of commercial recording/production processes. If a label can't sell the record, there is little reason to make it and there are financial consequences for performers and producers who cannot deliver a product that is sellable. A *master* is the original version of the recorded work and is the basis of all rights and values under copyright law.

22. The Recording Industry Association of America (RIAA) award certification "was launched in 1958 to honor artists and create a standard by which to measure sales of a sound recording." A "gold record" sold five hundred thousand copies and a "platinum record" sold a million. For more information about the RIAA and the awards see https://www.riaa.com/goldandplatinum .php?content_selector = historyx.

23. Don Cusic, "Acuff-Rose," *Tennessee Encyclopedia* (12–25–2009), ttp:// tennesseeencyclopedia.net/entry.php?rec = 4.

24. Kyle Coroneos [Trigger], "How Music Row and Acuff-Rose Killed the Everly Brothers," Saving Country Music (1–4–2014), http://www.savingcountry music.com/how-music-row-acuff-rose-killed-the-everly-brothers.

25. Julian Aberbach, "Biography," http://www.julianaberbach.com/biography.

26. Ibid.

27. David Sanjek, "Hill and Range," *Continuum Encyclopedia of Popular Music of the World: Performance and Production,* vol. 2, A&C Black (2003), 586.

28. Aberbach.

29. Ibid.

30. Ibid.

31. Howard B. Abrams, "Copyright's First Compulsory License," *Santa Clara High Technology Law Journal* 26.2 (2009), 222–225, http://digitalcom-mons.law.scu.edu/cgi/viewcontent.cgi?article=1499&context=chtlj.

32. Ibid.

33. In practice, the complexities of mechanical licensing, as well as other music licensing issues, have been monitored by the Harry Fox Agency, which issues licenses for records distributed in the United States. Established in 1927 by the National Music Publishers Association, HFA continues to license "the largest percentage of the mechanical and digital uses of music in the United States on CDs, digital services, records, tapes and imported phonorecords," according the company's website,

For more information about mechanical licenses, see Section 115 of US copyright law and the explanatory material in Circulars 73 and 22, available at www.copyright.gov. For more information about the Harry Fox Agency, see www.harryfox.com.

34. Lydia Hutchinson, "Alan Freed and the Radio Payola Scandal," *Performing Songwriter* (11–20–2013), http://performingsongwriter.com/alan-freed-payola-scandal/.

35. Ibid.

36. For example, see Lorne Manly, "How Payola Went Corporate," *New York Times* (07–31–2005), http://www.nytimes.com/2005/07/31/weekinreview /31manly.html?pagewanted = all&_r = 0.

37. William Serrin, "James Petrillo Dead: Led Musicians, *New York Times* (10–25–1984), http://www.nytimes.com/1984/10/25/obituaries/james-petrillo-dead-led-musicians.html.

38. Ibid. The available monies in the Music Performance Trust Fund (MPTF) declined significantly as the digital and file-sharing eras unfolded and revenues from the sale of recorded music decreased. In 2004, the MPTF was rebranded as the MPF and its initiatives were considerably scaled back. See http:// www.npr.org/blogs/therecord/2011/08/25/139951603/a-dwindling-trust-puts-free-concerts-on-the-rocks and http://www.ewire.com/news-releases/music-performance-fund-takes-a-new-name-charts-new-directions/.

39. For more details about CAMI and its history, see "CAMI History," http://www.cami.com/?topic = history.

40. Dennis McClellan, "Talent Manager Discovered 2 Teen Idols," *Los Angeles Times* (3–16–2011), http://articles.latimes.com/2011/mar/16/local/la-me-robert-marcucci-20110316.

41. See also Ed Christman, "Reversion Rights: Will 2013 Be a Game-Changer?" *Billboard* (12–27–2012), https://www.billboard.com/biz/articles/news /1483926/reversion-rights-will-2013-be-a-game-changer.

CHAPTER 7. SCALING AND SELLING LIVE PERFORMANCE

1. Paul K. Saint-Amour, *Modernism and Copyright,* Oxford University Press (2011), 115.

2. Ibid.

3. Blair Tindall, *Mozart in the Jungle,* Atlantic Monthly Press (2005), 47.

4. "In 1936, Edsel Ford—son of Henry, the founder of the Ford Motor Company—established the Ford Foundation with an initial gift of $25,000. During its early years, the foundation operated in Michigan under the leadership of Ford family members. Since the founding charter stated that resources should be used for 'scientific, educational and charitable purposes, all for the public welfare,' the foundation made grants to many kinds of organizations." From "About Us: History," Ford Foundation (2015), https://www.fordfoundation.org/about-us /history/.

5. Tindall, 150.

6. Donal Henahan, "Our Orchestras Are Splintering," *New York Times* (8–13–1987), http://www.nytimes.com/1987/09/13/arts/music-view-our-orchestras -are-splintering.html.

7. *2008 Survey of Public Participation in the Arts* (Research Report no. 49), National Endowment for the Arts (2009), https://www.arts.gov/sites/default /files/2008-SPPA.pdf.

8. More recent research, including work by the Pew Internet and American Life Survey, indicates that more and more adults of all ages are willing to obtain recorded music, of all kinds, via streaming or downloading. See, for example,

Mary Madden, "The State of Music Online: Ten Years after Napster," Pew Research Center (6–15–2009), http://www.pewinternet.org/2009/06/15/the-state-of-music-online-ten-years-after-napster/.

9. For example, the Metropolitan Opera Company's production of Stravinsky's *Prince Igor* during the 2013–2014 season cost $4.3 million. See Jennifer Maloney, "New York's Metropolitan Opera Opens Its Budget Curtain," *Wall Street Journal* (5–30–2014), http://www.wsj.com/articles/new-yorks-metropolitan-opera-opens-its-budget-curtain-1401416711.

10. Lance Freed, "My Father and the Moondog Coronation Ball," Rock and Roll Hall of Fame, http://rockhall.com/story-of-rock/features/all-featured/7487_alan-freed-the-moondog-coronation-ball-lance-freed/.

11. Ibid.

12. Jess Stearn, "Rock 'n' Roll Runs into Trouble," *New York Daily News* (4–12–1956), quoted by Linda Martin and Kerry Seagrave, *Anti-Rock: The Opposition to Rock 'n' Roll*, Da Capo Press (1993), 52.

13. For more information about Murray "the K" Kaufman, see "This Meeting of the Swingin' Soirée Is Now in Session!" Murray the K Archives and Rear-View Productions (2015), http://www.murraythek.com.

14. Chris Nickson, "All about Gig Package Tours," Ministry of Rock, http://www.ministryofrock.co.uk/GigPackageTours.html.

15. Ibid.

16. For more information about the history of Lollapalooza, see Allison Stewart, "Alternative Nation's Last Stand: Lollapalooza 1995, an Oral History," *Washington Post* (8–11–2015), https://www.washingtonpost.com/lifestyle/style/alternative-nations-last-stand-lollapalooza-1995-an-oral-history/2015/08/10/cb6857e4-3087-11e5-8f36-18d1d501920d_story.html; and "History of Lollapalooza," interview of Perry Ferrell by Sal Masakela, Red Bull TV (2014), http://www.redbull.tv/videos/1406233338765-1140746799/the-history-of-lollapalooza.

17. Donna Freydkin, "Lilith Fair: Lovely, Lively and Long Overdue," *CNN Interactive* (7–28–1998), http://www.cnn.com/SHOWBIZ/Music/9807/28/lilith.fair/.

18. Ibid.

19. Ben Patashnik, "Are Package Tours Helping or Hurting Live Music?" *Rock Sound,* http://www.rocksound.tv/features/read/are-package-tours-helping-or-hurting-music.

20. For information about the origins of Colonel Tom Parker, see Mike Dash, "Colonel Parker Managed Elvis' Career, but Was He a Killer on the Lam?" Smithsonian.com (2–24–2012), http://www.smithsonianmag.com/history/colonel-parker-managed-elvis-career-but-was-he-a-killer-on-the-lam-108042206/#QdSw1cFKLSwMMOUz.99.

21. Alice Echols, *Scars of Sweet Paradise: The Life and Times of Janis Joplin,* Macmillan (1999), 115ff.

22. Ibid., 118.

23. "Chet Helms (1942–2005)," Family Dog, http://www.familydog.com/content/chet-helms.

24. "Bill Graham Biography," Rock and Roll Hall of Fame, http://rockhall.com/inductees/bill-graham/bio/.

25. "History," San Francisco Mime Troupe, http://www.sfmt.org/company /history.php.

26. Echols, 119.

27. "Bill Graham Biography."

28. Joey Bunch and Ricardo Baca, "Barry Fey, Legendary Colorado Concert Promoter, Dies at 73," *Denver Post* (4–28–2013), http://www.denverpost.com /ci_23127822/legendary-colorado-concert-promoter-barry-fey-dies.

29. Ibid.

30. Ibid.

31. Ben Sisario, "Lollapalooza and Its Promoters Rise on the Stage of Chicago," *New York Times* (8–16–2010), http://www.nytimes.com/2010/08/07/arts /music/07lolla.html.

32. Ibid.

33. Ibid.

34. Ibid.

35. Matt Pollock, "How One Insanely Popular Music Festival Is Keeping You from Seeing Your Favorite Bands," Mic.com (6–6–2014), http://mic.com /articles/91181/how-one-insanely-popular-music-festival-is-keeping-you-from-seeing-your-favorite-bands#.uEfM4Fs9i.

36. Lars Brandie, "Live Nation Completes Deal for C3 Presents," *Billboard* (12–22–2014), http://www.billboard.com/articles/business/6414053/live-nation-completes-deal-for-c3-presents.

37. Ray Waddell, "Live Music's $20 Billion Year: Rolling Stones, One Direction, Live Nation Top Boxscore's Year-End," *Billboard* (12–12–2014), http:// www.billboard.com/articles/business/6406028/boxscore-top-tours-2014-rolling-stones-live-nation.

38. AEG Live, Los Angeles, http://www.aeglive.com/overview.

39. Live Nation Entertainment Inc., *New York Times,* http://topics.nytimes .com/top/news/business/companies/live-nation-inc/index.html?inline = nyt-org; Glenn Peoples, "Live Nation Revenue Up 8% to $5.8 Billion, Posts Significant Net Losses," *Billboard* (2–26–2013), http://www.billboard.com/biz/articles /news/global/1549948/live-nation-revenue-up-8-to-58-billion-posts-significant-net-losses; Ben Sisario, "Live Nation Cut Its Losses Last Year," *New York Times* (2–24–2014), http://www.nytimes.com/2014/02/25/business/media/live-nations-loss-declined-as-revenue-rose-in-2013.html.

40. Sisario, "Live Nation Cut Its Losses Last Year."

41. Brandie.

42. David Byrne, "David Byrne's Survival Strategies for Emerging Artists—and Megastars," *Wired* 16.1 (12–18–2007), http://archive.wired.com/entertainment /music/magazine/16-01/ff_byrne?currentPage = all.

43. Ibid.

44. For an assortment of venue capacity assessments see "Las Vegas Live Music Venues," http://www.poppermost.com/linksvegasvenues.html; "A Look at the Size of Capital Region Concert Venues," http://alloveralbany.com /archive/2013/03/08/a-look-at-the-size-of-capital-region-concert-venue; Andrea Swensson, "Infographic: Comparing Venue Sizes in the Twin Cities," *Current* (11–1–2013), http://blog.thecurrent.org/2013/11/infographic-comparing-venue-

sizes-in-the-twin-cities/; "Guide to Live Music Venues in Boston," http://boston
.cbslocal.com/guide/guide-to-live-music-venues-in-boston/; Indie on the Move
national database, http://www.indieonthemove.com/venues.

45. Steven Van Zandt, "A Crisis of Craft," originally presented at SXSW
(2009), archived at Little Steven's Underground Garage (2-2-2010), http://
undergroundgarage.com/essays-and-speeches/a-crisis-of-craft.html.

46. A term developed in relationship to the film industry, a *blockbuster* is an
extremely profitable movie. The idea, which was also relevant to the twentieth-
century-music industry, is that a few extremely successful artists/productions
generate the majority of industry profits (see also the Pareto principle, or the
80/20 rule). For a discussion of how blockbuster products have shaped the film
industry, see Stephen Heyman, "The Fast-Changing Economics of the Movie
Blockbuster," *New York Times* (7–8–2015), http://www.nytimes.com/2015/07/09
/arts/international/the-fast-changing-economics-of-the-movie-blockbuster
.html?_r = 0.

47. LiveNation announced (4-11-2011) that the 360° Tour was the most
successful concert tour in history. See http://www.prnewswire.com/news-releases
/live-nation-entertainment-announces-new-touring-record-u2-360-is-the-most-
successful-tour-of-all-time-119587979.html.

48. Ray Waddell, "U2's '360' Tour Gross: $736,137,344!" *Billboard* (7–29–
2011), http://www.billboard.com/biz/articles/news/touring/1176894/u2s-360-
tour-gross-736137344.

49. Andy Serwer, "Inside Rolling Stones, Inc.," *Fortune* (2002; reprinted
2-31-2013), http://fortune.com/2013/07/21/inside-rolling-stones-inc-fortune-
2002/.

50. Jonathan Gould, *Can't Buy Me Love: The Beatles, Britain, and America,*
Three Rivers Press (2007).

51. See, for example, Jacob Ganz, "Live Nation Stumbles over Summer Concert Sales," *NPR Music* (7–13–2010), http://www.npr.org/templates/story/story
.php?storyId = 128473078.

CHAPTER 8. VISUAL MEDIA

1. Marshall McLuhan's *Understanding Media: The Extensions of Man,*
McGraw-Hill (1964), is an early and influential study that includes a clear
exposition of the replication/modification principle for emerging media.

2. Al Kohn and Bob Kohn, *Kohn on Music Licensing,* 2nd ed., Aspen (1996),
1132–1133.

3. Carl Davis, "Charlie Chaplin's Film Music," *Guardian* (12–31–2010),
http://www.theguardian.com/culture/2011/jan/01/carl-davis-charlie-chaplin-
soundtracks.

4. Richard Abel and Charles Altman, *The Sounds of Early Cinema,* Indiana
University Press (2001), 143–150.

5. Elizabeth Fones-Wolf, "Sound Comes to the Movies: The Philadelphia
Musicians' Struggle against Recorded Music," *Pennsylvania Magazine of History and Biography* 118.1/2 (January/April 1994), http://journals.psu.edu/pmhb
/issue/view/2547.

6. James P. Kraft, "The 'Pit' Musicians: Mechanization in the Movie Theaters, 1926–1934," *Labor History* 35.1 (2–28–2007), 66–89.

7. "Those Theme Songs!" *New York Times* (8–4–1929).

8. Ibid.

9. Ibid.

10. Ibid.

11. Deborah Allison, "'Do Not Forsake Me: The Ballad of High Noon' and the Rise of the Movie Theme Song," *Senses of Cinema* (October 2003), http://sensesofcinema.com/2003/cinema-and-music/ballad_of_high_noon/#3.

12. Peter Ford, "Rock around the Clock and Me," http://www.peterford.com/ratc.html.

13. That said, many "live" concert performances are heavily edited in the studio to enhance the quality of the performance.

14. Steve Binder was a producer and director who spent much of his career working at NBC producing music specials. In addition to the *T.A.M.I Show,* he produced/directed the weekly music show *Hullabaloo,* the Elvis "Comeback" special in 1968, and many more "special" shows for artists such as Petulah Clark, Patti Labelle, Barry Manilow, Wayne Newton, and most intriguingly, Peewee Herman.

15. "Earliest 'Concert Film' Documentaries," IMDb, http://www.imdb.com/search/title?at = o&genres = documentary&keywords = concert-film&sort = year,asc&start = 51.

16. Joel Blitzstein, "Watch Martin Scorsese Break Down 'The Last Waltz,'" *Rolling Stone* (11–26–2014), http://www.rollingstone.com/movies/videos/martin-scorsese-talks-the-last-waltz-20141126#ixzz3wkx6jYM6.

17. "Music Concerts, 1984–Present," Box Office Mojo, http://www.boxofficemojo.com/genres/chart/?id = musicconcert.htm.

18. Marla Matzer, "These Days Soundtracks Can Be Sweet Music to Movie Marketers' Ears," *Los Angeles Times* (7–10–1997), http://articles.latimes.com/1997/jul/10/business/fi-11337.

19. Ibid.

20. Ibid.

21. Ibid.

22. Some have argued that film and television licensing are replacing traditional record label support.

23. Guild of Music Supervisors, "Role," http://www.guildofmusicsupervisors.com/role/.

24. Steve Binder, "Question: Primetime Variety—'Whatever Happened to It?' Answer: It's Alive and Well in the Hands of the Wrong People," *Caucus Journal* (Spring 2000), http://www.caucus.org/archives/oospr_primetimevariety.html.

25. Fiona Sturges, "The Rembrandts: 'So No One Told Me It Was Going to Be This Way,'" *Independent* (4–27–2004), http://www.independent.co.uk/arts-entertainment/music/features/the-rembrandts-so-no-one-told-me-it-was-going-to-be-this-way-6170741.html.

26. See, for example, the *Miami Vice* episode "Smugglers Blues" (season 1, episode 15, 1985), which featured the song "Smugglers Blues," written by Glenn Frey of the Eagles.

27. James Hughes, "Can't Get You out of My Head: The History of Advertising Jingles, a Truly American Art Form," *Slate* (9–7–2012), http://www.slate .com/articles/arts/books/2012/09/music_in_advertising_timothy_taylor_s_the _sounds_of_capitalism_reviewed_.html. For more on the Wheaties jingle specifically, see Monte Olmsted, "What Wheaties Did to Jumpstart Our Cereal Success." *Taste of General Mills* (2–24–2016), http://www.blog.generalmills .com/2016/02/what-wheaties-did-to-jumpstart-our-cereal-success/.

28. Timothy D. Taylor, *The Sounds of Capitalism: Advertising, Music, and the Conquest of Culture,* University of Chicago Press (2012), 168.

29. See Adtunes, http://adtunes.com.

30. Shelley DuBois, "Are Advertisers the New Record Labels?" *Fortune* (3–14–2012), http://fortune.com/2012/03/14/are-advertisers-the-new-record-labels/.

31. Ibid.

CHAPTER 9. ARTISTS, AUDIENCES, AND BRANDS

1. See, for example, Bernd H. Smith, David L. Rogers, and Karen L. Vrotsos, *There's No Business That's Not Show Business,* FT Press (2003).

2. Daniel Kreps, "Nipple Ripples: 10 Years of Fallout from Janet Jackson's Halftime Show," *Rolling Stone* (1–30–2014), http://www.rollingstone.com /culture/news/nipple-ripples-10-years-of-fallout-from-janet-jacksons-halftime-show-20140130#ixzz3CAKv8vvR .

3. Ibid.

4. Ibid. A more recent example of the "wardrobe malfunction" would be that experienced by Nicki Minaj onstage at the 2014 Video Music Awards (VMA). Though the artist claimed she "ran out of time" to zip her dress and was forced to perform holding the front of it together with one hand, it was widely reported as premeditated rather than an accident. See, e.g., http://www .torontosun.com/2014/08/31/nicki-minajs-vmas-wardrobe-malfunction-was-planned, http://time.com/3170169/vmas-2014-nicki-minaj-ariana-grande-jessie-j-performance-video/, among many other accounts.

5. Olivier Driessens, "Celebrity Capital: Redefining Celebrity Using Field Theory," *Theory and Society* 42.5 (September 2013), 556.

6. This concept—the democratization of celebrity—inevitably evokes Andy Warhol's observation (from a 1968 exhibition brochure) that "in the future, everyone will be world-famous for 15 minutes." For a detailed discussion of the provenance of this quote see Adam Sherwin, "Andy Warhol's 'Famous for 15 Minutes' Quote May Not Be His, Experts Believe," *Independent* (9–2–2014), http://www.independent.co.uk/news/people/news/andy-warhols-famous-for-15-minutes-quote-may-not-be-his-experts-believe-9249200.html.

7. Ibid.

8. Driessens, 547.

9. Ibid., 546.

10. Andy Serwer, "Inside Rolling Stones Inc.," *Fortune* (2002; reprinted 2–31–2013), http://fortune.com/2013/07/21/inside-rolling-stones-inc-fortune-2002/.

11. Ibid.

12. Ibid.

13. Ibid.

14. Michael Hahn, "How the Rolling Stones Became Music's Biggest Business," *Guardian* (5–22–2014), http://www.theguardian.com/music/musicblog /2014/may/22/how-the-rolling-stones-became-musics-biggest-business. For an example of how the Rolling Stones's age and capacity to tour are discussed, see Joe Levy, "Is There Such a Thing as 'Too Old to Rock'?" *Soundcheck Blog*, WNYC (1–23–2013), http://www.wnyc.org/story/264482-too-old-to-rock/.

15. Rachel Johnson, "Material Girls: There's One Huge Difference between Madonna and Beyoncé," *Quartz* (3–21–2014), http://qz.com/193390/theres-one-huge-difference-between-beyonce-and-madonna/. See also "Madonna's 'Confessions' Tour Sets Record," *Billboard* (9–20–2006), http://www.billboard .com/articles/news/57197/madonnas-confessions-tour-sets-record.

16. On Madonna's MDNA tour, see Johnson. On Madonna's 2013 income, see Zack O'Malley Greenburg, "The World's Highest-Paid Musicians, 2013," *Forbes* (11–19–2013), http://www.forbes.com/sites/zackomalleygreenburg/2013 /11/19/the-worlds-highest-paid-musicians-2013/.

17. O'Malley Greenburg, "The World's Highest-Paid Musicians, 2013."

18. "Madonna Close to Massive Deal with Live Nation," *Billboard* (10–11–2007), http://www.billboard.com/articles/news/1048285/madonna-close-to-massive-deal-with-live-nation.

19. Ethan Smith, "Madonna Heads for Virgin Territory," *Wall Street Journal* (10–11–2007), http://online.wsj.com/news/articles/SB119205443638155166.

20. Jan Blumentrath, "Interview with Jeff Hanson," Hit Quarters (9–13–2010), http://www.hitquarters.com/index.php3?page = intrview/opar/intrview _Jeff_Hanson_Interview.html.

21. Sonicbids and other twenty-first-century businesses that connect musicians to purchasers of music are discussed in more detail in chapter 11. Quotation from Kimbel Bouwman, "Interview with PANOS PANAY, CEO of Sonicbids," Hit Quarters (7–5–2010), http://www.hitquarters.com/index.php3?page = intrview /opar/intrview_Panos_Panay_Interview.html#ixzz3bFpp2Yxo.

22. Others suggest that the first 360-degree deal was developed in 2005 by Jeff Hanson on behalf of Paramore with Atlantic Records. See Blumentrath.

23. For more information about 360-degree deals see Tom Cole, "You Ask, We Answer: What Exactly Is a 360 Deal?" *Record, Music News from NPR* (11–24–2010), http://www.npr.org/sections/therecord/2010/11/24/131574836 /you-ask-we-answer-what-exactly-is-a-360-deal.

24. Joel Rose, "A Pricey Investment, Even for Jay-Z," NPR (4–11–2008), http://www.npr.org/templates/transcript/transcript.php?storyId=89565696.

25. O'Malley Greenburg, "The World's Highest-Paid Musicians, 2013."

26. Zack O'Malley Greenburg, "Toby Keith, Cowboy Capitalist: Country's $500 Million Man," *Forbes* (6–26–2013), http://www.forbes.com/sites /zackomalleygreenburg/2013/06/26/toby-keith-cowboy-capitalist-countrys-500-million-man/.

27. See Jack Conte and Nataly Dawn's TEDxStanford talk, "No Record Label Necessary, Just Pomplamoose," http://tedxtalks.ted.com/video/No-record-label-necessary-just.

28. Eriq Gardner, " 'American Idol' Winner Files Bold Legal Claim to Escape 'Oppressive' Contracts" (1–26–2015), *Hollywood Reporter,* http://www .hollywoodreporter.com/thr-esq/american-idol-winner-files-bold-767088.

29. Alan Attwood, "The King and the Colonel," *The Age* (8–2–1997), http:// newsstore.fairfax.com.au/apps/viewDocument.ac?page=1&sy=age&kw=the+k ing+and+the+colonel&pb=age&dt=selectRange&dr=entire&so=relevance&sf =text&sf=headline&rc=10&rm=200&sp=nrm&clsPage=1&docID=n ews970208_0279_0715.

30. Robert Hillburn, "Eternal Revenue: Elvis' Millions Were Disappearing When Priscilla Presley Took Charge and Rebuilt the King's Fortune," *Los Angeles Times* (6–11–1989), http://articles.latimes.com/1989-06-11/magazine/tm-2866_ 1_joseph-hanks-vernon-presley-films-or-records; Zack O'Malley Greenburg, "Elvis Presley Earnings 2015: $55 Million," *Forbes* (10–28–2015), http://www .forbes.com/sites/zackomalleygreenburg/2015/10/28/elvis-presley-earnings-2015-55-million/#6a343d613779.

31. P. Norman quoting John Lennon in *John Lennon: The Life,* Doubleday (2008), 547–548.

32. Sadly, both Cobain and Lennon suffered serious consequences from their fame. Cobain's mental and physical health deteriorated and he committed suicide in 1994 when he was arguably at the height of the success he had imagined when developing the musical and brand concept of Nirvana. Lennon, after years of struggling with the frustrations within the Beatles and a degree of backlash following their dissolution, had reconnected with audiences with his album *Double Fantasy,* released in November 1980. A month later, in a bizarre twist on celebrity, Lennon was shot by a deranged fan shortly after autographing a copy of his new album.

33. Alan Feuer and Jason George, "Internet Fame Is Cruel Mistress for a Dancer of the Numa Numa," *New York Times* (2–26–2005), http://www .nytimes.com/2005/02/26/nyregion/internet-fame-is-cruel-mistress-for-a-dancer-of-the-numa-numa.html?_r=0.

34. J.R. Raphael, "A Decade of Internet Superstars," *PC World* (10–7–2008), http://www.pcworld.com/article/151803/internet_superstars.html. For an analysis of the cultural and economic impact of the Backdorm Boys videos and other viral videos, see Donna Miller and David Bruenger, "Decivilization: Compressive Effects of Technology on Culture and Communication," *China Media Research* 3.2 (April 2007), 83–95.

CHAPTER 10. DIGITIZATION

1. "An Audio Timeline," Audio Engineering Society (6–13–2014), http:// www.aes.org/aeshc/docs/audio.history.timeline.html.

2. Douglas A. Boyd, "Digital Audio Recording: The Basics," in *Oral History in the Digital Age,* ed. Douglas A. Boyd, Steve Cohen, Brad Rakerd, and Dean Rehberger, Institute of Museum and Library Services (2012), http://ohda .matrix.msu.edu/2012/06/digital-audio-recording/.

3. Henry Pelham, "Vinyl Prices, 1982–1984," AudioKarma (4–15–2012), http://www.audiokarma.org/forums/showthread.php?t = 437593.

4. David Goldman, "Music's Lost Decade: Sales Cut in Half," *CNN Money* (2–3–2010), http://money.cnn.com/2010/02/02/news/companies/napster_music _industry/.

5. Jacob Ganz and Joel Rose, "The MP3: A History of Innovation and Betrayal," *The Record*, NPR (2–23–2011), http://www.npr.org/sections/therecord/2011/03 /23/134622940/the-mp3-a-history-of-innovation-and-betrayal.

6. Ganz and Rose quoting Brandenburg.

7. [Guest], "The History of File Sharing," *Torrent Freak* (4–22–2012), https://torrentfreak.com/the-history-of-filesharing-120422/.

8. Richard Nieva, "Ashes to Ashes, Peer to Peer: An Oral History of Napster," *Fortune* (9–5–2013), http://fortune.com/2013/09/05/ashes-to-ashes-peer- to-peer-an-oral-history-of-napster/.

9. Ibid.

10. Ibid.

11. Neda Ulaby, "2006 and the Death of Tower Records," NPR (12–29– 2009), http://www.npr.org/2009/12/29/121975854/2006-and-the-death-of-tower- records.

12. Michael Wilson-Morris, "Recording Industry Sues Napster for Copyright Infringement," *Music Dish* (12–15–1999), http://www.musicdish.com /mag/index.php3?id = 113.

13. Sean "Puffy" Combs, CEO, Bad Boy Entertainment Inc., quoted in Michelle Wilson Morris, "Recording Industry Sues Napster for Copyright Infringement," *Music Dish* (12–15–1999), http://www.musicdish.com/mag/index .php3?id=113.

14. Matt Richtel, "The Napster Decision: The Overview; Appellate Judges Back Limitations on Copying Music," *New York Times* (2–13–2001), http:// www.nytimes.com/2001/02/13/business/napster-decision-overview-appellate- judges-back-limitations-copying-music.html.

15. Ibid.

16. Ibid.

17. *Variety* staff, "ASCAP Seeks to Work with Napster," *Variety* (11–2– 2000), http://variety.com/2000/digital/news/ascap-seeks-to-work-with-napster- 1117788718/.

18. David Kravets, "Napster Trial Ends Seven Years Later, Defining Online Sharing Along the Way," *Wired* (8–31–2007), http://www.wired.com/2007/08 /napster-trial-e/.

19. Ibid.

20. ibid.

21. Ibid.

22. Amy Harmon, "The Napster Decision: The Reaction; Napster Users Make Plans for the Day the Free Music Dies," *New York Times* (2–13–2001), http://www.nytimes.com/2001/02/13/business/napster-decision-reaction-nap- ster-users-make-plans-for-day-free-music-dies.html.

23. Ibid.

24. Statement of Marybeth Peters, Register of Copyrights before the Subcommittee on Courts, the Internet and Intellectual Property of the House Committee on the Judiciary (2004), http://www.copyright.gov/docs/regstato31104.html.

25. Ibid.

26. Kellen Myers, "The RIAA, the DMCA, and the Forgotten Few Webcasters: A Call for Change in Digital Copyright Royalties," *Federal Communications Law Journal* 61.2 (2009), http://www.repository.law.indiana.edu/fclj/vol61/iss2/7/.

27. See also chapter 4, "Media Revolutions."

28. "Public Performance Right for Sound Recordings," Future of Music Coalition (11–5–2013), https://www.futureofmusic.org/article/fact-sheet/public-performance-right-sound-recordings.

29. Randy Lewis, "Fair Play, Fair Pay Act of 2015 Would Require Radio to Pay for Music," *Los Angeles Times* (4–13–2015), http://www.latimes.com/entertainment/music/posts/la-et-ms-fair-play-fair-pay-act-congress-radio-royalties-20150413-story.html. See also Emmauel Legrand, "Artists Press Congress to Pass the Fair Play Fair Pay Act," *Music Week* (5–12–2016), http://www.musicweek.com/news/read/artists-press-congress-to-pass-the-fair-play-fair-pay-act/064758.

30. Tomomi Harkey, "Bonneville International Corp. v. Peters: Considering Copyright Rules to Facilitate Licensing for Webcasting," *Berkeley Technology Law Journal* 20.1 (January 2005), http://scholarship.law.berkeley.edu/cgi/viewcontent.cgi?article=1542&context=btlj.

31. Myers.

32. "SoundExchange Is Celebrating 'Ten Years in Play,'" *Soundbyte* (10–9–2013), http://www.soundexchange.com/wp-content/uploads/2013/10/Soundbyte-10–9-13.pdf.

33. "CRB Appoints SoundExchange Sole 'Collective,'" *Billboard* (3–8–2007), http://www.billboard.com/biz/articles/news/publishing/1326173/crb-appoints-soundexchange-sole-collective.

34. "SoundExchange Fact Sheet" (7–29–2014), http://www.soundexchange.com/wp-content/uploads/2014/07/SoundExchange-Factsheet-07–29–14.pdf.

35. "International Partners," SoundExchange, http://www.soundexchange.com/about/international-partners/.

36. MRI was founded in 1995 to offer "a full spectrum of music rights administration services to clients including strategic consulting, copyright research, licensing, and royalty reporting. The company's clients include the world's most successful broadcasters, record labels, digital music services, wireless carriers, and consumer products companies." See http://www.musicreports.com/web/about.php. See also Ed Christman, "SiriusXM Attempting to License Directly from Labels," *Billboard* (8–11–2011), http://www.billboard.com/biz/articles/news/1176559/siriusxm-attempting-to-license-directly-from-labels.

37. Jeff Price, "Sirius-ly, It's Not One Size Fits All," *TuneCore* (blog) (11–10–2011), http://www.tunecore.com/blog/2011/11/sirius-ly-its-not-one-size-fits-all.html.

38. Ibid.

39. "Federal Copyright Protection for Pre-1972 Sound Recordings," Report of the Register of Copyrights (December 2011), http://www.copyright.gov/docs/sound/pre-72-report.pdf.

40. Hanna Karp, "Sirius Is Sued over Music Royalties for Pre-1972 Recordings," *Wall Street Journal* (8–26–2013), http://online.wsj.com/news/articles/SB1 0001424127887324591204579037260890310376.

41. Shirley Halperin and Eriq Gardner, "Major Labels Unite in Lawsuit against SiriusXM," *Hollywood Reporter* (9–11–2013), http://www.hollywoodreporter .com/thr-esq/major-labels-unite-lawsuit-siriusxm-627554.

42. Todd Spangler, "Sirius XM to Pay $210 Million to Record Companies for Pre-1972 Songs," *Variety* (6–26–2015), http://variety.com/2015/music /news/sirius-xm-settlement-record-companies-pre-1972-songs-1201529103/. Eriq Gardner, "Pandora Reaches $90 Million Settlement with Labels over Pre-1972 Music," *Billboard* (10–22–15), http://www.billboard.com/articles /business/6738203/pandora-settlement-record-labels-pre-1972-music-riaa.

43. Brian X. Chen, "April 28, 2003: Apple Opens iTunes Store," *Wired* (4–28–2010), http://www.wired.com/2010/04/0428itunes-music-store-opens/.

44. Long since removed by the company due to competition from DRM-free services and consumer complaints. For discussion of early DRM issues with iTunes purchases and the iPod player, see, for example, Josh Lowensohn, "Jury Finds Apple not Liable of Harming Consumers in iTunes DRM Case," *Verge* (12–16–2014), http://www.theverge.com/2014/12/16/7402695/jury-decision-in-iTunes-iPod-DRM-case.

45. Chen.

46. Alex Pham, "iTunes Market Share Still Dominant after a Decade (Research)," *Billboard Biz* (4–16–2013), http://www.billboard.com/biz/articles /news/1557486/itunes-market-share-still-dominant-after-a-decade-research.

47. SNOCAP, Shawn Fanning's post-Napster development, was a song registry and point-of-sale manager for web purchases. Ten years later, in 2014, Audiam (created by the founders of digital rights service TuneCore) enabled individuals to track user-produced covers or mashups of songs, sound recordings, and videos. Between the two, Soundcloud was established in 2007 as a collaborative platform for musicians, not as a "store." As it developed, however, Soundcloud's potential to integrate with Facebook and other social media made it an immensely valuable tool for promotion.

48. Josh Tyrangiel, "Radiohead Says: Pay What You Want," *Time Magazine* (10–1–2007), http://content.time.com/time/arts/article/0,8599,1666973,00 .html.

49. Eric Garland, "The 'In Rainbows' Experiment: Did It Work?" *NPR Music* (11–16–2009), http://www.npr.org/blogs/monitormix/2009/11/the_in _rainbows_experiment_did.html.

50. Adam Bychawski, "Radiohead Reveal How Successful 'In Rainbows' Download Really Was," NME (10–15–2008), http://www.nme.com/news/radio head/40444#wYJVSzrGTm1Zfb00.99..

51. Garland.

52. Stephen J. Dubner, "What's the Future of the Music Industry? A Freakonomics Quorum," *Freakonomics* (blog) (9–7–2007), http://freakonomics. com/2007/09/20/whats-the-future-of-the-music-industry-a-freakonomics-quorum/.

CHAPTER 11. STATE OF THE ART

1. John Cloud, "The YouTube Gurus," *Time Magazine* (12–25–2006), http://content.time.com/time/magazine/article/0,9171,1570795-5,00.html.

2. Todd Wasserman, "The Revolution Wasn't Televised: The Early Days of YouTube," Mashable (2–14–2015), http://mashable.com/2015/02/14/youtube-history/.

3. David Itzkoff, "Nerds in the Hood, Stars on the Web," *New York Times* (12–27–2005), http://www.nytimes.com/2005/12/27/arts/nerds-in-the-hood-stars-on-the-web.html.

4. Peter Kafka, "The Numbers behind the World's Fastest-Growing Web Site: YouTube's Finances Revealed," *All Things D* (3–19–2010), http://allthingsd.com/20100319/the-numbers-behind-the-worlds-fastest-growing-web-site-youtubes-finances-revealed/.

5. Leslie Kaufman, "Viacom and YouTube Settle Suit over Copyright Violations," *New York Times* (3–18–2014). http://www.nytimes.com/2014/03/19/business/media/viacom-and-youtube-settle-lawsuit-over-copyright.html?_r=0.

6. Greg Sandoval, "Source: Universal Music Group Plans 'Hulu-Like' Site," CNET (9–25–2008), http://www.cnet.com/news/source-universal-music-group-plans-hulu-like-site/.

7. Ibid.

8. Candace Lombardi, "YouTube Cuts Three Content Deals," CNET (10–9–2006), http://www.cnet.com/news/youtube-cuts-three-content-deals/.

9. Greg Sandoval, "Universal, YouTube Near Deal on Music Video Site," CNET (3–5–2009), http://www.cnet.com/news/universal-youtube-near-deal-on-music-video-site/.

10. Tom Lowry, "Vevo Aims to Help Music Companies Cash in on Video," *Business Week* (12–6–2009), http://www.businessweek.com/technology/content/dec2009/tc2009126_307441.htm.

11. Alex Pham, "YouTube Confirms Vevo Deal," *Billboard* (7–2–2013), http://www.billboard.com/biz/articles/news/digital-and-mobile/1568816/youtube-confirms-vevo-deal.

12. For more information about Merlin, see http://www.merlinnetwork.org/. For more information about the Worldwide Independent Network see http://winformusic.org/.

13. Hugh McIntyre, "YouTube Is About to Delete Independent Artists from Its Site," *Forbes* (6–18–2014), http://www.forbes.com/sites/hughmcintyre/2014/06/18/youtube-is-about-to-delete-independent-artists-from-its-site/.

14. Robert Cookson, "YouTube to Block Indie Labels as It Launches Paid Music Service," *Financial Times* (6–17–2014), http://www.ft.com/intl/cms/s/0/ea6728e2-f568-11e3-afd3-00144feabdco.html#axzz3D209sr42.

15. "Listen.com Buys TuneTo.com," *Ad Week* (4–5–2001), http://www.adweek.com/news/advertising/listencom-buys-tunetocom-47939.

16. Benny Evangelista, "Industry Starting to Endorse Net Music/Listen.com to Offer Songs from All Five Major Labels," *SF Gate* (7–1–2002), http://www.sfgate.com/business/article/Industry-starting-to-endorse-Net-music-2801248.php.

17. Curt Woodward, "Rhapsody at 10 Years: Surviving Long Enough to Face a Herd of New Competitors," *Xconomy* (1–30–2011), http://www.xconomy.com/seattle/2011/11/30/rhapsody-at-10/.

18. Ibid. For information about Rhapsody and its products today, see the company's website: www.rhapsody.com.

19. For more details on how the Music Genome works see Rob Walker, "The Song Decoders," *New York Times* (10–14–2009), http://www.nytimes.com/2009/10/18/magazine/18Pandora-t.html?pagewanted = all.

20. Amadou Diallo, "Pandora Radio's Dominance Built on Big Data Edge," *Forbes* (10–6–2013), http://www.forbes.com/sites/amadoudiallo/2013/10/06/pandora-radios-dominance-built-on-big-data-edge/.

21. Stephanie Clifford, "Pandora's Long Strange Trip," *Inc.* (10–1–2007), http://www.inc.com/magazine/20071001/pandoras-long-strange-trip_pagen_2.html.

22. Ibid.

23. "Pandora Announces September 2013 Audience Metrics," Pandora Pressroom (10–02–2013), http://press.pandora.com/phoenix.zhtml?c = 251764 &p = irol-newsArticle&ID = 1860867&highlight =.

24. Glenn Peoples, "Pandora Now Sharing Listener Data with Artists," *Billboard* (10–22–2014), http://www.billboard.com/articles/business/6289343/pandora-now-sharing-listener-data-with-artists.

25. Ibid.

26. Pandora recently moved to strengthen its data analytics dominance with the acquisition of Next Big Sound, a music analytics company specializing in tracking streaming and social media activity. See Glenn Peoples, "Pandora Acquires Next Big Sound," *Billboard* (5–19–2015), http://www.billboard.com/articles/business/6568814/pandora-acquires-next-big-sound.

27. Spotifysehr, "We've Only Just Begun!" Spotify (10–7–2008), https://news.spotify.com/us/2008/10/07/weve-only-just-begun/.

28. Brendan Greeley, "Daniel Ek's Spotify: Music's Last Best Hope," *Business Week* (7–13–2011), http://www.businessweek.com/magazine/daniel-eks-spotify-musics-last-best-hope-07142011.html.

29. Ibid.

30. Brendan Greeley, "Spotify's Ek Wins over Music Pirates with Labels' Approval," *Bloomberg Business* (7–14–2011), http://www.bloomberg.com/news/articles/2011-07-14/spotify-wins-over-music-pirates-with-labels-approval-correct-.

31. Irving Azoff, record executive and Live Nation CEO, quoted in Greeley, "Daniel Ek's Spotify."

32. Swedish musician Magnus Uggla quoted by Hellienne Lindvall, "Behind the Music: The Real Reason Why the Major Labels Love Spotify," *Guardian* (blog) (8–17–2009), http://www.theguardian.com/music/musicblog/2009/aug/17/major-labels-spotify.

33. Rebecca Rosen, "Forgotify: The Tool for Discovering Spotify's 4 Million Unheard Tracks," *Atlantic* (1–30–2014), http://www.theatlantic.com/technology/archive/2014/01/forgotify-the-tool-for-discovering-spotifys-4-million-unheard-tracks/283484/.

34. Jason Palmer, "Analytics at Spotify," Spotify Labs (5–13–2013), https://labs.spotify.com/2013/05/13/analytics-at-spotify/.

35. Ben Sisario, "As Music Streaming Grows, Spotify Reports Rising Revenue and a Loss," *New York Times* (11–25–2014), http://www.nytimes.com/2014/11/26/business/spotify-discloses-revenue-but-not-its-future-plans.html?_r = 0.

36. Ben Sisario, "Spotify's Revenue Is Growing, but So Are Its Losses," *New York Times* (5–8–2015), http://www.nytimes.com/2015/05/09/business/media/as-spotify-expands-revenue-rises-and-losses-deepen.html.

37. Sheehy quoted in Julia Greenberg, "Spotify Is Worth $8 Billion? It's Not as Crazy as It Sounds," *Wired* (4–14–2015), http://www.wired.com/2015/04/spotify-worth-8-billion-not-crazy-sounds/.

38. Ibid.

39. Bobby Owsinski, "Amazon Prime Adds Music: The Good and the Bad," *Forbes* (6–12–2014), http://www.forbes.com/sites/bobbyowsinski/2014/06/12/amazon-prime-adds-music-the-good-and-the-bad/.

40. Laurie Segall, "How Too-Early Startup Shazam Survived a Decade," *CNN Money* (3–6–2012), http://money.cnn.com/2012/03/06/technology/shazam/.

41. Devin Leonard, "Shazam Comes Out of the Shadows," *Fortune* (10–17–2008), http://archive.fortune.com/2008/10/15/technology/shazam.fortune/index.htm?postversion = 2008101705.

42. Farhad Manjoo, "That Tune, Named," *Slate* (10–19–2009), http://www.slate.com/articles/technology/technology/2009/10/that_tune_named.html.

43. Parmy Olson, "Shazam Hits 100 Million Active Users as It Gears Up for IPO," *Forbes* (8–20–2014), http://www.forbes.com/sites/parmyolson/2014/08/20/shazam-hits-100-million-active-users-as-it-gears-up-for-ipo/.

44. Segall.

45. Ibid.

46. Manjoo.

47. Laura Montini, "Shazam vs. Spotify: Which Startup Can Predict the Grammys?" *Inc.* (2–6–2015), http://www.inc.com/laura-montini/spotify-v-shazam-which-is-the-better-predictor-of-grammy-winners.html.

48. Eliot Van Buskirk, "Best Grammy Prediction Data: Shazam or Spotify?" *Evolver.fm* (2–11–2013), http://evolver.fm/2013/02/11/best-grammy-prediction-data-shazam-or-spotify/.

49. Max Willens, "Shazam and Spotify's Grammy Picks Are More Accurate Than Billboard's. Here's Why," *International Business Times* (2–6–2015), http://www.ibtimes.com/shazam-spotifys-grammy-picks-are-more-accurate-billboards-heres-why-1808170.

50. Marc Schneider, "Grammys 2015: Most Shazamed Moments Belong to ELO, Katy Perry, Ed Sheeran," *Billboard* (2–9–2015), http://www.billboard.com/articles/events/grammys-2015/6465702/most-shazamed-moments-grammys-elo-katy-perry-ed-sheeran.

51. Stuart Dredge, "Spotify Opens Up Analytics in Effort to Prove Its Worth to Doubting Musicians," *Guardian* (3–12–2013), http://www.theguardian.com/technology/2013/dec/03/spotify-analytics-musicians-streaming-music-artists-earn.

52. Sasha Frere-Jones, "If You Care about Music, Should You Ditch Spotify?" *New Yorker* (7–19–2013), http://www.newyorker.com/culture/sasmakingha-frere-jones/if-you-care-about-music-should-you-ditch-spotify.

53. Damon Krukowski, "Making Cents," *Pitchfork* (11–14–2012), http://pitchfork.com/features/articles/8993-the-cloud/.

54. Jeff Price, "The Democratization of the Music Industry," *Huffington Post* (5–25–2011), http://www.huffingtonpost.com/jeff-price/the-democratization-of-th_b_93065.html.

55. Ibid.

56. Pricing information from www.TuneCore.com.

57. Ed Christman, "Jeff Price, Peter Wells, TuneCore Co-Founders, Launch Audiam," *New York Times* (6–12–2013), http://www.billboard.com/biz/articles/news/digital-and-mobile/1566513/jeff-price-peter-wells-tunecore-co-founders-launch.

58. Ben Sisario, "Out to Shake Up Music, Often with Sharp Words," *New York Times* (5–6–2012), http://www.nytimes.com/2012/05/07/business/TuneCore-chief-shakes-up-music-with-his-own-words.html?pagewanted = all.

59. Paul Resnikoff, "I'm Jeff Price. And This Is My New Company, Audiam . . .," *Digital Music News* (6–12–2013), http://www.digitalmusicnews.com/permalink/2013/06/12/audiem.

60. Lora Kolodny, "Audiam Raises $2M to 'Get People Paid' for Use of Their Music on YouTube," *Wall Street Journal* (3–4–2014), http://blogs.wsj.com/venturecapital/2014/03/04/audiam-raises-2m-to-get-people-paid-for-use-of-their-music-on-youtube/.

61. Jake Smith, "Over the Past 12 Years, Streaming Services Have Failed to Pay $100 Million In Royalties . . . ," *Digital Music News* (9–3–2014), http://www.digitalmusicnews.com/permalink/2014/09/03/past-12-years-streaming-services-failed-pay-100-million-royalties.

62. The YouTube Partner Program allows content creators to monetize their content through advertising, subscriptions, and merchandise (through links to external vendors). The company provides users resources for building individual channels and audiences for them, as well as data via YouTube Analytics. See "What Is the YouTube Partner Program" at https://support.google.com/youtube/answer/72851?hl = en.

63. Joel Warner, "Fueled by Venture-Capital Funding and a Love for Unknown Bands, Can Boulder's Next Big Sound Predict the Next Rock Star?" *Westword* (10–7–2010), http://www.westword.com/music/fueled-by-venture-capital-funding-and-a-love-for-unknown-bands-can-boulders-next-big-sound-predict-the-next-rock-star-5110133.

64. Ibid.

65. Ibid.

66. Ibid.

67. "Unparalleled Music Intelligence for Brands," https://www.nextbigsound.com/brands.

68. "About—Why Next Big Sound?" https://www.nextbigsound.com/about#wrap.

69. Ibid.

70. Pandora announced the acquisition Next Big Sound on May 19, 2015. See Peoples.

71. Chris Reidy, "Sonicbids CEO Panos Panay Is Leaving the Company He Founded," *Boston Globe* (11–13–2013), http://archive.boston.com/business /innovation/blogs/inside-the-hive/2013/11/13/sonicbids-ceo-panos-panay-leaving-the-company-founded/SsxJty4SgwtRvINsjxtULP/blog.

72. Ibid.

73. Ben Sisario, "Backstage to Acquire Sonicbids" (1–30–2013), *New York Times,* http://mediadecoder.blogs.nytimes.com/2013/01/30/backstage-to-acquire-sonicbids/?_r = 0.

74. Backstage Staff, "Backstage Acquires Sonicbids" (1–30–2013, *Backstage,* http://www.backstage.com/news/backstage-acquires-sonicbids/.

75. "Kickstarter Crowdfunding Site Officially Launches in Canada," *CBC News* (9–10–2013), http://www.cbc.ca/news/business/kickstarter-crowdfunding-site-officially-launches-in-canada-1.1703774.

76. Andrew Flanagan, "YouTube Announces Crowdfunding, Donations, Free Music," *Billboard* (6–27–2014), http://www.billboard.com/biz/articles/news /digital-and-mobile/6140819/youtube-announces-crowdfunding-donations-free-music.

77. Sarah McKinney, "Patreon: A Fast-Growing Marketplace for Creators and Patrons of the Arts" (4–10–2014), *Forbes,* http://www.forbes.com/sites /sarahmckinney/2014/04/10/patreon-a-fast-growing-marketplace-for-creators-and-patrons-of-the-arts/.

78. Alvin Toffler, *Future Shock*, Random House (1970); William Deresiewicz, "The Death of the Artist and the Rise of the Creative Entrepreneur," *Atlantic* (January/February 2015), http://www.theatlantic.com/magazine/archive /2015/01/the-death-of-the-artist-and-the-birth-of-the-creative-entrepreneur /383497/.

79. Deresiewicz.

80. Ibid.

81. Janelle Brown, "The Jukebox Manifesto," *Salon* (11–13–2000), http:// www.salon.com/2000/11/13/jukebox/.

Bibliography

Abel, Richard, and Charles Altman. *The Sounds of Early Cinema.* Indiana University Press (2001).

Abrams, Howard B. "Copyright's First Compulsory License." *Santa Clara High Technology Law Journal* 26.2 (2009). http://digitalcommons.law.scu.edu/cgi/viewcontent.cgi?article=1499&context=chtlj.

Adweek Staff. "Listen.com Buys TuneTo.com." *Adweek* (4–5–2001). http://www.adweek.com/news/advertising/listencom-buys-tunetocom-47939.

Alexander, Scott. "The First Jazz Record." http://www.redhotjazz.com/jazz1917.html.

Allison, Deborah. "'Do Not Forsake Me: The Ballad of High Noon' and the Rise of the Movie Theme Song." *Senses of Cinema* (October 2003). http://sensesofcinema.com/2003/cinema-and-music/ballad_of_high_noon/#3.

Almind, Gert. "History of Coin-Operated Phonographs" (unpublished MS dated 2–23–2015).http://coin-o-phone.com/history.pdf.

Backstage Staff. "Backstage Acquires Sonicbids" (1–30–2013). Backstage. http://www.backstage.com/news/backstage-acquires-sonicbids/.

Barnum, P. T. *The Life of P. T. Barnum.* American Museum/P. T Barnum (1855).

Berlatsky, Norah. "Elvis Wasn't the First to Steal Black Music: 10 White Artists Who 'Borrowed' from R&B before the King." *Salon* (5–17–2014). http://www.salon.com/2014/05/17/elvis_wasnt_the_first/.

Billboard. "Madonna Close to Massive Deal with Live Nation." *Billboard* (10–11–2007). http://www.billboard.com/articles/news/1048285/madonna-close-to-massive-deal-with-live-nation.

Billboard. "Madonna's 'Confessions' Tour Sets Record." *Billboard* (9–20–2006). http://www.billboard.com/articles/news/57197/madonnas-confessions-tour-sets-record.

Binder, Steve. "Question: Primetime Variety—'Whatever Happened to It?' Answer: It's Alive and Well in the Hands of the Wrong People." *Caucus Journal* (Spring 2000). http://www.caucus.org/archives/oospr_primetimevariety .html.

Blitzstein, Joel. "Watch Martin Scorsese Break Down 'The Last Waltz.'" *Rolling Stone* (11–26–2014). http://www.rollingstone.com/movies/videos/martin-scorsese-talks-the-last-waltz-20141126#ixzz3wkx6jYM6.

Blumentrath, Jan. "Interview with Jeff Hanson" (9–13–2010). Hit Quarters. http://www.hitquarters.com/index.php3?page = intrview/opar/intrview_Jeff _Hanson_Interview.html.

Bourdieu, Bourdieu. "The Forms of Capital." In *Handbook of Theory and Research for the Sociology of Education,* edited by J. Richardson. Greenwood (1986).

Bouwman, Kimbel. "Interview with PANOS PANAY, CEO of Sonicbids" (7–5–2010). Hit Quarters. http://www.hitquarters.com/index.php3?page = intrview /opar/intrview_Panos_Panay_Interview.html#ixzz3bFpp2Yxo.

Boyd, Douglas A. "Digital Audio Recording: The Basics." In *Oral History in the Digital Age,* edited by Douglas A. Boyd, Steve Cohen, Brad Rakerd, and Dean Rehberger. Institute of Museum and Library Services (2012). http:// ohda.matrix.msu.edu/2012/06/digital-audio-recording/.

Brandie, Lars. "Live Nation Completes Deal for C3 Presents." *Billboard* (12–22–2014). http://www.billboard.com/articles/business/6414053/live-nation-completes-deal-for-c3-presents.

Brenner, Lisa. "Hear Thomas Edison's Earliest Known Recording from 1878 for the First Time (Audio)." KPCC (10–25–2012). http://www.scpr.org/blogs /news/2012/10/25/10712/hear-thomas-edison-sing-rare-1878-audio-restored-f/.

Broven, John. *Record Makers and Breakers: Voices of the Independent Rock 'n' Roll Pioneers.* University of Illinois (2009).

Brown, Janelle. "The Jukebox Manifesto." *Salon* (11–13–2000). http://www .salon.com/2000/11/13/jukebox/.

Bruenger, David. "Musical Experience as Transaction: Complexity, Adaptive Expertise, and Operative Concepts in the Music Business Curriculum." *MEIEA Journal* 15.1 (2015), 99–119. http://www.meiea.org/Journal/Vol.15 /Bruenger-MEIEA_Journal_2015_Vol_15_No_1_p99.pdf.

Bunch, Joey, and Ricardo Baca. "Barry Fey, Legendary Colorado Concert Promoter, Dies at 73." *Denver Post* (4–28–2013). http://www.denverpost.com /ci_23127822/legendary-colorado-concert-promoter-barry-fey-dies.

Bychawski, Adam. "Radiohead Reveal How Successful 'In Rainbows' Download Really Was." NME (10–15–2008). http://www.nme.com/news/radiohe ad/40444#wYJVSzrGTm1Zfboo.99.

Byrne, David. "David Byrne's Survival Strategies for Emerging Artists—and Megastars." *Wired* 16.1 (12–18–2007). http://archive.wired.com/entertain-ment/music/magazine/16–01/ff_byrne?currentPage = all.

Callahan, Mike, and David Edwards. "The Chess Story." Both Sides Now (11–4–2005). http://www.bsnpubs.com/chess/chesscheck.html.

Canadian Press. "Kickstarter Crowdfunding Site Officially Launches in Canada." *CBC News* (9–10–2013). http://www.cbc.ca/news/business/kickstarter-crowdfunding-site-officially-launches-in-canada-1.1703774.

Carroll, Michael. "The Struggle for Music Copyright" (Working Paper No. 2005–7). Villanova University School of Law, Public Law and Legal Theory. http://www.floridalawreview.com/wp-content/uploads/2010/01/Carroll-BOOK.pdf.

Chattman, Jon. "'It's Time' for Imagine Dragons: An Interview with Front Man Dan." *Huffington Post* (5–2–2012). http://www.huffingtonpost.com/jon-chattman/imagine-dragons_b_1468394.html.

Chen, Brian X. "April 28, 2003: Apple Opens iTunes Store." *Wired* (4–28–2010). http://www.wired.com/2010/04/0428itunes-music-store-opens/.

Christman, Ed. "Jeff Price, Peter Wells, TuneCore Co-Founders, Launch Audiam." *New York Times* (6–12–2013). http://www.billboard.com/biz/articles/news/digital-and-mobile/1566513/jeff-price-peter-wells-tunecore-co-founders-launch.

———. "Reversion Rights: Will 2013 Be a Game-Changer?" *Billboard* (12–27–2012). https://www.billboard.com/biz/articles/news/1483926/reversion-rights-will-2013-be-a-game-changer.

———. "SiriusXM Attempting to License Directly from Labels." *Billboard* (8–11–2011). http://www.billboard.com/biz/articles/news/1176559/siriusxm-attempting-to-license-directly-from-labels.

———. "U.S. Dept. of Justice to Review ASCAP and BMI Consent Decrees." *Billboard Biz* (6–4–2014). https://www.billboard.com/biz/articles/news/legal-and-management/6106492/us-dept-of-justice-to-review-ascap-and-bmi-consent.

Clifford, Stephanie. "Pandora's Long Strange Trip." *Inc.* (10–1–2007). http://www.inc.com/magazine/20071001/pandoras-long-strange-trip_pagen_2.html.

Cloud, John. "The YouTube Gurus" (12–25–2006). *Time Magazine*. http://content.time.com/time/magazine/article/0,9171,1570795-5,00.html.

CNN. "Sony, BMG Agree on Music Merger." CNN (11–7–2003). http://edition.cnn.com/2003/BUSINESS/11/06/sony.bmg.reut/.

Cole, Tom. "You Ask, We Answer: What Exactly Is a 360 Deal?" (11–24–2010). *Record, Music News from NPR*. http://www.npr.org/sections/therecord/2010/11/24/131574836/you-ask-we-answer-what-exactly-is-a-360-deal.

Conte, Jack, and Nataly Dawn. "No Record Label Necessary, Just Pomplamoose." *TEDxStanford* (6–11–2014). http://tedxtalks.ted.com/video/No-record-label-necessary-just.

Cookson, Robert. "YouTube to Block Indie Labels as It Launches Paid Music Service." *Financial Times* (6–17–2014). http://www.ft.com/intl/cms/s/0/ea6728e2-f568-11e3-afd3-00144feabdc0.html#axzz3D209sr42.

Coroneos, Kyle [Trigger]. "How Music Row and Acuff-Rose Killed the Everly Brothers." Saving Country Music (1–4–2014). http://www.savingcountrymusic.com/how-music-row-acuff-rose-killed-the-everly-brothers.

Cuff, Daniel F. "RCA Records Plans Bertelsmann Link." *New York Times* (6–13–1984). http://www.nytimes.com/1984/06/13/business/rca-records-plans-bertelsmann-link.html.

Cunningham, Hugh. *Leisure in the Industrial Revolution, c. 1780-c. 1880.* Taylor and Francis (1980).

Cusic, Don. "Acuff-Rose." *Tennessee Encyclopedia* (12–25–2009). http://tennesseeencyclopedia.net/entry.php?rec = 4.

Daniel, Wayne W. "Charlie D. Tillman (1861–1943)." *New Georgia Encyclopedia* (11–15–2013). http://www.georgiaencyclopedia.org/articles/arts-culture/charlie-d-tillman-1861–1943.

Davis, Carl. "Charlie Chaplin's Film Music." *Guardian* (12–31–2010). http://www.theguardian.com/culture/2011/jan/01/carl-davis-charlie-chaplin-soundtracks.

Deresiewicz, William. "The Death of the Artist and the Rise of the Creative Entrepreneur." *Atlantic* (January/February 2015). http://www.theatlantic.com/magazine/archive/2015/01/the-death-of-the-artist-and-the-birth-of-the-creative-entrepreneur/383497/.

Diallo, Amadou. "Pandora Radio's Dominance Built on Big Data Edge" (10–6–2013). *Forbes.* http://www.forbes.com/sites/amadoudiallo/2013/10/06/pandora-radios-dominance-built-on-big-data-edge/.

Dideriksen, Gabriella, and Matthew Ringel. "Frederick Gye and 'the Dreadful Business of Opera Management.'" *19th Century Music* 19.1 (Summer 1995), 3–30.

Dredge, Stuart. "Spotify Opens Up Analytics in Effort to Prove Its Worth to Doubting Musicians." *Guardian* (3–12–2013). http://www.theguardian.com/technology/2013/dec/03/spotify-analytics-musicians-streaming-music-artists-earn.

Driessens, Olivier. "Celebrity Capital: Redefining Celebrity Using Field Theory." *Theory and Society* 42.5 (September 2013), 543–560.

Dubner, Stephen J. "What's the Future of the Music Industry? A Freakonomics Quorum" *Freakonomics* (blog) (9–7–2007). http://freakonomics.com/2007/09/20/whats-the-future-of-the-music-industry-a-freakonomics-quorum/.

DuBois, Shelley. "Are Advertisers the New Record Labels?" *Fortune* (3–14–2012). http://fortune.com/2012/03/14/are-advertisers-the-new-record-labels/.

Durenberger, Mark. "Behind the Clear-Channel Matter." http://www.oldradio.com/archives/general/clears.htm.

Echols, Alice. *Scars of Sweet Paradise: The Life and Times of Janis Joplin.* Macmillan (1999).

Edwards, Gavin. "'We Are the World': A Minute-by-Minute Breakdown on Its 30th Anniversary." *Rolling Stone* (3–6–2015). http://www.rollingstone.com/music/features/we-are-the-world-a-minute-by-minute-breakdown-30th-anniversary-20150306.

Evangelista, Benny. "Industry Starting to Endorse Net Music/Listen.com to Offer Songs from All Five Major Labels." *SF Gate* (7–1–2002). http://www.sfgate.com/business/article/Industry-starting-to-endorse-Net-music-2801248.php.

Farber, Jim. "Beatles' Historic Arrival in New York City 50 Years Ago Gave Big Apple Unforgettable Lift." *New York Daily News* (1–24–2014). http://www.nydailynews.com/new-york/beatles-electrified-nyc-50-years-article-1.1590579.

Fisher, William Arms. *One Hundred and Fifty Years of Music Publishing in the United States*. Oliver Ditson (1933).

Flanagan, Andrew. "YouTube Announces Crowdfunding, Donations, Free Music." *Billboard* (6–27–2014). http://www.billboard.com/biz/articles/news/digital-and-mobile/6140819/youtube-announces-crowdfunding-donations-free-music.

Florida, Richard, and Scott Jackson. "Sonic City: The Evolving Geography of the Music Industry" (Working Paper, January 2008). Martin Prosperity Institute, University of Toronto. http://www-2.rotman.utoronto.ca/userfiles/prosperity/File/Sonic%20City%20RF3.w.cover.pdf.

Florida, Richard, Charlotta Mellander, and Kevin Solarik. "From Music Scenes to Music Clusters: The Economic Geography of Music in the U.S., 1970-2000" (Working Paper, June 2009). Martin Prosperity Institute, University of Toronto. http://martinprosperity.org/media/pdfs/Manuscript_Music_Scenes_to_Music_Clusters_June_2009.pdf.

Fones-Wolf, Elizabeth. "Sound Comes to the Movies: The Philadelphia Musicians' Struggle against Recorded Music." *Pennsylvania Magazine of History and Biography* 118.1/2 (January/April 1994). http://journals.psu.edu/pmhb/issue/view/2547.

Ford, Peter. "Rock around the Clock and Me." http://www.peterford.com/ratc.html.

Fowler, Gene, and Bill Crawford. "Border Radio." *Handbook of Texas Online*. http://www.tshaonline.org/handbook/online/articles/ebb01.

Francis, Joel. "The True Story of Cadillac Records: The Final Days and Legacy of Chess Records." *Daily Record* (12–12–2008). http://joelfrancis.com/2008/12/08/the-real-cadillac-records-three/.

Freed, Lance. "My Father and the Moondog Coronation Ball." Rock and Roll Hall of Fame. http://rockhall.com/story-of-rock/features/all-featured/7487_alan-freed-the-moondog-coronation-ball-lance-freed/.

Frere-Jones, Sasha. "If You Care about Music, Should You Ditch Spotify?" *New Yorker* (7–19–2013). http://www.newyorker.com/culture/sasmakingha-frere-jones/if-you-care-about-music-should-you-ditch-spotify.

Freydkin, Donna. "Lilith Fair: Lovely, Lively and Long Overdue." *CNN Interactive* (7–28–1998). http://www.cnn.com/SHOWBIZ/Music/9807/28/lilith.fair/.

Feuer, Alan and Jason George. "Internet Fame Is Cruel Mistress for a Dancer of the Numa Numa." *New York Times* (2–26–2005). http://www.nytimes.com/2005/02/26/nyregion/internet-fame-is-cruel-mistress-for-a-dancer-of-the-numa-numa.html?_r=0.

Future of Music Coalition. "Public Performance Right for Sound Recordings." *Future of Music Coalition* (11–5–2013). https://www.futureofmusic.org/article/fact-sheet/public-performance-right-sound-recordings.

Ganz, Caryn. "Lady Gaga 'Artpop' Review." *Rolling Stone* (7–13–2013). http://www.rollingstone.com/music/albumreviews/artpop-20131113.

Ganz, Jacob. "Live Nation Stumbles over Summer Concert Sales." *NPR Music* (7–13–2010). http://www.npr.org/templates/story/story.php?storyId = 128473078.

Ganz, Jacob, and Joel Rose. "The MP3: A History of Innovation and Betrayal." *The Record,* NPR (2–23–2011). http://www.npr.org/sections/therecord /2011/03/23/134622940/the-mp3-a-history-of-innovation-and-betrayal.

Gardner, Eriq. "'American Idol' Winner Files Bold Legal Claim to Escape 'Oppressive' Contracts." *Hollywood Reporter* (1–26–2015). http://www .hollywoodreporter.com/thr-esq/american-idol-winner-files-bold-767088.

———. "Pandora Reaches $90 Million Settlement with Labels over Pre-1972 Music." *Billboard* (10–22–15). http://www.billboard.com/articles/business /6738203/pandora-settlement-record-labels-pre-1972-music-riaa.

Garland, Eric. "The 'In Rainbows' Experiment: Did It Work?" *NPR Music* (11–16–2009). http://www.npr.org/blogs/monitormix/2009/11/the_in_ rainbows_experiment_did.html.

Gill, Andy. "Album Review: Lady Gaga, ARTPOP—It's Hard Not to Feel Underwhelmed." *Independent* (11–7–2013). http://www.independent.co.uk /arts-entertainment/music/reviews/album-review-lady-gaga-Artpop—its- hard-not-to-feel-underwhelmed-8926676.html.

Goldman, David. "Music's Lost Decade: Sales Cut in Half." *CNN Money* (2–3– 2010). http://money.cnn.com/2010/02/02/news/companies/napster_music_ industry/.

Gould, Jonathan. *Can't Buy Me Love: The Beatles, Britain, and America.* Three Rivers Press (2007).

Greeley, Brendan. "Daniel Ek's Spotify: Music's Last Best Hope." *Business Week* (7–13–2011). http://www.businessweek.com/magazine/daniel-eks-spotify- musics-last-best-hope-07142011.html.

———. "Spotify's Ek Wins over Music Pirates with Labels' Approval" (7– 14–2011). *Bloomberg Business.* http://www.bloomberg.com/news/articles /2011-07-14/spotify-wins-over-music-pirates-with-labels-approval- correct-.

Green, Stanley. "Jukebox Piracy." *Atlantic* (April 1962). http://www.theatlantic .com/magazine/archive/1962/04/jukebox-piracy/305829/.

Greenberg, Julia. "Spotify Is Worth $8 Billion? It's Not as Crazy as It Sounds" (4–14–2015). *Wired.* http://www.wired.com/2015/04/spotify-worth-8-billion- not-crazy-sounds/.

[Guest]. "The History of File Sharing." *Torrent Freak* (4–22–2012). https://tor- rentfreak.com/the-history-of-filesharing-120422/.

Hahn, Michael. "How the Rolling Stones Became Music's Biggest Business." *Guardian* (5–22–2014). http://www.theguardian.com/music/musicblog/2014 /may/22/how-the-rolling-stones-became-musics-biggest-business.

Halperin, Shirley. "RCA Execs Confirm Jive and Arista Labels Shut Down." *Hollywood Reporter* (10–7–2011). http://www.hollywoodreporter.com/news /rca-execs-confirm-jive-arista-245392.

Halperin, Shirley, and Eriq Gardner. "Major Labels Unite in Lawsuit against Sir- iusXM." *Hollywood Reporter* (9–11–2013). http://www.hollywoodreporter .com/thr-esq/major-labels-unite-lawsuit-siriusxm-627554.

Harkey, Tomomi. "Bonneville International Corp, v. Peters: Considering Copyright Rules to Facilitate Licensing for Webcasting." *Berkeley Technology Law Journal* 20.1 (January 2005). http://scholarship.law.berkeley.edu/cgi/viewcontent.cgi?article=1542&context=btlj.

Harmon, Amy. "The Napster Decision: The Reaction; Napster Users Make Plans for the Day the Free Music Dies." *New York Times* (2–13–2001). http://www.nytimes.com/2001/02/13/business/napster-decision-reaction-napster-users-make-plans-for-day-free-music-dies.html.

Henahan, Donal. "Our Orchestras Are Splintering." *New York Times* (8–13–1987). http://www.nytimes.com/1987/09/13/arts/music-view-our-orchestras-are-splintering.html.

Hewett, Ivan. "The Proms and the Promenerders." *Daily Telegraph* (London) (7–12–2007). http://www.telegraph.co.uk/culture/music/classicalmusic/3666494/The-Proms-and-the-Promenerders.html.

Heyman, Stephen. "The Fast-Changing Economics of the Movie Blockbuster." *New York Times* (7–8–2015). http://www.nytimes.com/2015/07/09/arts/international/the-fast-changing-economics-of-the-movie-blockbuster.html?_r = 0.

Hillburn, Robert. "Eternal Revenue : Elvis' Millions Were Disappearing When Priscilla Presley Took Charge and Rebuilt the King's Fortune." *Los Angeles Times* (6–11–1989). http://articles.latimes.com/1989-06-11/magazine/tm-2866_1_joseph-hanks-vernon-presley-films-or-records. http://articles.latimes.com/1989-06-11/magazine/tm-2866_1_joseph-hanks-vernon-presley-films-or-records.

Howard, John Tasker, Ray Lev, and Dorothy B. Commins. *A Treasury of Stephen Foster*. Random House (1946).

Howse, Pat, and Jimmy Phillips. "Godfather of Delta Blues: H. C. Speir." Originally published in *Peavey Monitor Magazine* (1995). http://www.bluesworld.com/SpierIntro.html.

Hughes, James. "Can't Get You out of My Head: The History of Advertising Jingles, a Truly American Art Form." *Slate* (9–7–2012). http://www.slate.com/articles/arts/books/2012/09/music_in_advertising_timothy_taylor_s_the_sounds_of_capitalism_reviewed_.html.

Hutchinson, Lydia. "Alan Freed and the Radio Payola Scandal." *Performing Songwriter* (11–20–2013). http://performingsongwriter.com/alan-freed-payola-scandal/.

Itzkoff, David. "Nerds in the Hood, Stars on the Web." *New York Times* (12–27–2005). http://www.nytimes.com/2005/12/27/arts/nerds-in-the-hood-stars-on-the-web.html.

Johns, Adrian. *Piracy: The Intellectual Property Wars from Gutenberg to Gates*. University of Chicago Press (2009).

Johnson, Rachel. "Material Girls: There's One Huge Difference between Madonna and Beyoncé." *Quartz* (3–21–2014). http://qz.com/193390/theres-one-huge-difference-between-beyonce-and-madonna/.

Kafka, Peter. "The Numbers behind the World's Fastest-Growing Web Site: YouTube's Finances Revealed." *All Things D* (3–19–2010). http://allthingsd.com/20100319/the-numbers-behind-the-worlds-fastest-growing-web-site-youtubes-finances-revealed/.

Kappers, Rogier. *Lomax, the Song Hunter.* PBS (8–22–2006). http://www.pbs.org/pov/lomax/.

Karp, Hanna. "Sirius Is Sued over Music Royalties for Pre-1972 Recordings." *Wall Street Journal* (8–26–2013). http://online.wsj.com/news/articles/SB10001424127887324591204579037260890310376.

Kaufman, Leslie. "Viacom and YouTube Settle Suit over Copyright Violations." *New York Times* (3–18–2014). http://www.nytimes.com/2014/03/19/business/media/viacom-and-youtube-settle-lawsuit-over-copyright.html?_r=0.

Kohn, Al, and Bob Kohn. *Kohn on Music Licensing.* 2nd ed. Aspen (1996).

Kolodny, Lora. "Audiam Raises $2M to 'Get People Paid' for Use of Their Music on YouTube." *Wall Street Journal* (3–4–2014). http://blogs.wsj.com/venturecapital/2014/03/04/audiam-raises-2m-to-get-people-paid-for-use-of-their-music-on-youtube/.

Kraft, James P. "The 'Pit' Musicians: Mechanization in the Movie Theaters, 1926–1934." *Labor History* 35.1 (2–28–2007), 66–89.

Kravets, David. "Napster Trial Ends Seven Years Later, Defining Online Sharing along the Way." *Wired* (8–31–2007). http://www.wired.com/2007/08/napster-trial-e/.

Kreps, Daniel. "Nipple Ripples: 10 Years of Fallout from Janet Jackson's Halftime Show." *Rolling Stone* (1–30–2014). http://www.rollingstone.com/culture/news/nipple-ripples-10-years-of-fallout-from-janet-jacksons-halftime-show-20140130#ixzz3CAKv8vvR.

Krukowski, Damon. "Making Cents." *Pitchfork* (11–14–2012). http://pitchfork.com/features/articles/8993-the-cloud/.

Kunhardt, Philip B., Jr., Philip B. Kunhardt III, and Peter W. Kunhardt. *P. T. Barnum: America's Greatest Showman.* Alfred A. Knopf (1995).

Landrum, Gene N. *Paranoia and Power: Fear and Fame of Entertainment Icons.* Morgan James Publishing (2007).

Law, Benjamin. "Troye Sivan, the Most Famous Teenager You've Never Heard of." *Sydney Morning Herald* (2–27–2015). http://www.smh.com.au/good-weekend/troye-sivan-the-most-famous-teenager-youve-never-heard-of-20150209-13a11r.html.

Lebrecht, Norman. "The Future of Music is Free." *La Scena Musicale* (1–23–2008). http://www.scena.org/columns/lebrecht/080123-NL-future.html.

Leonard, Devin. "Shazam Comes out of the Shadows." *Fortune* (10–17–2008). http://archive.fortune.com/2008/10/15/technology/shazam.fortune/index.htm?postversion=2008101705.

Lewis, Randy. "Fair Play, Fair Pay Act of 2015 Would Require Radio to Pay for Music." *Los Angeles Times* (4–13–2015). http://www.latimes.com/entertainment/music/posts/la-et-ms-fair-play-fair-pay-act-congress-radio-royalties-20150413-story.html.

Lieberman, Marvin B., and David B. Montgomery. "First-Mover Advantages." *Strategic Management Journal* 9 (Summer 1988), 41–58.

Lindvall, Hellienne. "Behind the Music: The Real Reason Why the Major Labels Love Spotify." *Guardian* (blog) (8–17–2009). http://www.theguardian.com/music/musicblog/2009/aug/17/major-labels-spotify.

Linkon, Sherry Lee. "Reading Lind Mania: Print Culture and the Construction of Nineteenth-Century Audiences." *Book History* 1.1 (1998), 94–106.

Lippman, Andrew, and David Reed. "Viral Communications." Media Laboratory Research (5–19–2003). http://dl.media.mit.edu/viral/viral.pdf.

Lombardi, Candace. "YouTube Cuts Three Content Deals." CNET (10–9–2006). http://www.cnet.com/news/youtube-cuts-three-content-deals/.

Lowensohn, Josh. "Jury Finds Apple Not Liable of Harming Consumers in iTunes DRM Case." *Verge* (12–16–2014). http://www.theverge.com/2014/12/16/7402695/jury-decision-in-iTunes-iPod-DRM-case.

Lowry, Tom. "Vevo Aims to Help Music Companies Cash in on Video." *Business Week* (12–6–2009). http://www.businessweek.com/technology/content/dec2009/tc2009126_307441.htm.

Maloney, Jennifer. "New York's Metropolitan Opera Opens Its Budget Curtain." *Wall Street Journal* (5–30–2014). http://www.wsj.com/articles/new-yorks-metropolitan-opera-opens-its-budget-curtain-1401416711.

Manjoo, Farhad. "That Tune, Named" (10–19–2009). *Slate*. http://www.slate.com/articles/technology/technology/2009/10/that_tune_named.html.

Manly, Lorne. "How Payola Went Corporate" (7–31–2005). *New York Times*. http://www.nytimes.com/2005/07/31/weekinreview/31manly.html?pagewanted = all&_r = 0.

Martin, Linda, and Kerry Seagrave. *Anti-Rock: The Opposition to Rock 'n' Roll*. Da Capo Press (1993).

Matzer, Marla. "These Days Soundtracks Can Be Sweet Music to Movie Marketers' Ears." *Los Angeles Times* (7–10–1997). http://articles.latimes.com/1997/jul/10/business/fi-11337.

McClellan, Dennis. "Talent Manager Discovered 2 Teen Idols." *Los Angeles Times* (3–16–2011). http://articles.latimes.com/2011/mar/16/local/la-me-robert-marcucci-20110316.

McClennan, Douglas. "Hail the Amateur, Loved by the Crowd." *New York Times* (6–10–2011). http://www.nytimes.com/2011/06/12/arts/music/amateur-musicians-and-crowd-sourced-talent-competitions.html?pagewanted = all&_r = 0.

McLuhan, Marshall. *Understanding Media: The Extensions of Man*. McGraw-Hill (1964).

McIntyre, Hugh. "YouTube Is About to Delete Independent Artists from Its Site." *Forbes* (6–18–2014). http://www.forbes.com/sites/hughmcintyre/2014/06/18/youtube-is-about-to-delete-independent-artists-from-its-site/.

McKinney, Sarah. "Patreon: A Fast-Growing Marketplace for Creators and Patrons of the Arts." *Forbes* (4–10–2014). http://www.forbes.com/sites/sarahmckinney/2014/04/10/patreon-a-fast-growing-marketplace-for-creators-and-patrons-of-the-arts/.

Miller, Donna, and David Bruenger. "Decivilization: Compressive Effects of Technology on Culture and Communication." *China Media Research* 3.2 (April 2007), 83–95.

———. "The Rise and Fall of YouTube: How Compressive Effects of Technology and Digital Capitalism Shape Social Media." Paper presented at the

International Association for Intercultural Communication Studies Conference, Harbin, China, 2007.

Montini, Laura. "Shazam vs. Spotify: Which Startup Can Predict the Grammys?" *Inc.* (2–6–2015). http://www.inc.com/laura-montini/spotify-v-shazam-which-is-the-better-predictor-of-grammy-winners.html.

Morris, Michelle Wilson. "Recording Industry Sues Napster for Copyright Infringement." *Music Dish* (12–15–1999). http://www.musicdish.com/mag/index.php3?id=113.

Mullen, Peter. "Everyone Knows Henry Wood Set Up the Proms: But Who Remembers the Man Who Hired Him to Do It?" *Independent* (London) (7–21–1995). http://www.independent.co.uk/arts-entertainment/music/everyone-knows-henry-wood-set-up-the-proms-but-who-remembers-the-man-who-hired-him-to-do-it-by-peter-mullen-1592519.html.

Myers, Kellen. "The RIAA, the DMCA, and the Forgotten Few Webcasters: A Call for Change in Digital Copyright Royalties." *Federal Communications Law Journal* 61.2 (2009). http://www.repository.law.indiana.edu/cgi/viewcontent.cgi?article=1534&context=fclj.

Nickson, Chris. "All about Gig Package Tours." Ministry of Rock. http://www.ministryofrock.co.uk/GigPackageTours.html.

Nieva, Richard. "Ashes to Ashes, Peer to Peer: An Oral History of Napster." *Fortune* (9–5–2013). http://fortune.com/2013/09/05/ashes-to-ashes-peer-to-peer-an-oral-history-of-napster/.

Norman, Phillip. *John Lennon: The Life.* Doubleday (2008).

O'Malley Greenburg, Zack. "Elvis Presley Earnings 2015: $55 Million." *Forbes* (10–28–2015). http://www.forbes.com/sites/zackomalleygreenburg/2015/10/28/elvis-presley-earnings-2015-55-million/#6a343d613779.

———. "Toby Keith, Cowboy Capitalist: Country's $500 Million Man." *Forbes* (6–26–2013). http://www.forbes.com/sites/zackomalleygreenburg/2013/06/26/toby-keith-cowboy-capitalist-countrys-500-million-man/.

———. "The World's Highest-Paid Musicians, 2013." *Forbes* (11–19–2013). http://www.forbes.com/sites/zackomalleygreenburg/2013/11/19/the-worlds-highest-paid-musicians-2013/.

Olson, Parmy. "Shazam Hits 100 Million Active Users as It Gears Up for IPO." *Forbes* (8–20–2014). http://www.forbes.com/sites/parmyolson/2014/08/20/shazam-hits-100-million-active-users-as-it-gears-up-for-ipo/.

Owsinski, Bobby. "Amazon Prime Adds Music: The Good and the Bad." *Forbes* (6–12–2014). http://www.forbes.com/sites/bobbyowsinski/2014/06/12/amazon-prime-adds-music-the-good-and-the-bad/.

Palmer, Jason. "Analytics at Spotify." Spotify Labs (5–13–2013). https://labs.spotify.com/2013/05/13/analytics-at-spotify/.

Paradise, Paul R. *Trademark Counterfeiting, Product Piracy, and the Billion Dollar Threat to the U.S. Economy.* Greenwood (1999).

Patashnik, Ben. "Are Package Tours Helping or Hurting Live Music?" *Rock Sound.* http://www.rocksound.tv/features/read/are-package-tours-helping-or-hurting-music.

Patry, William F. "England and the Statute of Anne." In *Copyright Law and Practice.* Bureau of National Affairs (1994). http://digital-law-online.info/patry/patry2.html.

Pelham, Henry. "Vinyl Prices, 1982–1984." AudioKarma (4–15–2012). http://www.audiokarma.org/forums/showthread.php?t = 437593.

Peoples, Glenn. "Live Nation Revenue Up 8% to $5.8 Billion, Posts Significant Net Losses." *Billboard* (2–26–2013). http://www.billboard.com/biz/articles/news/global/1549948/live-nation-revenue-up-8-to-58-billion-posts-significant-net-losses.

———. "Pandora Acquires Next Big Sound" (5–19–2015). *Billboard*. http://www.billboard.com/articles/business/6568814/pandora-acquires-next-big-sound.

———. "Pandora Now Sharing Listener Data with Artists." *Billboard* (10–22–2014). http://www.billboard.com/articles/business/6289343/pandora-now-sharing-listener-data-with-artists.

Petridis, Alexis. "Lady Gaga: Artpop—Review." *Guardian* (11–7–2013). http://www.theguardian.com/music/2013/nov/07/lady-gaga-Artpop-review.

Pham, Alex. "iTunes Market Share Still Dominant after a Decade (Research)." *Billboard Biz* (4–16–2013). http://www.billboard.com/biz/articles/news/1557486/itunes-market-share-still-dominant-after-a-decade-research.

———. "YouTube Confirms Vevo Deal." *Billboard* (7–2–2013). http://www.billboard.com/biz/articles/news/digital-and-mobile/1568816/youtube-confirms-vevo-deal.

Price, Jeff. "The Democratization of the Music Industry." *Huffington Post* (5–25–2011). http://www.huffingtonpost.com/jeff-price/the-democratization-of-th_b_93065.html.

———. "Sirius-ly, It's Not One Size Fits All." *TuneCore* (blog) (11–10–2011). http://www.tunecore.com/blog/2011/11/sirius-ly-its-not-one-size-fits-all.html.

Raphael, J.R. "A Decade of Internet Superstars." *PC World* (10–7–2008). http://www.pcworld.com/article/151803/internet_superstars.html.

Rath, Derek. "The Success and Undoing of Vee-Jay Records." *Day to Day*, NPR (8–21–2007). http://www.npr.org/templates/story/story.php?storyId = 18112344.

Register of Copyrights. "Federal Copyright Protection for Pre-1972 Sound Recordings." A Report of the Register of Copyrights (December 2011). http://www.copyright.gov/docs/sound/pre-72-report.pdf.

Resnikoff, Paul. "I'm Jeff Price. And This Is My New Company, Audiam . . ." *Digital Music News* (6–12–2013). http://www.digitalmusicnews.com/permalink/2013/06/12/audiem.

Richtel, Matt. "The Napster Decision: The Overview; Appellate Judges Back Limitations on Copying Music." *New York Times* (2–13–2001). http://www.nytimes.com/2001/02/13/business/napster-decision-overview-appellate-judges-back-limitations-copying-music.html.

Rogers, Francis. "Jenny Lind." *Musical Quarterly* 32.3 (July 1946), 437–448.

Rose, Joel. "A Pricey Investment, Even for Jay-Z." NPR (4–11–2008). http://www.npr.org/templates/story/story.php?storyId = 89565696.

Rosen, Jody. "Oh! You Kid! How a Sexed-Up Viral Hit from the Summer of '09—*1909*—Changed American Pop Music Forever." *Slate* (6–2–2014). http://www.slate.com/articles/arts/culturebox/2014/06/sex_and_pop_the_forgotten_1909_hit_that_introduced_adultery_to_american.html.

Rosen, Rebecca. "Forgotify: The Tool for Discovering Spotify's 4 Million Unheard Tracks." *Atlantic* (1–30–2014). http://www.theatlantic.com /technology/archive/2014/01/forgotify-the-tool-for-discovering-spotifys-4-million-unheard-tracks/283484/.

Ross, Alex. "The Record Effect: How Technology Has Transformed the Sound of Music." *New Yorker* (6–6–2005). http://www.newyorker.com/archive /2005/06/06/050606crat_atlarge?currentPage = all .

Rutherford, Kevin. "Lady Gaga Discounts Rumors, Hints at Deception in Website Vent." *Billboard* (6–5–2014). http://www.billboard.com/articles/ news/5862267/lady-gaga-discounts-rumors-hints-at-deception-in-website -vent.

———. "OneRepublic Extends Summer Tour, Talks 'Counting Stars' Success." *Billboard* (2–17–2014). http://www.billboard.com/articles/news/5900971 /onerepublic-extends-summer-tour-talks-counting-stars-success.

Saint-Amour, Paul K. *Modernism and Copyright.* Oxford University Press (2011).

Sandoval, Greg. "Source: Universal Music Group Plans 'Hulu-Like' Site." CNET (9–25–2008). http://www.cnet.com/news/source-universal-music-group -plans-hulu-like-site/.

———. "Universal, YouTube Near Deal on Music Video Site." CNET (3–5–2009). http://www.cnet.com/news/universal-youtube-near-deal-on-music-video-site/.

Sanjek, David. "Hill and Range." *Continuum Encyclopedia of Popular Music of the World: Performance and Production.* Vol. 2. A&C Black (2003).

Scherer, F. M. "The Emergence of Musical Copyright in Europe From 1709 to 1850" (Faculty Research Working Papers Series). John F. Kennedy School of Government, Harvard University (2008).

Schneider, Marc. "Grammys 2015: Most Shazamed Moments Belong to ELO, Katy Perry, Ed Sheeran." *Billboard* (2–9–2015). http://www.billboard.com /articles/events/grammys-2015/6465702/most-shazamed-moments-gram- mys-elo-katy-ed-sheeran.

Scott, Derek B. *Sounds of the Metropolis: The Nineteenth-Century Popular Music Revolution in London, New York, Paris, and Vienna.* Oxford University Press (2008).

Scott, Hugh Arthur. "London's Earliest Public Concerts." *Musical Quarterly* 22.4 (October 1936), 446–457.

Segall, Laurie. "How Too-Early Startup Shazam Survived a Decade." *CNN Money* (3–6–2012). http://money.cnn.com/2012/03/06/technology/shazam/.

Serrin, William. "James Petrillo Dead: Led Musicians. *New York Times* (10– 25–1984). http://www.nytimes.com/1984/10/25/obituaries/james-petrillo-dead- led-musicians.html.

Serwer, Andy. "Inside Rolling Stones, Inc." *Fortune* (2002; reprinted 7– 21–2013). http://fortune.com/2013/07/21/inside-rolling-stones-inc-fortune- 2002/.

Sherwin, Adam. "Andy Warhol's 'Famous for 15 Minutes' Quote May Not Be His, Experts Believe." *Independent* (9–2–2014). http://www.independent .co.uk/news/people/news/andy-warhols-famous-for-15-minutes-quote-may- not-be-his-experts-believe-9249200.html.

Sisario, Ben. "As Music Streaming Grows, Spotify Reports Rising Revenue and a Loss." *New York Times* (11–25–2014). http://www.nytimes.com/2014/11/26/business/spotify-discloses-revenue-but-not-its-future-plans.html?_r = 0.

———. "Backstage to Acquire Sonicbids" (1–30–2013). *New York Times.* http://mediadecoder.blogs.nytimes.com/2013/01/30/backstage-to-acquire-sonicbids/?_r = 0.

———. "EMI Is Sold for $4.1 Billion in Combined Deals, Consolidating the Music Industry." *New York Times* (11–11–2011). http://www.nytimes.com/2011/11/12/business/media/emi-is-sold-for-4–1-billion-consolidating-the-music-industry.html?_r = 2&.

———. "From One Mine, the Gold of Pop History." *New York Times* (10–30–2012). http://www.nytimes.com/2012/10/31/books/360-sound-celebrates-columbia-records-125th-anniversary.html?_r = 0.

———. "Live Nation Cut Its Losses Last Year." *New York Times* (2–24–2014). http://www.nytimes.com/2014/02/25/business/media/live-nations-loss-declined-as-revenue-rose-in-2013.html.

———. "Lollapalooza and Its Promoters Rise on the Stage of Chicago." *New York Times* (8–16–2010). http://www.nytimes.com/2010/08/07/arts/music/07lolla.html.

———. "Out to Shake Up Music, Often with Sharp Words." *New York Times* (5–6–2012). http://www.nytimes.com/2012/05/07/business/TuneCore-chief-shakes-up-music-with-his-own-words.html?pagewanted = all.

———. "Spotify's Revenue Is Growing, but So Are Its Losses." *New York Times* (5–8–2015). http://www.nytimes.com/2015/05/09/business/media/as-spotify-expands-revenue-rises-and-losses-deepen.html.

Skirboll, Aaron. "The Next Page: Stephen Foster's Sad End." *Pittsburgh Post-Gazette* (3–1–2014). http://www.post-gazette.com/opinion/Op-Ed/2014/03/02/Next-Page-Stephen-Foster-s-sad-end/stories/201403020083.

Smith, Bernd H., David L. Rogers, and Karen L. Vrotsos. *There's No Business That's Not Show Business.* FT Press (2003).

Smith, Ethan. "Madonna Heads for Virgin Territory." *Wall Street Journal* (10–11–2007). http://online.wsj.com/news/articles/SB119205443638155166.

Smith, Jake. "Over the Past 12 Years, Streaming Services Have Failed to Pay $100 Million in Royalties . . . ." *Digital Music News* (9–3–2014). http://www.digitalmusicnews.com/permalink/2014/09/03/past-12-years-streaming-services-failed-pay-100-million-royalties.

"SoundExchange Is Celebrating 'Ten Years in Play.'" *Soundbyte* (10–9–2013). http://www.soundexchange.com/wp-content/uploads/2013/10/Sound-byte-10-9-13.pdf.

Sousa, John Philip. "The Menace of Mechanical Music." *Appleton's Magazine* 8 (1906). http://explorepahistory.com/odocument.php?docId = 1-4-1A1.

Spangler, Todd. "Sirius XM to Pay $210 Million to Record Companies for Pre-1972 Songs." *Variety* (6–26–2015). http://variety.com/2015/music/news/sirius-xm-settlement-record-companies-pre-1972-songs-1201529103/.

Spotifysehr. "We've Only Just Begun!" Spotify (10–7–2008). https://news.spotify.com/us/2008/10/07/weve-only-just-begun/.

Sturges, Fiona. "The Rembrandts: 'So No One Told Me It Was Going to Be This Way.'" *Independent* (4–27–2004). http://www.independent.co.uk/arts-entertainment/music/features/the-rembrandts-so-no-one-told-me-it-was-going-to-be-this-way-6170741.html.

Swensson, Andrea. "Infographic: Comparing Venue Sizes in the Twin Cities." *Current* (11–1–2013). http://blog.thecurrent.org/2013/11/infographic-comparing-venue-sizes-in-the-twin-cities/.

Taylor, Timothy D. *The Sounds of Capitalism: Advertising, Music, and the Conquest of Culture.* University of Chicago Press (2012).

Thorne, Mike. "The Recording Studio." Chapter posted from *Music in the Machine* (unpublished MS). http://www.stereosociety.com/recordingstudio.shtml.

Tindall, Blair. *Mozart in the Jungle.* Atlantic Monthly Press (2005).

Toffler, Alvin. *Future Shock.* Random House (1970).

Trav, S. D. *No Applause, Just Throw Money: The Book That Made Vaudeville Famous.* Macmillan (2005).

Tucker, Jeffrey A. "The End of the US Piano Industry." *Mises Daily* (12–10–2008). https://mises.org/library/end-us-piano-industry.

Tussey, Deborah. "Music at the Edge of Chaos: A Complex Systems Perspective on File Sharing." *Loyola University Chicago Law Journal* 37 (2005), 147–212.

Tyrangiel, Josh. "Radiohead Says: Pay What You Want." *Time Magazine* (10–1–2007). http://content.time.com/time/arts/article/0,8599,1666973,00.html.

Ulaby, Neda. "2006 and the Death of Tower Records." NPR (12–29–2009). http://www.npr.org/2009/12/29/121975854/2006-and-the-death-of-tower-records.

Van Buskirk, Eliot. "Best Grammy Prediction Data: Shazam or Spotify?" (2–11–2013). *Evolver.fm* at http://evolver.fm/2013/02/11/best-grammy-prediction-data-shazam-or-spotify/.

Van Zandt, Steven. "A Crisis of Craft." Originally presented at SXSW (2009); archived at Little Steven's Underground Garage (2–2–2010). http://undergroundgarage.com/essays-and-speeches/a-crisis-of-craft.html.

Waddell, Ray. "Live Music's $20 Billion Year: Rolling Stones, One Direction, Live Nation Top Boxscore's Year-End." *Billboard* (12–12–2014). http://www.billboard.com/articles/business/6406028/boxscore-top-tours-2014-rolling-stones-live-nation.

———. "U2's '360' Tour Gross: $736,137,344!" *Billboard* (7–29–2011). http://www.billboard.com/biz/articles/news/touring/1176894/u2s-360-tour-gross-736137344.

Wald, Elijah. *Escaping the Delta: Robert Johnson and the Invention of the Blues.* Amistad (2004).

Walker, Rob. "The Song Decoders." *New York Times* (10–14–2009). http://www.nytimes.com/2009/10/18/magazine/18Pandora-t.html?pagewanted = all.

Ward, Ed. "How the Bristol Sessions Changed Country Music." NPR (4–19–2011). http://www.npr.org/2011/04/19/134173199/how-the-bristol-sessions-changed-country-music.

Warner, Joel. "Fueled by Venture-Capital Funding and a Love for Unknown Bands, Can Boulder's Next Big Sound Predict the Next Rock Star?" *West-*

word (10–7–2010). http://www.westword.com/music/fueled-by-venture-capital-funding-and-a-love-for-unknown-bands-can-boulders-next-big-sound-predict-the-next-rock-star-5110133.

Wasserman, Todd. "The Revolution Wasn't Televised: The Early Days of YouTube." Mashable (2–14–2015). http://mashable.com/2015/02/14/youtube-history/.

Weber, W. E., ed. *The Musician as Entrepreneur, 1700–1914: Managers, Charlatans, and Idealists.* Indiana University Press (2004).

Willens, Max. "Shazam and Spotify's Grammy Picks Are More Accurate than Billboard's. Here's Why" (2–6–2015). *International Business Times.* http://www.ibtimes.com/shazam-spotifys-grammy-picks-are-more-accurate-billboards-heres-why-1808170.

Wilson-Morris, Michael. "Recording Industry Sues Napster for Copyright Infringement." *Music Dish* (12–15–1999). http://www.musicdish.com/mag/index.php3?id = 113.

Woodward, Curt. "Rhapsody at 10 Years: Surviving Long Enough to Face a Herd of New Competitors." *Xconomy* (1–30–2011). http://www.xconomy.com/seattle/2011/11/30/rhapsody-at-10/.

Wynne, Ben. *In Tune: Charley Patton, Jimmie Rodgers, and the Roots of American Music.* Louisiana State University Press (2014).

Young, William H., and Nancy K. Young. *Music of the Great Depression.* Greenwood (2005).

Index